WALK RIGHT BACK

The Story of the Everly Brothers

Roger White

Plexus, London

This book is dedicated, with love, to my wife Rita for her patience
and understanding, and to our two boys Graeme and Kevin, who
mean so much to me.

All rights reserved including the right
of reproduction in whole or in part in any form
Text copyright © 1984 by Roger White
This edition copyright © 1984 by Plexus Publishing Limited
Published by Plexus Publishing Limited
30 Craven Street
London WC2N 5NT
First printing 1984

White, Roger
    Walk right back.
    1. Everly Brothers 2. Rock musicians
    United States   Biography
    I. Title
    784.5'0092'2   ML421.E9

    ISBN 0–85965–099–5
    ISBN 0–85965–081–2 Pbk

Cover and book design by Ken Kitchen

Printed and bound in Great Britain by
Hollen Street Press Limited, Slough, Berks

CONTENTS

I am pleased to be able to write a few words to introduce this
book to you.

I am very proud of the success Don and I achieved when Rock n Roll
was in its infancy and flattered that so many stars of today have
said that we were a direct influence on their careers.

This book has been compiled by one of the many fans who have remained
loyal to the music of Don and Phil Everly over the past 25 years.
You will see that our story has been told with the use of press
articles, show programmes and other memorabilia and has been
fascinating to read as I have not previously seen many of the articles.

I would like to take the opportunity of thanking everybody who has
bought our records over the past quarter of a century and hope that
this book will be seen not only as a celebration of the past but an
introduction to the future.

Phil Everly

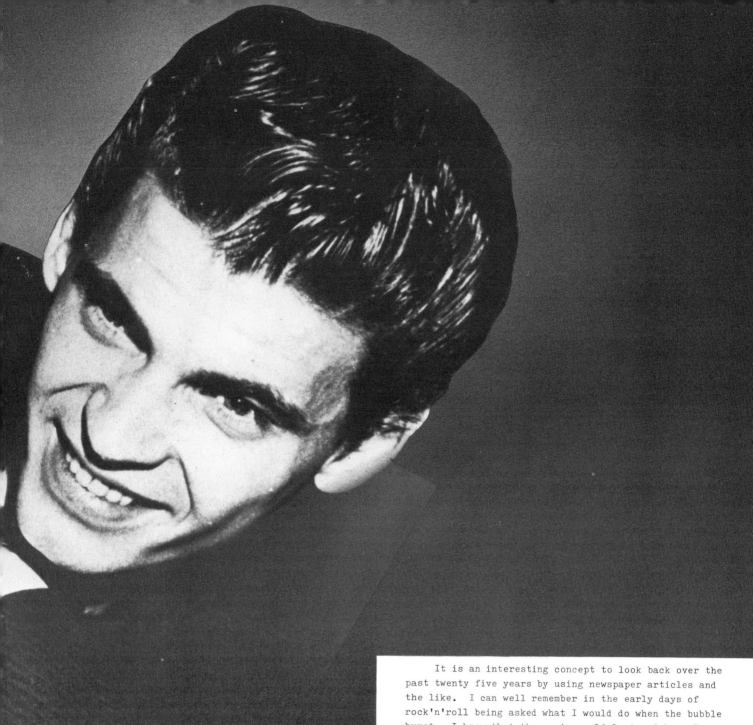

It is an interesting concept to look back over the past twenty five years by using newspaper articles and the like. I can well remember in the early days of rock'n'roll being asked what I would do when the bubble burst. I knew that the music would last and here I am still producing rock music today.

The music Phil and I produced over the years still sounds fresh to me today as can be seen by the number of new releases of our songs.

I thank everybody who has supported our music over the years and to the continued support we get from the fans for our solo careers.

Enjoy the book - it is the history of rock 'n' roll up to the present day.

Don Everly

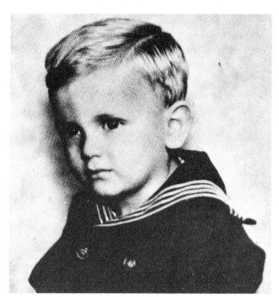

1
Kentucky, Illinois and Iowa

Kentucky
You are the dearest land outside of heaven to me
Kentucky
Your laurel and your redbud trees

Kentucky
I miss the old folks singing in the silv'ry moonlight
Kentucky
I miss the hound dog chasing coon
Kentucky by Carl Davis

Anyone who has heard the Everly Brothers sing *Kentucky* knows of the emotion they convey in the song of their home state. Although the length of time they have actually lived in Kentucky is minimal, Don and Phil are clearly Kentuckians by birthright. The origins of the Everly family are unclear, but it seems certain that Don and Phil's ancestors were British. The name Everly has appeared in Ireland, Scotland and, perhaps most interestingly, there is evidence of a village named Everly in Oxfordshire in the eighteenth century.

The Everly ancestors who settled in Kentucky became substantial landowners. However, Don and Phil's great great great grandfather wanted more excitement and decided to 'drive hogs down to New Orleans' but, alas, he died of yellow fever on the way. Before he left home he had signed over his property to his brother. This meant that Don and Phil's side of the family was penniless thereafter and it was inevitable that they would become coal miners, mining being the principal industry in a state requiring substantial manpower.

The sentimental views of *Kentucky*, and even Don and Phil's own song *Green River*, probably reflect the mental attitudes of early twentieth-century Kentuckians rather than the practicalities that faced the workers in a mining community of that time. For the miners were exploited by the coal companies. They were poorly paid for spending long hours in the dark each day miles underground bent in a strained crouch, their eyes for ever looking upward, searching for signs of 'horse backs' – treacherous slate flakes that would drop without warning and crush whatever was beneath. This danger, along with blowouts, was an

Early photographs of the Everly Brothers: Top: *Don, aged four, and two year old Phil.* Centre: *Phil in a sailorsuit, aged three.* Below: *Outside the KMA offices with their parents in 1945, one of the first Everly family portraits.*

everyday hazard and there were many who continued to work after losing limbs in mining accidents. Others lost their lives.

Don and Phil's grandfather, Melford Everly, was a union organiser and not too popular with his employers. Nevertheless, Melford was regarded as an honourable man by both the employers and the miners, and was judged the right man to settle disputes between the two sides. Despite constant poverty, Melford and his wife had a large family – five sons and five daughters. Ike (Don and Phil's father) was the fourth child. He was born on 29 April 1908 in Ohio, just over the Kentucky border, but soon the family moved to Muhlenburg County in Kentucky where there was a concentration of coal mines. As soon as they were old enough and provided they were fit, the boys were expected to start work down the mines. Ike started at the age of thirteen and worked at Powderly, Cleaton Drakesboro and Brownie. In those days the mines were reliant on manual labour and at one mine Ike and his brother Roland held the record for loading eighteen tons of coal in a day's shift 'for the company store', conjuring up echoes of Merle Travis' *Sixteen Tons*.

Like the miners of South Wales, the Kentucky miners would spend their spare time making music with their families. Melford was a left-handed fiddler and his wife played too. As well as 'front-porch picking' there would be Saturday night dances where the whole community would get together. Phil Everly's fondest memories are of his father recounting stories from those early days. Ike, along with all his brothers, learned to play the guitar and became highly accomplished at playing a thumb-pick style which was common in the area. Phil described the style as 'The thumb strokes the bass pattern in two/four time while the forefinger, or sometimes the index finger, picks out the lead.' Ike had been taught by a negro called Arnold Schultz who also taught the Monroe Brothers. Although there were many guitar players in the district, Ike was considered by neighbour Merle Travis as the best there was, along with a man called Mose Regar. Travis, who was fourteen years old at the time, idolised Ike, and would go to parties where he played just to listen. He became a great personal friend to Ike and to his brothers Chuck and Leonard. Ike taught Travis how to play guitar with the thumb-pick style, and Travis went on to develop that style and in turn to influence, among others, Chet Atkins and Scotty Moore, both leading guitarists of rock'n'roll.

Although an accomplished guitar player, Ike never really thought of making a living out of music. He began to perform in the evening after his day's work at the mine. His first musical employment was with WGBS in Evansville, Indiana, which was a natural progression for someone who loved country music.

In 1929 Ike left the mines and went with Chuck and Leonard to Chicago where they worked on a small radio station one day a week. There was a large community of Southerners in Chicago – people from Tennessee, Kentucky and the Carolinas – so there was a demand for country music of the type played by Ike and his brothers. But he soon felt homesick and headed back to Brownie. He kept playing for fun and joined a band as guitarist and singer. On 31 August 1935 Ike married the girl next door – Margaret Embry. Margaret came from the large coal-mining family of Blueatrice Embry. Her brothers were named Zerkel, Shirley, Prock (who was christened after the first word he ever spoke) and Kenneth, and her sisters were called Dimple and Melta. Margaret was born on 25 November 1919, so she was not quite sixteen years old when she and Ike got married. Ike was twenty-seven. They had known each other since Margaret was a child. It was a courtship typical of the time and the place; Ike had even carried her books home from school.

Ike and Margaret stayed on in Brownie after their marriage and their first son Isaac Donald was born there on 1 February 1937. But soon after Don's birth the family took the train to Chicago with a view to Ike working full time as a musician. When Don was twelve the family returned on holiday to Brownie to show Don where he was born, only to find that the mining company had demolished the smokestack and the town was no more.

The importance of Ike and Margaret's decision to exchange mining for show business cannot be underestimated. Phil Everly has written a song called *My Family's All Kentucky, My Grandad's Name was Blue* which includes the line '. . . If it wasn't for that guitar I'd've been down in that dirty hole . . .'. In taking that giant step, Ike generated his family out of the mining context which still envelops many of Don and Phil's cousins today. While strip mining has now replaced the pits, the Kentucky mining community has remained historically untouched.

Soon after their arrival in Chicago Ike and Margaret had an addition to their family. Phillip Everly was born in Cook County Hospital on 19 January 1939. Ike began working the nightclubs in the Madison Street and Maxwell Street district which was full of honky tonks and bars. Ike owned the first electric guitar in Madison Street and the bar owners would open their doors and place the amplifier in the entrance in order to attract customers. His status as an accomplished guitarist meant that he soon became known around Chicago. Eventually he worked for WJ-JD and WLS radio stations and appeared on the celebrated Barndance road show and worked with, among others, Red Foley and George Gobel, who were popular at the time.

Despite Ike's ever-growing status in the music industry, there were still occasions when he was obliged to take on other work to support his family. During the early war years he worked a full day in an asbestos factory and then would go play guitar in a bar until the small hours of the morning. Phil describes one occasion when Ike Everly was playing in a nightclub in Calumet City, a town outside Chicago. Across the street a then unknown Boudleaux Bryant was playing jazz fiddle in a bar where the bartender was Wesley

Above: *The site at Brownie, Kentucky in 1983. The town was actually demolished in 1945.*

Above: *Phil's birth certificate, indicating that he was born in Chicago, and not Brownie as so often stated.*

Rose, later to become head of Acuff Rose Publishing.

Apart from its many famed attributes, Chicago also has the distinction of being the location of the first recording session to involve either of the Everly Brothers. When Don was about five, Ike took him down to a booth where talking records could be made by soldiers to be sent home. From the radio Don had learned *Paper Doll*, the Mills Brothers hit record, and he sang it with Ike backing him on guitar. Unfortunately Don couldn't remember all the song and before the end said 'aw shucks' and left it at that. He later referred to the record as his first flop!

By the autumn of 1944 Ike had established himself as an entertainer in Chicago but he and Margaret decided to make the first of their sacrifices for the benefit of their children. They wanted Don and Phil to grow up in the clean rural environment of a small town, away from the dirt and bustle of city life. They moved to Waterloo, Iowa, where Ike worked with four other musicians as the Blackhoff Boys on Radio Station KASL. Margaret recalls that the band would rehearse at home and Don and Phil would be encouraged to take part. Phil, who by this time was five, already had a high voice which the band would encourage. Don, at seven, was having difficulty keeping time. His father told him that he couldn't play with a boy who broke time. Don went off by himself and came back eventually, saying, 'Dad, I won't break time this time' and he never did again. Margaret doesn't know what Don did to learn how to keep time.

The Everlys spent one cold winter in Waterloo and then moved down to the deep south west of Iowa to the town of Shenandoah, some sixty miles from Omaha. Shenandoah was a fairly small town of some 6,500 inhabitants but boasted two powerful radio stations. The town was known as the nursery centre of the world and the radio stations were owned by two

seed companies who between them ran the town. The May Seed Company did, and still do, own KMA (Keep Millions Advised) while the Field Company owned the KFNF station.

Ike joined KMA as a staff artist and stayed until 1951 before moving over to KFNF for a short period. The staff artists were not paid much during the years of austerity that followed World War II and many were also on the May Seed Company payroll. Merl Roulstone was with KMA for many years under the name of Merl Douglas. He remembers that when he first went to Shenandoah to work for KMA he was offered a job with the May Company sewing seed sacks to which he replied, 'No, sir. I want to be an entertainer!' Similarly, Ike didn't work for the May Company and relied on supplementing the $40/50 a week he earned from KMA with bookings at fairs, dances, weddings and other functions.

The mid-west radio stations had a special place in the community. Not only did they provide the information service the farmers required but they also created a 'family' for the listeners. Ike became Cousin Ike Everly to the listeners of KMA. He had a daily fifteen-minute radio show of his own, and being a staff artist, he also took part in other shows, with regular parts in 'Cargill Calling', 'Morning Roundup', 'Green Mountain Boys' and 'RFD 960'. The shows were usually informal, early-morning programmes with singing, news and comedy. Warren Neilson, who often MC'd, remembers being involved with Ike on the 'Stump Us Gang Show': 'Listeners would write in asking the musicians to play a particular song. If the gang between them didn't know the song the writer would get a free packet of the crackers sold by the programme's sponsors – they were called Waldorf Crackers. We would get hundreds of letters each week from the listeners with songs that were very obscure and the musicians, particularly Ike, would try and trick me and say, "Oh yeah, it goes like this" and make something up and try and lead me up the wrong road, so I had to be on my guard.'

KMA extended the family atmosphere between the station and its listeners by producing a monthly magazine called the *KMA Guide*, which featured articles about the May family who owned the station, as well as the staff artists and their families. It also contained recipes, garden news, announcements of the birthdays and anniversaries of the artists and their families, as well as a full programme guide for the month. Some of the articles about the Everlys are reproduced and give a good impression of the kind of life Don and Phil had in their childhood years.

Ike Everly rented two-roomed places for his family to live in. Ike saw himself as a bit of a farmer, so there would always be land on which he would grow vegetables for the family to eat. Margaret, like a good Southern wife, would bottle and store their home-grown tomatoes. Ike's only vice, reveals his close friend Merl Douglas, was his fighting chickens. The family loved to hunt and they would spend whole days out in the countryside on a shoot. Don and Phil lived an open-air life and a full one. A former neighbour, Jim Androy, remembers that for a time the Everlys occupied a house at the bottom of his father's garden which he likens to an overgrown chicken house. Don and Phil would sneak over the fence and take a ride on Jim's horse. Clair Johnson was about Don's age and used to do a paper round with them delivering the *Evening Sentinel* to supplement the family income. Mr. Johnson remembers that when the papers were late they would all play on the Elk Lodge yard, making pea shooters out of large straws that could 'fire' a mouthful of peas at once.

Don began to be interested in photography, painting and cooking (Albert Lee swears that Don makes the best pizza in Nashville), hobbies that he has retained to this day. Don remembers how his interest in cooking began: 'I think it came about from my childhood in Chicago where we lived in an Italian neighbourhood and I was really influenced by that. I also remember going to Chinese restaurants in Chicago none of which was indigenous to Kentucky. So when we were in Iowa I wasn't content with all that old-type Southern cooking which we normally had. I was always complaining that we didn't have enough pasta and other ethnic foods. It was hard keeping everybody interested in it.' Phil, on the other hand, was more athletic. He was a sprinter and a member of the school basket-ball team as well as helping his father farm their land. For both of them, however, music was of prime importance and everything else took second place when it came to practising their singing or playing. Don remembers: 'I knew that my career was going to be in music.'

As soon as Ike began his radio show for KMA he

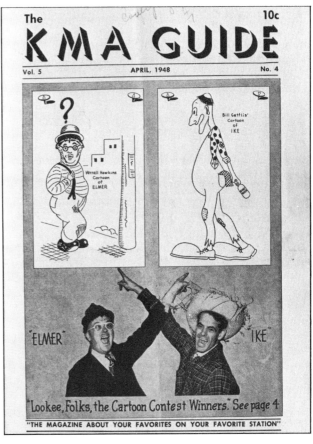

Above: Ike in the KMA studios in 1947 and *below:* Ike was a regular favourite in the monthly KMA Guide.

Above left: *The Everlys lived in this house in Shenandoah and 'didn't have enough room to change their minds', according to a neighbour.* Centre left: *Thirteen year old Don cooks shrimp Creole with his mother.* Below left: *Phil and Don practise with their father at home.* Above right: *The family go on a hunting trip, 1946.* Centre right: *Phil (third from left on the back row) in the Shenandoah Junior High basketball team.* Below right: *Ike Everly is flanked by fellow KMA staff artists Harpo Richardson (left) and Wayne Van Horn (right).*

11

introduced Don and Phil into the act whenever the programme didn't interfere with their school. Don would sing solos and Phil, at six years old unable to hold the tune, would tell jokes with Ike as the straight man. There was always an occasion over the Christmas period, usually Christmas Day, when the children of staff artists would perform on the radio. Like all the programmes at that time the shows would be broadcast live which caused some problems. Warren Neilson would MC the programmes and he has fond memories of one Christmas programme when Phil's song didn't go quite as planned and he started to cry in the studio and Ike had to calm him down. A recording of the 1946 Christmas Show has survived in which Don, aged nine, sings *Santa Claus is Coming to Town* and Phil, aged seven sings *Silent Night*. During the programme it is revealed that the previous night Margaret had heard Phil making noises in bed and had gone in to the bedroom to find that he was singing in his sleep the song that he was to perform the next day. Other practical problems of live radio were revealed by Charles Ingram who occasionally played with Ike. Both Don and Phil had to stand on chairs to reach the microphone. On one occasion Don was standing on a folding canvas chair which collapsed as he was singing. Ike had to catch him as he fell. Another time all the lights went out in the studio while Phil was singing. On both occasions they continued singing without a break, like true professionals.

Articles over the years have stated that Don was given his own programme, 'The Little Donnie Show'. A thorough search of the KMA Guides has failed to reveal any programme of that name. The probable reason for the confusion is answered by Margaret Everly: 'A boy by the name of Little Joe Parish had a Saturday afternoon show and Don was invited down to sing a solo on that show. Well, it was kinda nice to have him there and he liked it so they invited him back each Saturday for a few weeks and he got to singing the theme song for them which was *I'm Free Little Birdie as I Can Be*.' There was a strong listener reaction to Don's appearances on these programmes as well as Ike's shows so that some photographs of Don were

Above: *Don's first paid performance in 1946.*
Below: *Relaxing on a family picnic in 1950.*

taken and sold by the boys for 50c each. The good response also led to Don's first paid performances.

There was a regular Saturday night programme called 'The KMA Country School', a light-hearted romp set in a classroom with the artists being given improbable names, which involved most of the staff artists. In the autumn of 1946 it was decided to extend the show's format with a series of live programmes called 'The Corn Belt Jamboree' to be broadcast from an auditorium in Council Bluffs, some sixty miles from Shenandoah, near Omaha. Ike was a regular on the programme and was due to attend. However, in an article in *Country and Western Jamboree*, published in the summer of 1958, Ike said, 'A good friend of ours, Lou Black, came over from KMA. I'll never forget what Lou said: "Of all the talent, the most popular act on this station with nineteen acts is Little Donnie Everly who

Above: *Don and Phil playing in a garden jam session with a couple of friends, circa 1950.*

is going to be the star of this show and we are going to have to pay him".' Don was paid $5 a week for this one show which, at his parents' suggestion, he shared with Phil, along with the receipts for the sale of the photographs.

Throughout the middle to late 1940s, Don and Phil were developing their musical skills. Both tried to learn the violin but without success and switched to the guitar. Phil also learned the mandolin, bass fiddle and flute. Phil says: 'I could barely play the bass fiddle and the flute was more what you'd call the recorder. I learned that at school which, incidentally, was where I learned to read music. I took mandolin lessons from a musician in Shenandoah and I can still chord a little.' They were taught by their father which accounts for them playing right-handed while they are naturally left-handed. Ike didn't know any other way. He told Don, 'They'll always call you "lefty" and it will be difficult for you to tune guitars.' Ike was also teaching them songs. In fact, all the training came from their father. To start with, Don was taught to sing harmony and then, as Phil grew, because his voice was naturally higher, he took over the harmony parts. But the songs were not limited to two-part harmony. The family also worked on three- and four-part songs with Margaret joining in, although as Phil says: 'We had to watch Mother because she would sometimes drift into one of

the other parts.' Ike had a Wilcox Gay recorder which was a little home disc recorder; there was no tape in those days. The boys practised and gradually worked up a repertoire of songs. Ike not only taught them the songs, but also the basics of singing that were to hold the brothers in good stead in later years.

Don and Phil were also exposed to the musical tastes of the other KMA staff artists. Despite their small house Ike would still invite the other musicians round for jam sessions, and Merl Douglas remembers how the boys were interested in all the different musical styles to which they were exposed. They listened to commercial radio stations as well as the tremendous selection of records disposed of by the radio station, including those of the Bailes Brothers, the Delmore Brothers, the Milo Twins and the York Brothers. As Phil recalls, 'They were the harmony singers that Dad equated Don and me with but he never said at any time, "Hey, you should become the Everly Brothers". He was more or less teaching us.'

Their training was continuous and their appearances on Ike's radio show increased. Don and Phil began working on a regular basis in 1949. Don was twelve and Phil was ten. Ike suggested to KMA that his show become a family show. The station had received a lot of mail praising the show which not only included the boys and Ike but also Margaret who gave out cookery tips and read the sponsors' advertisements. The problem was that all this work was being done for no extra money. Phil says, 'Dad threatened to quit unless they hired us as well. They wanted him so badly that they took us on.' The first official Everly Family Show was on the air in 1950 and provided the family with a substantial increase in their weekly earnings – from $50 to $75 a week.

The establishment of the family show fixed a routine for Don and Phil that was to remain with them right through their schooling until they moved to Nashville. During school time they would be up early to get down to the radio station for their 6.00–6.30 a.m. show which was broadcast live each morning except Sunday. In addition they did a slot on Saturday afternoon. The show would be made up of solos sung by any of the family, including country songs and hymns, duets, trios, guitar solos from Ike, comedy, home tips from Margaret and, of course, the sponsors' advertisements. There was no set pattern to the music or the way it was presented. If Don had a solo, he would usually sing a Hank Williams song (only recently Don admitted that when he was little he dreamed of growing up to be Hank Williams). The early morning programme didn't suit everybody. One of their neighbours, Mrs. Jack Funk, remembers Don and Phil waking everybody up by strumming their guitars and singing on the back porch of their house after they had done their show and before they ate their breakfast and went off to school.

Warren Neilson reveals that it was Margaret's dream to have a family show and the KMA programme worked well for a year or so, although it was only an extension of the type of programme that Ike had already been doing for years. In 1952 the family moved to the smaller KFNF station and it was there that the family act really got going. Merl Douglas feels

that they moved because Margaret believed that at a smaller station they would have a better chance of developing the act. Extracts of one of the 1952 KFNF shows feature on Don and Phil's Warner Brothers 1968 album *Roots*. The *Roots* tapes reveal that there were family shows each day at 7.15 while Mum and Dad did their show at 10.15 in which the boys sometimes took part.

It is interesting to consider how Don and Phil reacted to being radio performers. Don, in 1971 on an Australian TV show, *Hippies with Money*, described himself as a precocious child: 'I think any kid is gonna be precocious if they are told that however many thousand people are listening to them on radio.' Phil regards himself as being an easy child who just drifted along, anticipating that his life would be in music. Even as children they had little in common, but their ages were close enough for their parents to dress them identically. Philip Norman's article in the London *Sunday Times* in 1971 reveals that Don had to wait for his first sports jacket until Phil was old enough for one, too. This treatment, together with Don having to share with Phil the money he had earned, must have been tough for a young boy to accept and it would not be surprising if Don had emphasised his two-year seniority.

Above: This 1950 publicity photograph was taken when the Ike Everly Family Show first appeared on KMA. Left: Phil, aged eleven, and Don, thirteen, were now established as a performing duo.

There is one area, however, in which Don and Phil were, and probably still are, vehemently in agreement. For their shows and publicity shots they wore cowboy suits which they detested. The suits confirmed the views of the other young people of Shenandoah that Don and Phil were very hillbilly. Mary Reddington remembers: 'I was in seventh grade (about twelve years old) and Phil, who I knew, was in eighth grade and Don in tenth grade. At the time, the boys and their parents had a daily radio programme singing country and western music. To be honest, the local teenagers at that time did not appreciate that type of music and so Don and Phil were not considered as any kind of celebrities and consequently little attention was given to their singing.' Phil agrees: 'Nobody thought anything positive about what we were doing. It was country music which was put down by everyone. They were into Eddie Fisher.' Don feels that the changing sources of entertainment had something to do with it: 'When I started on radio singing songs my Dad taught me, my friends knew I was on radio because it was right before the movies took off after the war, so radio and the theatre were all there was. When it became the Everly Family Show early in the morning, none of my contemporaries knew I was on radio so I was influenced during that period by what they were listening to on radio and records.'

The Everlys spent nine years in Shenandoah, a period of stability in a notoriously unstable industry. However, that impression of security is misleading. As Phil explains: 'Shenandoah, Iowa, is in the American cornbelt region and the radio station was geared to the farming community. During the severe winters there was little for the farmers to do so there was a full programme service from the radio station. In the summer, though, the farmers would be out in the fields all day so that even our six o'clock show was too late for them. So the station would fire us each year and we would be forced to do something else. It was very depressing because we had to spend each summer job hunting.' The family would load up the car with food and instruments and travel all over the country stopping in parks to eat and sleep, auditioning at radio stations and playing at town halls and fairs. As the years passed, live radio began to die out. Warren Neilson explains why. 'Although the staff artists weren't paid a great deal for their radio work, it was expensive to retain the staff that KMA had. With the development of the record industry, management realised that they could buy records cheaper.' The result, as far as the Everlys were concerned, was that they would have to travel farther each year to get jobs for the summer.

The gradual rundown of live radio reached its nadir in the summer of 1952 when the Everlys packed up their '46 Chevy and auditioned at, as Phil says, 'just about every radio station between Iowa and Arkansas – a journey of four or five hundred miles, maybe a thousand miles we travelled. We had a couple of offers

Right: Phil, aged eleven, was attracting his own fans as this publicity shot indicates.

but not enough to survive.' The act could buy time on a radio station for a show but it was then up to the act to obtain sponsorship to cover the cost of the programme and, hopefully, provide something to live on. In the summer of 1952 the Everlys finally found a job at Evansville, Indiana for only $55 a week. Their sponsors were the None Better Milling Company and the family played their fairs around Evansville. It was there that Don and Phil first caught the attention of young girls. It was on stage in Evansville that they first signed autographs. They were attracting an audience but they were making so little that they were starving. As autumn approached, the family returned to Iowa.

It may have been the audience response in Evansville that convinced Ike and Margaret that it was time to move on. Merl Douglas says that 'Margaret felt that they had gone as far as they could and it was time to move to where the action was. They had some war bonds and they cashed them all in and sold all their furniture to make this trip which eventually ended at Knoxville, Tennessee. They moved on in the summer of 1953.'

There is no doubt that Shenandoah provided Don and Phil with the type of childhood Ike and Margaret had wanted for them. It was a close-knit rural community with the advantage of an influential radio station where Don and Phil gained valuable experience of working both on live radio and performing before audiences. It implanted a professionalism in their work which was a cornerstone of their future success. Let Margaret Everly have the final word – 'Shenandoah is a beautiful town which will always have a soft spot in my heart because it gave my sons so much.'

2
Knoxville to Nashville — Out On Their Own

In the summer of 1953 the Everly family left Shenandoah, travelling farther and farther south, until they finally settled in Knoxville, Tennessee, where there was still a number of radio stations providing live entertainment. The Everlys signed with WROL, a country and western station owned by Cass Walker, who also owned a chain of grocery stores in the area. Walker was also the Everlys' sponsor and paid them $90 a week for their radio programmes which he MC'd himself. Phil remembers that Don did an advert for a pinto pony which was a plastic blow-up which was supposed to support a two-hundred-pound man. 'Mail in your four dollars and we'll send it to you', was the slogan of the radio advertisement. Don recalls, 'We weren't making that much. It was really just enough to get the necessities of life.'

For $90 a week the family would do two shows a day, in the morning before school and at noon, and on Wednesdays they also did an evening programme. The style of programme was similar to those in Shenandoah but there was a difference in the way Don and Phil sang. Dan Bailey, who worked on the station at that time, recalls, 'Their dad played guitar really well. The music the boys sang was on the border line of *Bye Bye Love*. This was the time when Elvis Presley was starting and the boys' music was drifting away from country music. They were very talented boys and we knew they would make it big one day.' The family would also do live shows for Mr. Walker, and the station secretary, Pearl Mantooth, who worked with them on those shows confirms that even then Don and Phil sang in perfect harmony.

The musical education of Don and Phil continued. They worked regularly in the new medium of television and were exposed to different influences. Although black gospel music had been important to them, mainly because Ike liked it and listened to it at home, their musical direction had been towards the country music provided by the best mid-western entertainers. Here in Knoxville they could listen to the best southern singers and musicians. There was bluegrass; the Osborne Brothers worked in the city; and there was black rhythm and blues. Don especially liked the sound of rhythm and blues and was particularly attracted to the guitar styling of Bo Diddley. Phil remembers, 'We were a conglomerate. We were influenced by r'n'b and we did some pop things and a lot of country.'

Don and Phil attended West High School, situated

16

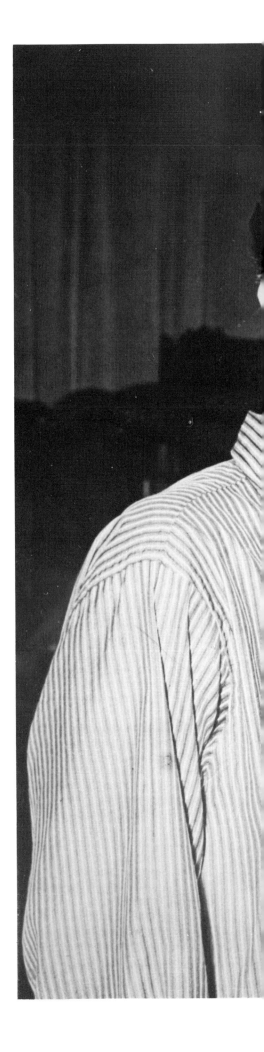

by the railroad. Like so many areas divided by a railroad, the people living on one side were very poor while on the other they were extremely rich. The High School's pupils came from both communities, which created a great social gulf. Don and Phil wore their long hair combed into ducktails (which style they had adopted in Shenandoah), their collars turned up, and pegged or tapered trousers. There was only one other kid in the school with ducktails, a red-headed boy called Will Hutchinson who went to Hollywood to be a movie star and was never heard of again. The three of them had to run the gauntlet from all the teachers and the other pupils. Phil recalls that 'Everybody was on your case about it. You were considered a rebel. It was the normal thing to think you were funny – you know everybody thought you were at least a little gay to have long hair.'

Phil applied to join the school choir but the combination of his appearance and his musical background meant that his involvement was short-lived. 'We just stuck out like sore thumbs and they weren't singing anything like I sang. I'd always had trouble with music teachers. I was singing professionally and maybe the teachers resented it and I had a different attitude about what we were doing.'

Things started to change during 1954/5. Phil says that he spent half his sophomore year regarded as an ugly delinquent and the other half of the year being called handsome. He and Don found that people were gradually moving over to ducktails and tapered trousers. The boys from the rich side of the track were having their trousers tailormade in the new style. Phil says wryly: 'To get your pants down from eighteen inches to thirteen was a big deal.' So, while Don and Phil didn't invent the fashions, like Elvis, they were in the forefront of the changing scene.

With all the developments in their lives it is not surprising that the change was reflected in Don and Phil's music. It was moving towards rock'n'roll. They wanted to do more songs with a beat, and they started making music that Ike had difficulty following on the guitar. Events reached a stage where the family act wasn't accepted as well as it used to be. One sponsor called Don and Phil 'bobby soxers!' They sometimes tried to sing their new music in front of strictly country audiences and didn't get as good a reception as their parents received. Cass Walker liked 'real country music' and felt that it was that type of music that sold groceries to the older people whereas Don and Phil's music appealed only to the young people.

The result was that the Everly family were fired from WROL during 1954 and were unable to get another job around Knoxville. Ike and Margaret had seen the writing on the wall and had both enrolled in classes – Ike to be a barber, Margaret to be a beautician – which they attended between their radio shows. Unfortunately they had not finished their courses when they were sacked which meant they had to re-think their lives. Don was in his last year in high school and Ike and Margaret refused to take him away at such a critical time.

They decided that they needed to conserve what cash they had so they moved out of their house into an apartment, where, to make ends meet, Ike was the cleaner/caretaker and Margaret cleaned the stairs and hallways. Both Ike and Margaret finished their studies and got jobs but it didn't make much difference financially because they had so few customers. It was a difficult time for the family and it scared Don and Phil. On the day the family was sacked, Don said, with a strange look in his eyes, 'Gee, Phil, maybe we'll starve to death.'

When things were at their lowest ebb encouragement was forthcoming, in the form of Chet Atkins. Chet had been made aware of Ike by Merle Travis because they played a similar style of guitar. They had corresponded over the years so that when Chet was booked to appear in Knoxville, Ike decided to consult him about Don and Phil. By this time, the Everlys did not have the admission price so they had to stay outside the enclosure. Ike got word to Chet that he was outside and would like to see him. Chet's memory of that day is seeing Ike the other side of the wire fence with two handsome boys standing shyly behind him. Ike explained to Chet the family's situation and, as Don and Phil had talent and some good songs, he asked whether Chet would help the boys get known in Nashville. Chet said if they went to Nashville he would listen to them and if he thought they had talent he would help them.

Both Don and Phil had been writing songs since their days in Shenandoah. Don, probably trying to fulfil his ambition to be the next Hank Williams, was the more prolific. His first song, *Lightening by Glove*, was written when he was thirteen or fourteen, which he can't now remember. 'I wrote novelty things first. I was amazed I could even write a song and then I got more serious about it.' He became a serious writer in Knoxville and it was some of these later songs that he showed to Chet Atkins when he and Phil went to Nashville.

Chet Atkins' role in Don and Phil's story cannot be over-stated. Here was an established musician, one of the famous 'Nashville Sound' which was a hallmark of so many records coming out of Nashville in the 1950s and 1960s, a record producer and performer in his own right, a busy man who took time out to help two budding entertainers. He listened to Don's songs and arranged for some of them to be recorded, the most notable being *Thou Shalt Not Steal* which was a hit for Kitty Wells in November 1954. Don says: 'I find it kinda weird that I wrote a song called *Thou Shalt Not Steal Another Man's Wife* when I was sixteen.' This song was published by Chet's company – Athens Music – but there was no signed agreement between them.

Don and Phil did not move to Nashville immediately. They were both still at school and, following their parents' policy throughout their childhood, school came first. Chet kept in touch with Don either by letter or by telephone, helping him with his song writing, suggesting ways in which songs could be structured, continuing to encourage. While still in

Knoxville, Don received his first royalty payment for *Thou Shalt Not Steal*, some $600. Although money was tight, the Everlys kept the cheque to use when Don and Phil were to move to Nashville. Some of the money was invested in stage suits; part of it enrolled them into the Musicians' Union, but that was the extent of their financial backing.

At the end of the term year of 1955, when Don graduated, the irrevocable decision was taken to abandon the family act and see whether Don and Phil would make it as the Everly Brothers. In 1976 Don declared, 'We didn't make the decision (to stop the family act). It was stopped because there was no longer a demand for it. The next logical step was try to push the Everly Brothers, and actually Phil and I could have had solo careers. When you look back over the period of time you think, "Well, gee whizz – did I

Above: Don practises with the school orchestra. He began his serious songwriting in Knoxville. Left: The bestselling Country and Western record chart of December 1954, with Don's composition at number 14.

19

really do what I wanted or was it really just what my mother and father wanted?" and it could've been.' Phil sees it another way: 'There were a lot of solo singers around and I guess we thought we'd be a little different. I also remember my father taking a stick and breaking it. He then put two sticks together and said, "You can't break that".' The fateful step was thus taken for Don and Phil to go to Nashville to try their luck. Margaret went with them, and they rented a place in Madison where she got a job. Ike stayed, for the time being, in his barber's job in Knoxville.

When Don and Phil arrived in Nashville, Chet Atkins was as good as his word and started introducing them to people in the industry, among them music publisher Troy Martin. Troy Martin's first priority was to get the boys a record contract, which was essential if they were to become known. Nashville was, and still is, very much a record-orientated society. Young hopefuls gravitate to Nashville because it is where all the major companies and publishers are based, but when Don and Phil went to Nashville most record companies still operated from New York and the music publishers were the talent scouts. The budding star was obliged to have a portfolio of his own songs which he hoped would be recorded either by himself or an established country and western act. It was not possible to succeed merely as a performer. Nashville was not a 'performing' city like New York, Los Angeles or London where you could have a career without a hit record. Without a hit record in Nashville you were nothing, and without good songs you couldn't get a recording contract.

Martin was able to fix a deal with Columbia Records. It may well have been that Columbia were interested because they liked Don's songs. But he already had a track record with *Thou Shalt Not Steal*; *Here We Are Again*, recorded by Anita Carter and Wanda Jackson, and *The Life I Have To Live* and *It Takes a Lot o'Heart* by Justin Tubb. 'I wrote *Here We Are Again*,' says Don, 'for Kitty Wells as a follow-up to *Thou Shalt Not Steal*. I thought "Well, I got a hit, let's do another one." It's a real cheating song about two married people meeting in a restaurant. It's a lot better country song I think. We got on Columbia because I had original songs. I gave half a dozen to Troy's publishing company so I could get a recording session and I went into the session with what Troy wanted.' Phil, however, feels there was another contributing factor. The audition with the head of Columbia Country Division, Don Law, took place in a hotel room with Law's girlfriend present. Phil says: 'I could give you a load of stories about how it happened but I really think it was because we sang for them in this hotel suite and she said, "Ain't they cute" and we were on records. We weren't of any consequence to anyone at that time and we wouldn't have been recording at all if it wasn't for that girl. We were lucky to get that.'

The recording contract was signed on 8 November 1955 and four sides were recorded at the Old Tulane Hotel in Nashville the next morning. The result was hardly monumental. Four country songs of Don's were recorded: *The Sun Keeps Shining/Keep a'Lovin' Me/If Her Love isn't True* and *That's the Life I Have to Live*. Don and Phil were backed by Carl Smith's Tunesmiths who had driven in from California that morning after a 2,000-mile journey. They had not even had time to go to their homes and so were in no mood to delay the session. The consequence was that all four sides were recorded in twenty-two minutes on the basis of a practice run and then a live recording. To Don and Phil it was like nothing had happened. All the struggling over the years had been aimed at getting to Nashville and making records and there, at the culmination of all their youthful ambition, they were rushed through the session. Phil felt that he sang sharp on three of them. Don remembers, 'It was hardly a session; it was so quick. We didn't have much say. We were told to go into the studio and cut as quickly as possible which is what they wanted at that time. We couldn't direct the style at all. I wanted a pedal steel guitar on it very badly but we didn't get it.' Phil joins in, 'When we left, Don and I were walking around just like you do when you first get laid, you know, like you're surprised that there is so much talk about it. In fact it was probably more like a French whorehouse, a real professional job. I asked Don, "Do you think they'll think it's a new sound with all that sharp singing I did?"'

By this time Ike had found a barber's job in Madison and had left Knoxville to join the family. Don and Phil were clearly disappointed in the session and their feelings were shared by their father when they took home the dub that evening. He felt that Don and Phil were capable of much more. Margaret, however, regarded the session as another stage in the boys' musical education. The irony was that Don and Phil, in obtaining the contract from Columbia, were obliged to record material that was pure country and not what they liked or would perform for choice. To obtain the contract in the first place Don had written the songs specifically for the country market knowing that it was the only way he and Phil would become accepted in Nashville. Columbia insisted on the style of the records and it was necessary for Don and Phil to stick to the rules. Thus Don and Phil were recording four country waltzes while Elvis Presley was singing *Heartbreak Hotel*.

Columbia issued *The Sun Keeps Shining* backed by *Keep a'Lovin' Me* on 6 February 1956. Columbia were initially enthusiastic about the record and wrote to Don and Phil expressing how pleased they were with the record and how well they thought it was going to do. It didn't take long, though, to judge the public's reaction to the record and recognise that the pessimism of Don and Phil and their father was justified. The songwriter himself said 'It was like only twelve

Opposite above: The Everly's first Nashville publicity shot. Below left: Ernest Tubb's record store in Nashville. Ernest Tubb's daughter, Elaine, was Don and Phil's manager for a time. Centre: The first Everly release came in February 1956, but was unsuccessful. Below right: Elvis Presley, on stage in Los Angeles in 1956. Don Everly pointed out that it was Elvis who 'blew it all apart'.

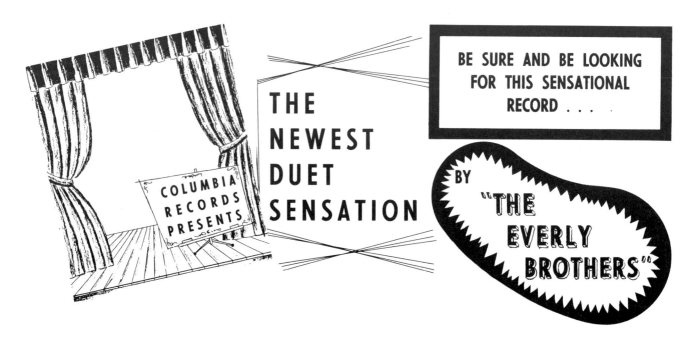

THE NEWEST DUET SENSATION

COLUMBIA RECORDS PRESENTS

BE SURE AND BE LOOKING FOR THIS SENSATIONAL RECORD . . . .

BY "THE EVERLY BROTHERS"

weeks before the publishing company was willing to give us brand new cars,' to spare them any disappointment.

As soon as they realised that the record was a flop, Don and Phil started auditioning again. Chet Atkins introduced them to Steven Scholes of RCA Victor who turned them down: 'At that time they were doing strictly country stuff, nothing that was similar to their hits so it's understandable.' That rejection was one of many the Everlys were to face over the next eighteen months. A producer at Capitol told them 'to come back in two years when your voices have matured'. Even Archie Bleyer's Cadence label turned them down only six months before *Bye Bye Love.* Don says, 'We would be going into an office or a hotel room or a studio and the head of the record company would be sitting there while we were standing. If he said he liked you, he signed you. If he didn't, he didn't. That was the opportunity we had. Phil and I were so young. We were in our teens and pretty immature really. We were considered as a kid act. There's a lot of luck involved in these things. The record business, especially at that time, was unpredictable. There was rock'n'roll, pop, country. They were all going in different directions and people weren't aware of what records were going to do. Neither was I. Basically, there was nothing Phil and I could emulate. The Louvins had the country thing covered and by then I was into pop music. My favourites were Hank Williams, Bo Diddley, Little Richard and Lefty Frizzell, and what we were doing was bringing the styles together. We had a period of just over a year when we were turned down by everybody. Either our hair was too long or we were too be-bop. But that's not too long. It's a lot longer today.'

They may not have been able to please the Nashville establishment but they were beginning to build up a following of young fans. One particular enthusiast was Elaine Tubb, daughter of the famous Ernest Tubb. Elaine (called by her nickname Scooter Bill – 'though

Above: Extracts from the publicity handouts prepared by the Everlys and Elaine Tubb to promote the second Columbia single, which ultimately was not released. There were also publicity photographs of Don and Phil released around this time, illustrated opposite.

not to my face') had first seen Don and Phil on the Joe Allison morning country TV show on which the cast was made up of established singers and people (like the Everlys at that time) trying to get on in the business. 'Just after that I ran into them at the back of the Grand Ole Opry and told them how impressed I was with them. I introduced them to my dad and got them on his midnight show and generally introduced them around to the right people.'

Elaine was eighteen years old and she became Don and Phil's manager. She arranged a song-writing contract with Hill and Range (a New York music publishing company) and negotiated a $200 advance. 'I knew Mr. Law at Columbia Records and I asked him if the second release would be coming yet. When he said yes, Don, Phil and I got together and, with the two hundred dollars, drew up an advert and got two thousand printed and then mailed them to all the disc jockeys and other people in the industry but the record never did get issued.' That record was expected to be the other two sides recorded the previous November but the lack of success of *The Sun Keeps Shining* resulted in the Everlys' recording contract being terminated. (It was thought for many years that the masters were destroyed but they appeared on an extended 12″ EP in 1981 titled 'Nashville Tennessee 9th November 1955' issued by the German label, Bear Family Records.)

Elaine Tubb believes that the only constructive thing she did was to build up Don and Phil's confidence. The whole of 1956 and the beginning of 1957 was to be the bleakest period of all for Don and Phil. Work was hard to come by and was not necessarily well paid as Phil remembers: 'If we worked five times during that

period I'd be surprised. They might offer you ten dollars which was a lot of money and you'd drive two hundred miles to earn that money and if the crowd was bad they'd give you five dollars and if the crowd was really bad you'd get nothing. We had a '52 Chevvy which we ran on the money that Dad sent down to us but in time we couldn't even keep that going and we had to start hitching to get about.'

Ike and Margaret had discovered that they couldn't keep the family going on the money they were earning in Madison. They moved up to Hammond, Indiana, where Ike, now forty-seven years old, took a job with a construction company. Margaret found a job as a beautician and between them they managed to make enough to pay their bills and send money down to Don and Phil in Nashville.

Even so, every economy had to be made. Phil completed his junior year in school but graduated by working through a correspondence course which was cheaper, and enabled Don and Phil to play any dates that might be offered. Phil highlights the difficulties: 'Don and I got down to a point where we didn't have anything to eat. What little money Mum and Dad could send we just couldn't manage to stretch out long enough. We wound down till all we had in the house was a stick of butter and half a box of cornmeal. Don made eight muffins, threw all the butter on them and we had four each. I've never tasted anything as good as that since. I started going steady with a girl named Mildred and I'd go over to her house for dinner as often as I could – at least every other night. We were always proud and even then I felt like a gigolo.' Other

"GREAT GRAN'DAD AND CHET ATKINS WERE GOOD FRIENDS" MY GREAT-GRAND CHILDREN WILL BOAST
Merle Travis '65

friends, like Chet Atkins, would help when they could, as Don fondly remembers: 'Chet gave me so much encouragement. I could always phone him or see him at the radio stations or call in at his home for a coffee and pie.'

Throughout all the hardships Elaine would be 'introducing them to the right people, who would have confidence in them', including bass player Floyd 'Lightning' Chance: 'I believed in them. People said their appearance was wrong with their long hair and their sound was wrong, but I liked it. Their harmonies were good and they were different. Good singers are a dime a dozen, it's those with style that make it, and Don and Phil had a lot of style. They were developing the music, and the resentment towards them came from the old timers, the basic three chord types who wanted to stick with things as they were.' Lightning's remarks meant a great deal to Don and Phil because they came from a professional who worked at the shrine of all country musicians, the Grand Ole Opry.

The Grand Ole Opry was staged at the Ryman Auditorium on 5th Avenue North in Nashville. There were shows on both Friday and Saturday nights but it was the Saturday show that was broadcast live on WSM radio station. Every budding musician would gravitate to the auditorium in the hope of getting noticed. Phil remembers: 'Every Friday and Saturday night we went down to WSM and hung out in the alley where the entertainers walked out of the Ryman Auditorium across to Tootsies which was a beer joint. All the deals were done in that alley. That's where you got noticed. We were known, and as the stars came out some would say "Hello". Chet Atkins would say "Hello" but you couldn't bother him, but you were there. You were still alive.'

Behind the Ryman Auditorium Don met a young secretary called Sue Ingraham and they started dating. In view of Don's tight cash position they spent their times together either at home where Don and Phil

Above left: *The Ryman Auditorium, Nashville, for many years the home of the Grand Ole Opry.* Above right: *Chet Atkins (left) and Merle Travis.* Opposite above: *Tootsies Lounge is the building second from the left along Nashville's Broadway.* Below: *Don gazes at his first wife, Sue Ingraham. They met behind the Ryman Auditorium and eloped across the county line to Georgia to be married.*

would play and sing, or in coffee bars. George Hamilton remembers that the first time he met Don was in a coffee bar: 'I was in the Clarkson Hotel Coffee Shop and someone played my record A Rose and a Baby Ruth on the juke box and as there was only a young couple sitting by themselves, I went over and introduced myself and thanked them for playing my record. A couple of years later I was with the Everly Brothers, Don sat smiling at me in a strange way and said, "Don't you remember me?" He told me he was the fella and the girl with him was Sue.'

Only a short time was to elapse before Don and Sue felt that they had to get married despite the uncertain future. Tennessee State Law insisted that parental consent was necessary for anyone under the age of twenty-one to marry. Don and Sue didn't want to approach their parents so they decided to elope across the county line into Georgia. They were married in Ringo on 22 November 1956, Phil giving Don $5 to buy the licence: 'It's not true to say I lent Don money. If I gave him five dollars it is because it was jointly owned and it was just in my pocket.' The immediate practical result of the marriage was that Sue moved in with Don and Phil and, by keeping her secretarial job, was able to help cover the day-to-day costs.

In October of 1956 Don and Phil had signed Eddie Crandell as their manager. He also handled Marty Robbins. Crandall was successful and liked Don and Phil, although Phil does not regard him as the kindest man in the world. He criticised their appearance, saying that they would not be successful while they wore

ducktails, tapered trousers and chartreuse green shirts all of which were considered effeminate by and unacceptable to the influential people in Nashville. Others were more forthright, as Phil remembers: 'Everyone thought we looked peculiar. We got a lot of hassle about it. They didn't just say, "You're not gonna make it"; it was much worse. They'd say, "You're gonna get arrested, you're really out of it".' Despite their manager's advice, Don and Phil decided to resist the pressure to change even though it affected the amount of bookings Crandall was able to get for them.

They continued to try for a recording contract, but without success. Even a demonstration tape sent to Cadence, the small independent New York company, had been rejected. Phil says: 'Eddie Crandall had a girlfriend who was about a year older than Don, and seemed to like us. She was quite nice and I always fancied her. She knew someone with a studio and arranged for us to record this audition tape. After we'd done the tape she explained to him that we didn't have the money. How she sorted it out I'll never know but she did. When we came out we found the police had towed our car away and that it would cost fifteen dollars to get it back. She then went back to the guy and got him to lend us the money. An amazing woman. The tape was sent to Archie Bleyer who promptly rejected it. That devastated us.'

Their continued failure was making Don and Phil feel they should give up and move back with their parents who had relocated to Chicago. But they still pursued every chance of a job and, early in 1957, they were asked by Dick MacAlpine to audition for a TV show. After the audition, MacAlpine was enthusiastic about the show and wanted to use Don and Phil. Every time they contacted him he said, 'It will be put together in a couple of weeks' and things staggered along for about three months without anything happening. The delay was fortuitous because the big break was just around the corner. Had it not been for MacAlpine and his promise the Everlys would have left Nashville. As it was, they were about to break upon an unsuspecting world.

The Everlys' early experiences in Nashville, their tenacity and commitment, together with the support of their parents, are an example to every budding musician. Phil says: 'Anyone who wants to succeed in this industry must have the tenacity to stand out on your own and have that support to survive. We weren't always *the* Everly Brothers – we were the Everly Brothers. You have to drive for it if you want it. You've got to work your tail off and believe in yourself.'

That Don and Phil did survive has much to do with the complementary personalities of their parents who gave Don and Phil the right attitudes towards their profession. Every person who has been connected with Ike and Margaret has described them as being devoted to their boys, and the family was regarded as being close knit. Merl Douglas says: 'Everything Ike and Margaret did was for their kids – they sacrificed themselves so that the boys could get on.' Chet Atkins adds: 'They were a really handsome couple which is probably why Don and Phil turned out as well as they did.' Merle Travis remembers: 'I have love for the Everlys as dear friends and Margaret as a great lady. Ike and Margaret worked so hard for their boys and were so proud of the success they achieved.' Warren Neilson contributes: 'Ike was a tremendously talented musician who was in love with music. That family show that success can happen to nice people. Ike was the great thing to the boys, they idolised him. There was plenty of love in that family and not much else. The drive came from Margaret. Her attitude was that "If you have that much talent you should make money". She used to say "We're going to be successful come heck or highwater".'

Ike is described as being a laid-back type of person. As long as he was able to play guitar he was happy. He had little personal ambition. He was, in Merl Douglas's opinion, 'a fine gentleman and performer with a personality that bubbled over. He really made you laugh.' Phil, in a 1959 article, described his father as 'the world's most easy-going man. When he makes up his mind it's not that he changes it easily but instead of making a big incident he'll step back to avoid an argument.' Ike would always be prepared to look after people less fortunate than himself. There would always be some musician needing help. Merl Douglas says 'I left KMA a couple of times to take different jobs and once I came up to Shenandoah to try and get a job. The trip took the last dollars I had and there was no job for me. I had to get back to Missouri but the cost of the coach was seven or eight dollars. I asked Ike if he could lend me the money but all he had was a cheque for forty-eight dollars and he gave me that. That man gave me his last cheque – that's the kind of man he was.' Don regards his father as his greatest influence: 'He taught me how to play guitar. He really discouraged me from learning to play the way he did. He taught me how to sing and keep time. He was *the* influence really.'

Margaret was the exact opposite to Ike. She was always optimistic, regardless of the circumstances, whereas Ike would get despondent if things weren't going well. Margaret was the businesslike member of the family. It was her dream to have a family show, and it was she who decided when to move from KMA to KFNF and when it was time to leave Shenandoah. Felice Bryant, who remains a close friend of Margaret, describes her as 'the balls of that act. She was ambitious for the boys, she had the push and desire to be successful.' Ike Everly said of Margaret: 'I was often ready to give up but Margaret always had that faith. She always had more faith than any one person I ever knew. Don and Phil would get disgusted and I would too – but Margaret would say "It's getting good now. It just can't miss. Don and Phil are getting better every day. They are going to be great stars one day."'

Phil says: 'Mother, in the tradition of southern women, had a continually positive attitude. I never considered anything negatively because my mother would always say, "Everything's going to be A", and

she was really the mainstay in the household in that respect. It was like if you had a hole in your pants it was the perfect place to have a hole. As I got older I became more conscious that she was telling me that to keep me with a positive attitude. It became irritating because you'd say ''It's still a hole''. So while Dad instilled the music into us, Mother instilled this positive attitude in me so that at eighteen, when we

Above: Don and Phil, aged nineteen and seventeen, their faces full of youthful optimism.

recorded *Bye Bye Love*, I didn't even think in terms of, ''Well, this record might not make it.'' I never considered that it would make it either. It just seemed okay. Things seemed all right and that attitude has been an important aspect of my life.'

27

ELVIS-STYLE EVERLYS

EVERLY BROTHERS: Bye Bye, Love/ I Wonder If I Care As Much (London 45-HLA8440).

HERE'S a release that offers two Elvis Presleys for the price of one!

The Everly Brothers affect the same stuttering, tortured style as Elvis—a factor that has undoubtedly helped their way to the top of the American best-seller list.

"Bye Bye, Love" is a disc that should soon repeat its Stateside success here. The song has all the ingredients necessary for a hit, and the Brothers give it a beaty rendering that is bound to click with the blue-jean and pony-tail element.

The Brothers are in their most maudlin mood on the reverse.

BEST SELLING POP RECORDS IN THE U.S.

Last Week	This Week		
1	1	All Shook Up	Elvis Presley
4	2	Love Letters In The Sand/ Bernardine	Pat Boone
3	3	School Day	Chuck Berry
2	4	Little Darlin'	Diamonds
5	5	White Sport Coat	Marty Robbins
8	6	So Rare	Jimmy Dorsey
7	7	I'm Walkin' / A Teenager's Romance	Ricky Nelson
10	8	Come Go With Me	Del Vikings
6	9	Gone	Ferlin Husky
8	10	Round And Round	Perry Como
11	11	Dark Moon	Gale Storm
12	12	Dark Moon	Bonnie Guitar
13	13	Rock-A-Billy	Guy Mitchell
20	14	Four Walls	Jim Reeves
—	15	Start Movin'	Sal Mineo
16	16	Young Blood/Searchin'	Coasters
—	17	Bye Bye Love	Everly Brothers
—	18	It's Not For Me To Say	Johnny Mathis
18	19	Fabulous	Charlie Gracie
14	20	Party Doll	Buddy Knox

The American charts are published by courtesy of "Billboard"

3
Bye Bye Love

While Dick MacAlpine continued to postpone the TV series, Don and Phil decided they couldn't stay in Nashville any longer and would go to Chicago to get work in the hope that someone would pick up their songs.

They were preparing to leave when a friend and fellow performer, suggested that they go to see his publisher, Hal Smith: 'I was representing Dave Rich who mentioned that he knew the Everlys on a number of occasions and thought they would be very good and after a while I said, "Okay, arrange for them to come and see me". One morning they came in and I recognised them straight away. It transpired they lived a couple of blocks down the street and I used to pass them on my way to work as they hitched into town. They were very impressive. I explained that I was in music publishing and didn't have the wherewithal to organise a recording session. In those days we had no real organisation in Nashville and we were obliged to do all our recording with the companies back east. I told them that there was only one person I knew of who had the backing that they would need and that was Wesley Rose and that if they liked I would 'phone him while they were in the office. This I did and I explained to Wesley how good I thought the Everlys were and were worth a record contract. He said that if I thought that way it was okay to send the boys over.'

Wesley Rose was, and still is, head of Acuff Rose Music Publishing Company, the largest music publisher in Nashville. Although the company had a strong base, notably from the royalties from the Hank Williams' catalogue, Wesley was acutely aware of the benefits of developing artists, and was one of the first publishers to make master records for leasing to record companies as an alternative to promoting an Acuff Rose song or artist. He even had his own label – Hickory Records.

Of that first meeting with the Everlys, Wesley Rose says, 'About a year prior to that meeting people had been trying to have me talk to the Everly Brothers but I believed they were under contract to somebody else and I never see anyone that's under contract. Hal phoned me and told me the boys were going to leave town and go home to their parents in Chicago. I said "Are they under contract?" and he said, "No." I said, "If you have them with you send them over." They

Opposite page: *Archie Bleyer presents gold records to the Everly Brothers.* Right: *The scene in the recording studios with Chet Atkins seated in the centre.*

29

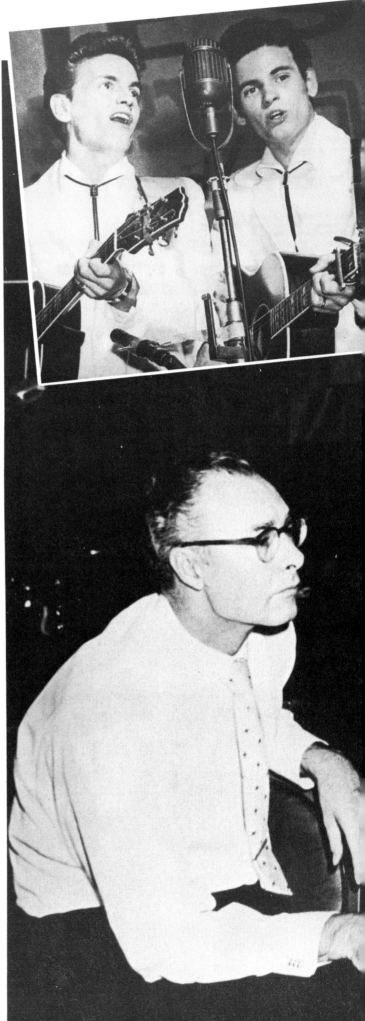

came into the office and I was very impressed with them. The material they were writing was good, their harmony was quite unique and there was a magnetism about the way they interpreted lyrics. Their style of guitar playing was quite out of the ordinary and I felt we really had something. We put them in the studio to cut a demonstration tape and after I heard it I told them to cancel those tickets to Chicago.'

Wesley Rose immediately contacted Archie Bleyer, with whom he had been talking for some time trying to get him involved in the country field, and recommended that Cadence give a contract to the Everlys. Archie remembered the earlier tape that had been submitted and said that he was not too impressed. Wesley replied by suggesting that he send a tape to New York for consideration. This time Archie *was* impressed and agreed to sign up Don and Phil for a three-year recording contract. The Everlys were to spearhead Cadence's move into the country market along with two other established country acts recommended by Wesley Rose, a country fiddler called Gordon Terry and Johnny Cash's sister-in-law, Anita Carter.

Cadence Records was one of a multitude of small independent record companies operating in the United States during the 1950s. Many are now mentioned in hallowed terms when the development of rock'n'roll is being discussed. Cadence was in a slightly different position to the other independents because unlike Sam Phillips' Sun label it did not rely on one type of music for its catalogue. The reason for the difference must be in the label owner.

Archie Bleyer was born on 12 June 1909. His life had

Above left: With Wesley Rose, their manager in the 1950s and right: on stage at the Grand Ole Opry, in classic stage outfits. Opposite: Don and Phil in the studios with Archie Bleyer, during the recording of Bye Bye Love.

30

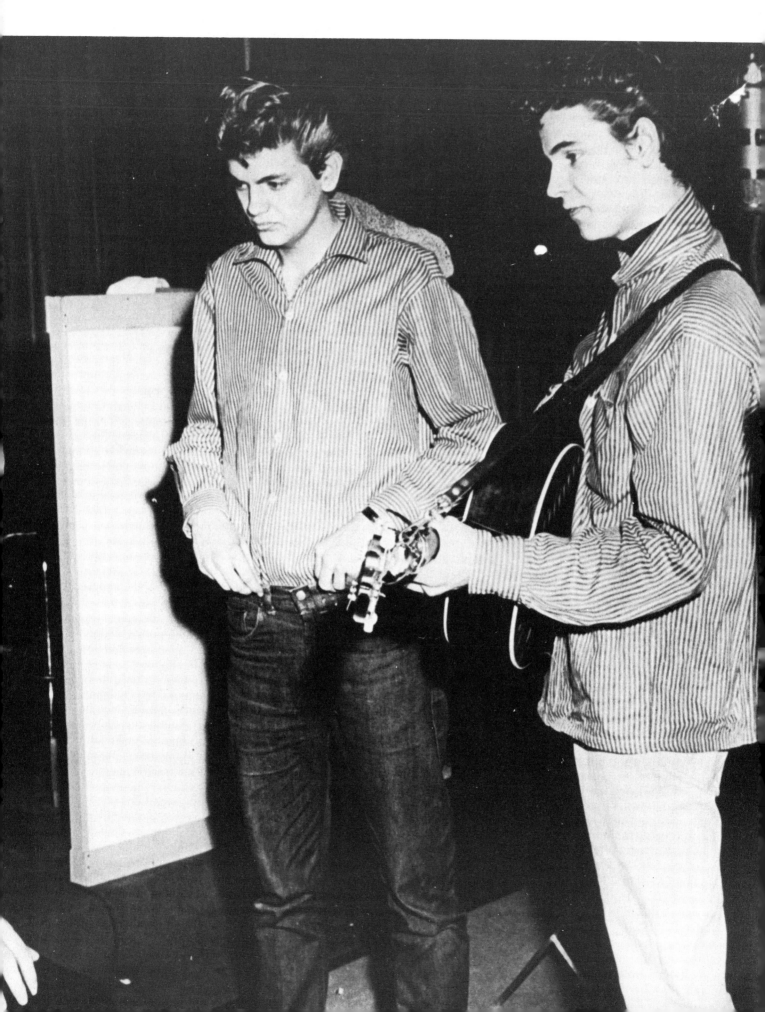

been spent in show business. He was a band leader, a producer and, in the early 1950s, musical director of the prestigious Arthur Godfrey TV show. He formed Cadence Records in 1953: 'Due to a very large extent to the success of Julius La Rosa on the Arthur Godfrey show. Julius used to receive a lot of mail while on the show asking, "When are you going to record?". I felt so strongly in the potential of Julius that I started the company and we released two of the songs that he used to sing on the show and we had a good hit on our hands.'' Godfrey and Bleyer parted company about that time and Archie worked full-time looking for acts that would sell records. He had an extremely good ear for a hit record and consequently the list of artists which qualified for gold records is varied. Apart from Julius La Rosa there were the Chordettes, Bill Hayes (*The Ballad of Davy Crockett*), Archie Bleyer himself, Andy Williams, Johnny Tillotson, Eddie Hodges, the Everlys (who were to earn seven gold records during their time with the label) and finally the LP *The First Family*, a satirical look at the Kennedys by Vaughn Meader.

It is interesting to consider why a perceptive man like Archie Bleyer should turn down the Everlys and then sign them six months later. It could be that Wesley Rose's recommendation carried weight or the demonstration tape was that much better. It could well have been that there was generally a greater awareness of rock'n'roll. The term rock'n'roll was coined by Alan Freed, a New York disc jockey, to describe the beat music that was attracting the young kids of America. Elvis Presley was clearly the first to reach a wide audience. His full impact began in 1956 and Phil is quick to give Elvis a great deal of credit: 'We were constantly getting all this hassle about our music and our appearance and then Elvis Presley came along and blew it all apart.' Presley's ability to combine the raw energy of black rhythm and blues and white country music had a charismatic effect on the young listeners he was singing to. Phil says: 'I was a junior in high school when I first became aware of Elvis Presley. I didn't hear him until one day the prettiest girl in my class, you know the one with the best body and the tightest skirt, brought in one of his LPs. When I heard that record I knew straight away what he was doing. We'd been in Nashville a year by then and getting nowhere and we went down to the Country Music Awards and all of a sudden if you had long hair you were a star. They didn't know who you were but you couldn't get into the place without getting mobbed. There were pockets all around the country – Holly, Buddy Knox and Jimmy Bowen in Texas; Cochrane on the West Coast; Gene Vincent in Philadelphia; Don and I in Nashville. We each had our own influences. They were there before Elvis came along so he didn't influence us but his charisma meant that the kids became switched on to what others were doing. I had great respect for him. Thank God he knocked the door down. If he hadn't maybe nobody would've made it.'

Once they had a recording contract arranged it was necessary for Don and Phil to organise their song-writing contract. They were still signed to Hill and Range but felt that they would do better with a company operating out of Nashville. Wesley Rose was also keen to sign up the young men who had so impressed him. Elaine Tubb persuaded her father to contact Hill and Range and he was successful in arranging for the contract to be cancelled.

The recording contract was finally signed on 21 February 1957 and, with the business side settled, a recording session was quickly arranged for 4 March. Archie Bleyer flew to Nashville to meet all the artists he had signed in order to manage their first sessions. When Wesley Rose had been trying to convince Archie to enter the country market, he had sent a portfolio of songs penned by various Acuff Rose staff writers. Among the songs was *Bye Bye Love*, written by husband and wife team Boudleaux and Felice Bryant. The song had been written eight months before and had been turned down by thirty artists. Archie Bleyer liked the song and was convinced that it was hit material. He had tried it in rehearsals with several of the acts on Cadence but it didn't seem to work out. Archie was determined to persevere with the song and included it among those he would show his country acts.

Meetings were arranged for Bleyer to meet the artists to discuss material the day before the sessions were to take place. It was natural for the Acuff Rose staff writers to be present and Boudleaux Bryant was among them. Gordon Terry was regarded as the big star of the three acts, so he met Bleyer in the morning to have the pick of the material. When Terry heard *Bye Bye Love* he rejected it and asked if the Bryants had anything stronger. Don and Phil met Archie Bleyer and Boudleaux Bryant for the first time that afternoon. It is highly likely that *Bye Bye Love* was the only song they heard during that session. Don Everly recalls: 'They sang *Bye Bye Love* to me. At that point I wasn't trying to pick out a hit song. I was thinking about the recording money that I was going to get from the

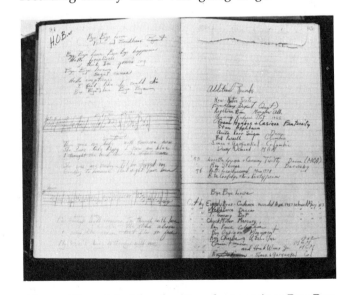

Above: The original handwritten sheet music to Bye Bye Love *by Felice and Boudleaux Bryant.*

session. I was probably more interested in doing my own material but I didn't say that. It isn't the kinda thing you pipe up and say when you're twenty years old.' Phil agrees: 'We went into cut for the sixty-four dollar session fee – that's what I wanted. A quick sixty-four dollars to buy some hamburgers. We had very little money and I think we would've recorded anything.'

It was decided that the next day the Everlys would record *Bye Bye Love* and one of Don's songs, *I Wonder if I Care as Much*. That they were restricting the session to two songs was unusual as the union would allow up to four songs to be recorded in a three-hour session. Archie Bleyer had strong views on the subject: 'It was my view that you were lucky enough to find one song that was of hit potential so I made it a rule that we would only record two songs at each session.' This policy meant that apart from the hastily recorded filler tracks on the Everlys' first album, and the special circumstances surrounding the *Songs Our Daddy Taught Us* album, all their recorded output during the Cadence period was aimed at the singles market. For the session Don and Phil were to have the cream of Nashville's session men working. The full line up was: guitars: Chet Atkins, Ray Edenton, James Clayton Day; stand up bass: Floyd 'Lightning' Chance; drums: Buddy Harman. These supporting musicians, with the exception of Buddy Harman (at that particular time), were regulars on the Grand Ole Opry. They were, with Floyd Cramer and Hank Garland who played on the later Everly sessions, the instigators of the famous Nashville Sound. We can only wonder how Don and Phil were feeling when they came into the session. Memories of that session are now very dim because, as Lightning Chance says: 'At the time we didn't realise we were making history. We were just enjoying ourselves.' For all that, he recalls that Don and Phil were 'shy, timid and introverted' while Buddy Harman remembers them as a 'couple of scared kids'.

One of the strengths of the record is its introduction. Boudleaux Bryant says: 'We had been working on the session for some time and although the boys were singing the song really well there seemed to be something missing. We were having a break and Don started strumming something which made me listen. I asked him to repeat the phrase twice. Don then did it in another tempo and I said, "That's it, put that on as the introduction".' Phil remembers: 'The introduction was off a song Don had written called *Give Me A Future* which we had used on the audition for Wesley, strangely enough. It wasn't until that introduction went on that the song came alive. It made people pay attention to it and I think it was that aspect that made it happen.'

The reaction of Don and Phil after the session differed from everyone else's. Don: 'The success of *Bye Bye Love* was a big surprise to Archie Bleyer, Wesley Rose and the Everly Brothers. I don't think anyone realised the potential.' Phil: 'I was just stumbling along. It was all a mystery to me. *Bye Bye Love* was the next project we had to keep us in the industry. I knew

that making music was better than working all day. Chet Atkins: 'I had a good feeling about the record. I thought we had a hit.' Felice Bryant: 'We went to the Grand Ole Opry the weekend after the song was recorded and there was a lot of talk about the session. It had got round that something special had been recorded.' Archie Bleyer: 'When we finished the session I was convinced that this was a hit.'

Coming away from the session Boudleaux gave Don and Phil a lift home and they invited him in. He was shocked when they told him that their financial situation was so desperate, that the only food in the house was a can of chilli. They had done little work for the best part of a year but, with the help of a friend of Phil's, Pat Kelly, they were booked on a Bill Monroe 'Grand Ole Opry' tent show being promoted by Pat's father. The tour was the biggest the Everlys had ever been involved in and lasted three weeks through Mississippi, Alabama and Florida for which they were paid $90 a week. 'We thought it was hot stuff,' Phil remembers. 'We'd only gotten the work because Pat, who was a rock'n'roll singer on the tour, had talked his father into it. It was a real carny operation. The stage was just a platform and back stage was like outside the tent. This was in the south in the 1950s. It was fifty cents to get in and another quarter to sit in the segregated part, otherwise you'd have to sit with the blacks and so to make sure you got seventy-five cents from every white there were three or four black workers with the carny and they would sit in the black section so that nobody sat there. The first five rows would fill up with all the rough kids in town because they threatened to cut the tent down unless you let them in free. Don and I played the country section and then they charged everybody another quarter to see the rock'n'roll show which was all of us again doing rock'n'roll songs. It was very hard to put over. Most of the time you rolled at night, "hit and run" they call it, sleeping in the limos. If we didn't sleep in the cars

Below: *Chet Atkins teaches Don a chord, while Phil and Archie Bleyer look on.*

we'd be in real seedy places where you wouldn't want to use the toilet.'

Although Eddie Crandall had had little success getting bookings for Don and Phil, the tent show was an indication that things were on the upturn, irrespective of a hit record, as Don recalls: 'At the time of the record we were beginning to get noticed a bit. We were starting to work the road and that would've happened without the record. I wasn't prepared for anything else. For five or six years I had been working towards being a songwriter and performer. There was nothing else I thought about doing or could do.' Immediately they returned from the Bill Monroe tour and before the record really took off, they found themselves booked on a similar Tom Kelly tour, headlined by Brenda Lee and George Jones.

While on the tour they heard that Webb Pierce had covered *Bye Bye Love*. The story goes that Pierce heard the Everlys record on his car radio as he was driving in for a session and had asked for a copy of the song and had then recorded it straight away. Pierce was a big country star in Nashville at the time and had a record of some twenty-four hits in a row. Mel Tillis, who was on the tour with Don and Phil, had suffered as a performer because Pierce had regularly covered his songs and when he heard Pierce had recorded *Bye Bye Love* he said: 'Well, that's it boys.' This time, though, Pierce was not going to have the bigger seller. His version sold well, but it was the Everlys' version that was really catching on.

Rumours began to circulate that their record was beginning to make it but it was some surprise to the brothers when they got back to Nashville to hear that their record was at Number Seven in the country charts on its way to the very top. The record was also beginning to receive attention on the pop stations, due to Archie Bleyer having contacted twenty-five of the top disc jockeys in the country. He explains: 'Although we did sign the Everlys as a country act, the minute we were through with the record I felt very strongly that the Everlys could become a pop act. They had so many non-country influences in their music. I was convinced that we had a hit but knew that it would be difficult to get the record played by the pop jockeys. I called up the top jockeys and told them the story about the Everlys and this record we had cut. I said, "This is not a 'please play my record' call. If you flip over it play it, otherwise throw it in the waste basket."'

At that time Bill Randall was probably one of the most influential DJs in the United States. He had 'discovered' Gene Vincent and had been one of the first to play Elvis Presley records. He worked in Cleveland, Ohio, with his radio programme and TV show. He played *Bye Bye Love* and there was such strong audience reaction that he asked if the Everlys could make an appearance on his TV show.

Two days after their return from the Brenda Lee tour, Don and Phil were on a Greyhound bus to Cleveland for their first major TV appearance. Archie Bleyer and his wife flew down from New York and Archie remembers Phil saying: 'If this record does a little

something, I'm going to get me a new guitar case.'

The record was gathering pace. It entered the Billboard Top 100 pop chart on 15 May 1957 and interest in the Everlys was immediate. The first sign Phil noticed that things were happening was when he had thumbed his way over to his girlfriend's house to find a message waiting for him. Ed Sullivan's office had called! The change from playing tent shows in the deep south to being contacted by Ed Sullivan occurred over a matter of days and was clear evidence that the entertainment machine was oiling itself for a new phenomenon. 'When *Bye Bye Love* was successful the act was taken over immediately,' recalls Don. 'The first thing they wanted to do was to take you and dress you and put you in a brand-new car which, of course, was the thing that you want when you're very young and worked all your life for just those things. So when it's offered to you it's very tempting.' Phil says: 'We had just come back from the tent show where we were making very little money. They gave us five thousand dollar advances and the money for a '57 Oldsmobile and we put the two guitars inside and drove out of Nashville to St. Louis, Missouri, to start a promotional tour with Johnny Cash. We were on our way.'

Bye Bye Love was not the first record to cross over from the country to the pop charts but its success did cause some misgivings for Wesley Rose. Archie Bleyer remembers: 'I know that for a while Wesley Rose was unhappy at the record being such a big hit in the pop field as he felt a country artist had a better chance of lasting. There was an occasion when I was talking to Wesley and Boudleaux and I said to Wesley "Look, the public has made the decision for us now".'

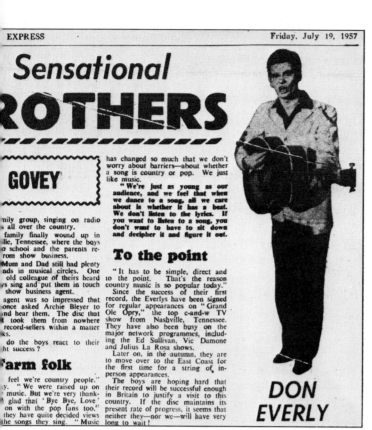

EXPRESS   Friday, July 19, 1957

Sensational
ROTHERS

GOVEY

mily group, singing on radio
all over the country.
family finally wound up in
lle, Tennessee, where the boys
o school and the parents re-
rom show business.

Mum and Dad still had plenty
nds in musical circles. One
old colleague of theirs heard
vs sing and put them in touch
show business agent.

agent was so impressed that
once asked Archie Bleyer to
nd hear them. The disc that
took them from nowhere
record-sellers within a matter
ks.

do the boys react to their
ht success ?

'arm folk

feel we're country people."
y. "We were raised up on
music. But we're very thank-
glad that 'Bye Bye, Love'
on with the pop fans too."
they have quite decided views
the songs they sing. "Music

has changed so much that we don't
worry about barriers—about whether
a song is country or pop. We just
like music.

"We're just as young as our
audience, and we feel that when
we dance to a song, all we care
about is whether it has a beat.
We don't listen to the lyrics. If
you want to listen to a song, you
don't want to have to sit down
and decipher it and figure it out.

To the point

"It has to be simple, direct and
to the point. That's the reason
country music is so popular today."

Since the success of their first
record, the Everlys have been signed
for regular appearances on " Grand
Ole Opry," the top c-and-w TV
show from Nashville, Tennessee.
They have also been busy on the
major network programmes, including the Ed Sullivan, Vic Damone
and Julius La Rosa shows.

Later on, in the autumn, they are
to move over to the East Coast for
the first time for a string of, in-
person appearances.

The boys are hoping hard that
their record will be successful enough
in Britain to justify a visit to this
country. If the disc maintains its
present rate of progress, it seems that
neither they—nor we—will have very
long to wait !

DON EVERLY

Of all their years in the business the Everlys'
remembrances of their most successful period are their
haziest. From doing little or no work, they were
catapulted into a hectic round of recording sessions,
package tours, TV and radio appearances. After the
promotional tour with Johnny Cash, *Bye Bye Love*
began to make headway in the pop charts; by then it
was high in the country music Top Ten with the result
that Don and Phil would no longer be bottom of the
bill. The success of the record meant that they were
able to fulfil their ambition to play on the Grand Ole
Opry. They first appeared at the Ryman Auditorium
on the 'Friday Night at the WSM Frolics' on 10 May
and the audience response was so great that they were
immediately booked to appear on the Grand Ole Opry
the next night, where once again they received a great
ovation after singing *Bye Bye Love*. Lightning Chance
backed the Everlys on the Opry shows and remembers
that 'they were timid and shy. The people were stamp-
ing and screaming for more while Don and Phil tried to
get off stage as quickly as possible. I blocked Don
getting off on one side while Ray Edenton stopped Phil
and I whispered to Don, "Get out there and milk
them".'

The Nashville press gave the Everlys rave reviews,
and W. D. Kirkpatrick, General Director of the Opry,
recognising their potential, signed them up as Opry
regulars. This meant they were obliged to appear at
the Opry one weekend out of four. Their first appearances under this arrangement took place on 1 June
1957. Also on the bill that night was their father's good
friend, Merle Travis, who flew in from California for
the show: 'They sounded so fresh and looked real

good that I can understand why the country liked
them. To me, I felt like an uncle to them. I remember
the time they were born and I remember them growing
up so it was good for me to see them being so successful.'

The Everlys' period as Opry regulars lasted only two
years; by 1959 they had outgrown Nashville and could
no longer fit regular Opry appearances into their busy
schedule. Don remains proud of being an Opry regular: 'When I was little Donnie my ambition was to be
on the Grand Ole Opry and when I had just turned
twenty I made it. It was one of my biggest thrills.
Everything after that was gravy as far as ambition was
concerned.'

When they became regulars Don and Phil broke two
Opry traditions. They appeared in suits rather than
the bright 'cowboy' clothes worn by most country acts.
This was not an intended swipe at convention; in fact
they only owned one outfit each. Breaking the other
tradition was to have far-reaching effects. Don and
Phil were the first act at the Opry to use drums on
stage. Buddy Harman backed them at first with just a
snare drum, eventually with a full drum kit. Until that
time drums had not been considered necessary to
country music. Harman had worked extensively in big
bands but, as the influence of that music waned, Harman found himself in Nashville doing session work
and using the snare drum to fill out the backing. Once
the use of drums became accepted he was able to
develop it so that drums contributed to the sound of
the record. Harman is quick to give Don and Phil credit
for introducing and developing the use of drums in
Nashville.

While being signed to the Opry as regulars meant
that the Everlys were now regarded as established
country performers, the entry of *Bye Bye Love* in the
pop charts opened up country-wide interest in the
duo. Within a week of signing for the Opry, Don and
Phil were contracted to appear on five networked TV
shows, including three prestigious Ed Sullivan TV
shows. It was clear by this time that their career was
going to need direction. Wesley Rose remembers:
'They started to get big and Archie Bleyer said, "They
are going to need managing and it will have to be
someone they can live with. The kids trust you." So I
talked to Don and Phil and they were happy with the
set-up. It took time to run the publishing company and
so forth and when we got into it we got carried away. It
was very exciting. It taught me something about managing. It taught me that there is more to the business
than just staying in an office – and I've always thought
international. So we directed the Everly Brothers
around the world and I sort of adopted them as my
sons which, I would say, shouldn't be done. It was
very exciting because we were doing things at that
time.' To handle the practical side of touring Wesley's

Following pages: Left to right: *A Cadence Records advertisement; Don and Phil on stage in 1960; the Everlys performing on stage at the renowned Ryman Auditorium in
Nashville.*

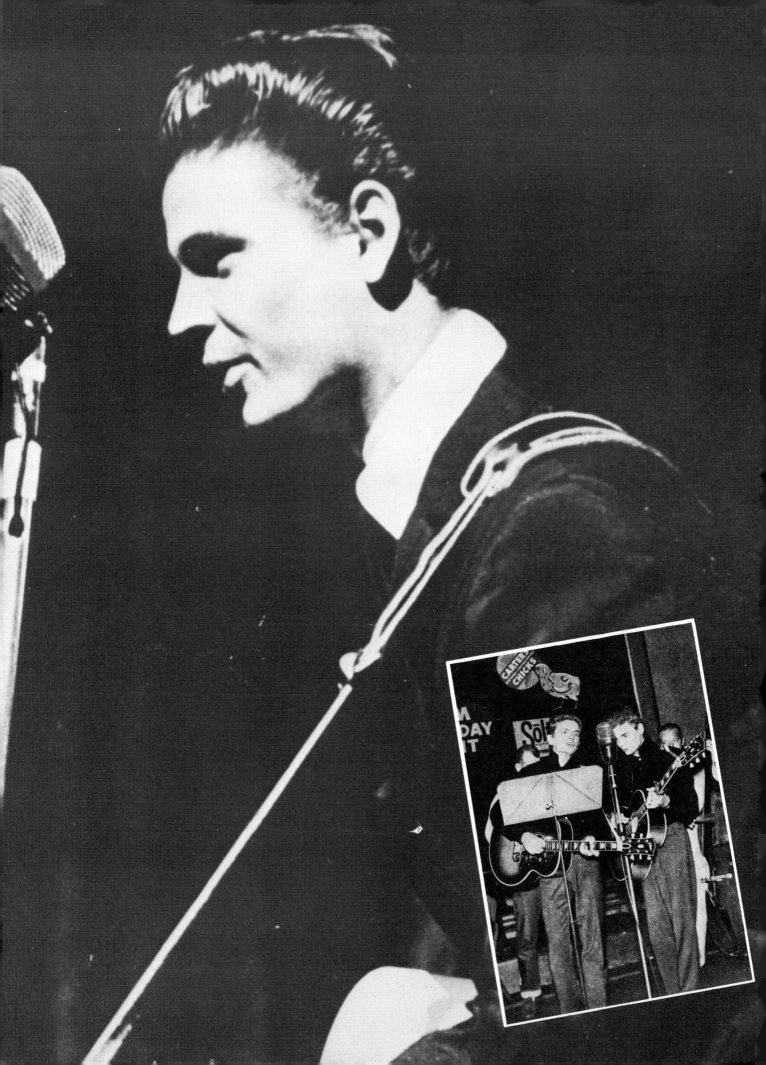

brother, Lester, was appointed road manager, a position he was to hold right through to 1961.

The success of *Bye Bye Love* also earned Don and Phil their first nationwide tour which was arranged by Alan Freed. The July tour, Alan Freed's Summer Festival, was headlined by Lavern Baker, Chuck Berry and Fats Domino but, like all Freed tours, was packed with acts which were 'hot' at that particular time. Of the sixteen acts, the majority were coloured; only Don and Phil and Teddy Randazzo were white and they appeared low on the bill. The tour was typical of many Don and Phil were to join during the 1950s. At that time, the record companies regarded tours as the best way of achieving necessary exposure, and promotion for the artist's latest material. Each act would perform for about ten minutes, running through two or three numbers. The most famous tours were arranged by

PROGRAM
LA VERN BAKER
CLYDE McPHATTER
CHUCK BERRY
THE TEENAGERS
featuring FRANKIE LYMON
THE MOONGLOWS
BIG JOE TURNER
SCREAMIN' JAY HAWKINS
JODIE SANDS
LEWIS LYMON
and TEEN CHORDS
EVERLY BROTHERS
JOHNNIE and JOE
TEDDY RANDAZZO
THE DUBS
ALAN FREED
AND HIS
ROCK 'N ROLL
ORCHESTRA
featuring
SAM "The Man" TAYLOR
BIG AL SEARS
PANAMA FRANCIS

Alan Freed, Irving Feld and later Dick Clark (of American Bandstand fame) and were extensive, usually running for fifty, sixty or even ninety consecutive days, playing the big cities across the United States.

In retrospect, the greatest value to come from these mammoth tours were the friendships and interchange of ideas among the artists. There could be over 100 people on those tours, all in their late teens and early twenties, both black and white, who would spend the many hours between dates singing and playing together on the tour buses and even sharing a changing room.

Those formative years created the foundation upon which the rock industry of today was built. There was little colour prejudice among the artists, although many came from the southern states, and generally the acts got on well together despite spending up to three months at a stretch in confining circumstances on the road. Phil recalls: 'We'd all be on the same bus except the headliners who travelled independently. We slept where we could. Paul Anka and Frankie Lymon were the ones that were small enough to sleep up in the racks. We were doing one-nighters and motoring constantly but it was fun all the time. We were young and strong.'

Firm friendships were established as they drank and gambled together, although Phil is quick to point out: 'Everybody drank a bit but there wasn't too much drunkenness on the road. The basic policy of most rockers was that you drank after the show.' Card and dice games whiled away the time, and Phil had to be given a budget of $20 a day by Lester Rose because he kept losing all his money. There were a lot of high spirits, and stories abound of jokes played on each other. Like Paul Anka putting ice cubes in Don and Phil's beds and, much later, Bobby Vee arranging a press conference for them at four o'clock in the morning. Extrovert Phil regards the years of the tours as the golden period of rock'n'roll when the artists enjoyed just making music, and big business had not seen the full potential of the new phenomenon: 'You got paid a lot less. The first tour we went on was two hundred dollars a night. And that went on until, after about a year, we worked up to about two thousand dollars. But we were fortunate enough to have enough hit records. In those days they talked about you being a one-record act, so being a star wasn't full of money. But most of your money was from record sales where now it's probably half and half. Then you were working on three, four or five per cent which is laughable when ten per cent is normal now. The best part of it was creating the music and achieving something and hanging out with Holly and, you know, we had a lot of friends. I had a delightful time.'

The more introverted Don has a slightly different view: 'I didn't want to work the road that much but I was constantly pushed to do it by Archie and Wesley. They felt it was selling the records but I didn't and I still don't because I remember going out on a promotional tour and wherever we went the record was Number One anyway. There was nothing held exclusively

Above: *Phil, Margaret, Ike and Don in 1957. The family resemblance is particularly noticeable in this shot.*

about touring. We just peddled our music.'

Don and Phil were to do two other packages during 1957. It was on 'the biggest show of stars for 1957' when they first met Buddy Holly and the Crickets and introduced them to the sophistication of New York. 'When Phil and I first hit New York we were still wearing baggy pants. It was the first time we ever saw shoes without laces or socks that came up your leg.' By the time they met Buddy and the others in Montreal they were already dressing in the fashion and drew cries of 'gee whizz'.

Buddy Knox recalls: 'When we got to New York the guys from my area all started hitting so it didn't take us long to get friendly. Like when the Everly Brothers came in – they were weird guys we thought, but they were just two or three years ahead of everybody else and we got to be good friends with them.' Lester Rose remembers one particular date on the tour: 'We were in Florida and the band booked to back Don and Phil just couldn't get it right and the boys were very unhappy about it and didn't want to do the show. So Buddy Holly said that he would like to back them and that's what happened.' It must have been very special because it is one of the few dates that both Don and Phil can remember. Don: 'The band they'd hired sounded terrible. They couldn't read our charts and we didn't know what to do. Well, Buddy said "I'll play behind you" and we said "Great". Needless to say that was one of the most unforgettable concerts I ever did. It was really marvellous. That's the kind of guy that Buddy was.' Phil goes farther: 'Buddy opened the second half and was blowing it apart. He was followed by Jerry Lee Lewis who rock'n'rolled it up one way and down the other. Without Buddy and the Crickets behind us Don and I would've had trouble handling it, but he *was* playing with us and I've never had such a good time on stage because we just had power.'

The third package was the Alan Freed Christmas Jubilee which played at the New York Paramount for ten days with up to ten shows a day for which the audience would pay $2.50 each. The shows started at nine o'clock in the morning and ran straight through until three the next morning. Everybody's act was severely restricted and the cue sheets showed that Don and Phil, as one of the headline acts, had seven minutes to perform three songs. There was always a big finale with all the acts singing *When the Saints Go Marching In*, watching the balcony shake. *Variety* reported the shows thus: 'Rock'n'roll still shows its strength for the very young. The jives all but create riots in and out of the house and probably wouldn't stop at that but for the tremendous number of uniformed police . . . The acts sound and look alike. It was difficult to distinguish either acts or numbers. With the kids bobbing up and screeching continually, neither sound or sight was permitted in any quarter of the house.'

By the end of 1957 the Everlys had established a work pattern they were to follow for the next four years: two or three long arduous tours each year and then a few smaller ones (Don and Phil were to follow the Paramount show with a seventeen-day tour as headliners with Buddy Holly and many of their friends from the previous year plus a young Eddie Cochran); then there would be selected dates where they would play a forty-five minute or one-hour set; and fitted between the touring would be TV and radio dates and other recording sessions.

Bye Bye Love remained in the Billboard Hot Hundred pop chart for twenty-seven weeks, peaking at number two and selling well over one million copies. Its success relieved the pressure for releasing a new record while paradoxically increasing that of finding the right song to record if they were not to be billed as 'one-hit wonders'.

Above: *Phil and Don strum their guitars while Wesley Rose and Boudleaux Bryant listen in.*

4
The Cadence Years

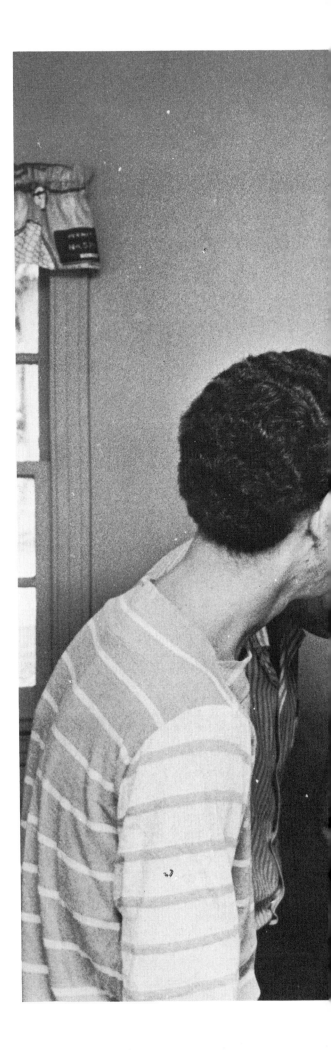

A great deal of effort went into choosing that second release. Don and Phil went through the whole Acuff Rose catalogue but found nothing suitable. Wesley Rose did not encourage songs from other publishers and finally, much to Archie Bleyer's astonishment, told the Bryants to go write another *Bye Bye Love*. 'That was just not done. Songs are inspirational rather than to order'. However, the Bryants came up with a whole string of them. *Wake Up Little Susie* was the first song written specifically with the Everlys in mind and was to be one of the more difficult songs for Boudleaux and Felice to complete. Boudleaux remembers: 'I couldn't sleep and went downstairs and started tinkering with the song. Felice woke up and heard me playing it and was attracted enough to come down to see what I had written. I had to tone down my own lyrics a bit.' Felice: 'He had them in the drive-in but I had them falling asleep to get it more straightened out why the kids were up so late. They were bored so they fell asleep and that cleaned it up some.'

Archie Bleyer, along with everyone else, liked the song as soon as he heard it, although he had some doubts about the attitude of some radio stations to the lyrics – with good reason as it turned out. Felice recalls: 'Some stations got the wrong idea and wouldn't play it. The Catholic Church got it banned from their radio stations. In Germany they put the sheet music out with a cartoon picture of a girl in bed and two guys looking through the door – can you imagine that? Including the words "Ooh-la-la" made the song sound dirty, but that was not strictly intended.'

It was decided that *Wake Up Little Susie* would be the second release, backed by another Don Everly song, a lilting country ballad called *Maybe Tomorrow*. The recording session was fixed for 15 and 16 August at the RCA Victor studios in Nashville. The success of *Bye Bye Love* meant that a hit formula had been established and was to be maintained throughout the Everlys' stay with Cadence. Only two sides would be recorded at the session, one fast and one slow to attract as large an audience as possible. The songs, contrary to most country songs, would not be aimed at death, divorce or drinking, but more juvenile subjects such as parents, school and young love. Don and Phil would pick the songs and would first rehearse the song together. If the song was a Bryant song they would work with Boudleaux. The sound would then be developed with the other musicians, everybody pitching in ideas, then Don would arrange the rhythmic

patterns for the song. Chet Atkins says of those rhythm patterns: 'Don and I used to dig a lot of the rhythm and blues things and we especially liked what Bo Diddley was doing. Don said to me, "When we get a recording contract will you play some Bo Diddley stuff with us?" and I said, "Sure". So we threw in a little Bo Diddley lick here and there and I think that helped to make those records hits because it made them more acceptable to the pop market.' Don says: 'Chet showed me the G tuning and the E tuning that Bo Diddley used and I liked the sound Chet got on a piece called *Blue Mountain Rag* that he played in G. So I started writing in those tunings in the style of rhythmic fields and that basically is how we came about with the arrangement sounds of the Everly Brothers.'

The recordings were all cut 'live' on two channel consoles in conditions that would be considered antiquated today. The engineer was vital, as Phil remembers: 'Selby Coffeen, the engineer, I marvel now at his ability to ride the panel. In those days the engineer had to play the board almost like playing an instrument because he had to bring up the guitar at each interval for the little lead rhythmic fills.'

The recording procedure must have been strained to the limit on *Wake Up Little Susie* because of the difficulty in getting a cut with which Archie Bleyer was happy. Boudleaux reckoned that: 'Archie didn't think it was coming off and we worked and worked at it. Everyone else thought it was pretty good. This was one time when Archie was absolutely wrong. Anyway, Archie got miffed and went back to New York saying, "Do what you want. Send it up and we'll print it." And that's just what we did. The song was recorded in two takes the next day.' Phil agrees: 'There were lots of hassles and lots of mistakes. We just couldn't get it at all. There were words between Archie and Don and I. We cut it the next day when Wesley was in the studio.' Archie Bleyer's views were: 'I just didn't like the way it was going at first. It wasn't until it was recorded the second time that I finally realised that it was a strong record.'

The record was released early in September 1957 and quickly entered the Billboard pop, country and rhythm and blues charts. Everything was now geared to the pop market from a promotional point of view, and the success of the record was enormous. Whether or not Don's views on touring are right the facts prove that the record was to sell nearly two and a half million copies and reach the Number One spot in the charts in a twenty-six-week stay, achieved while Don and Phil were undertaking those prolonged one-nighters. The effort was justified; it established the Everlys as leading rock'n'roll performers. From March to December 1957 they had gone from being close to starvation with very little work to an act with two million sellers headlining sell-out shows across the nation.

It is interesting to consider how the rapid change in fortunes affected Don and Phil. Don bought a house for himself and Sue, while Ike retired and returned to Nashville with Margaret to live in a house bought for

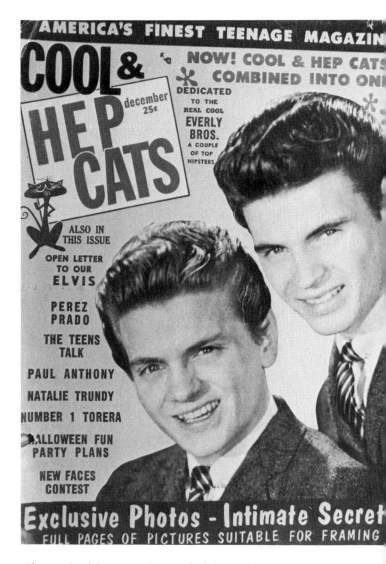

Above: *As rising stars, Don and Phil were frequently on the covers of fan magazines.* Opposite: *Don and his wife Sue, sharing a brief moment of relaxation in a hectic life of touring and recording.*

them by their sons. Phil moved in with his parents and Margaret lives in that house today, keeping Phil's room as he had it all those years ago. Don and Sue's marriage was less than six months old when things began to move; after that Don's time at home was limited to a few days between tours.

In line with the times, no mention was made in the early press articles of the fact that Don was married on the grounds that it was thought to be bad for business if a rock star admitted he was married and therefore 'unavailable'. But it was not long before Don was mentioning his wife in interviews and pictures of them together appeared in the music press and fan magazines. Phil feels that the special relationship with their fans had something to do with the fact that this disclosure became possible: 'There was one absolutely fantastic thing about being a duet and brothers and that is you're always in balance with each other so it keeps you from getting too "Oh Jesus, I'm really something" because you're not individually, so it keeps you level-headed. Don and my approach was not so much as idols so we didn't have that extra problem of tremendous screaming fans – we had a solid following. The money we made was made in a gradual process.' Don agrees: 'Elvis Presley was the Numero Uno of rock'n'roll. They called him the King of Rock. But the audience was teenage girls. It was hard for them to relate to the Everly Brothers as a single emotional entity. We had more guy fans than Elvis did. Back then it was all right to like the Everly Brothers but the guys resented Elvis. As a result we were allowed to appeal to other people than just teenage girls.'

It is hard to appreciate just how much the music machine consumed the Everlys. 'It ran us completely from the start,' Don remembers. 'You were out working and earning phenomenal fees. The first year I paid income tax I probably paid more in tax than my father, grandfather and great-grandfather had earned in their lives. It meant nothing to me because I was on the road living in hotels. You'd call down for food and drinks. You'd never pay for it. It's all on the bill so you just live it.' Phil agrees: 'You get a distorted sense of the value of money. We didn't have money as such. We had a little bit to tip people but that was all. They mostly paid the bills, you more or less went along with the programme rather than people come along and push money in your pocket. But, you know, it never takes long to adapt to having money. You soon get used to it.' Probably the best indication comes from Margaret, whose feelings were quite different. 'It was so frightening because it was like a snowball rolling down a hill and it was gathering speed as it went. I would try to slow everything down but it seemed that I was on top of a house and I could look down and see things

that were happening around me and I wished I couldn't see them because they were thrown into situations that they weren't up to handling because they were so young.'

During the whole of 1957 all the Everlys' efforts were aimed at securing a stronghold in the USA. In fact the instant appeal of *Bye Bye Love* knew no national boundaries and became a worldwide hit. Britain was, and probably still is, the second most important market for Americans to crack. The homegrown 'pop' market was in its infancy and in the main relied for success on copies of American hits. In those times of restricted television and limited 'needletime' on the national radio network there was little opportunity for record promotion other than package tours on the lines of the American tours and playing the records on Radio Luxembourg, the commercial radio station where programmes are transmitted in English during the evenings, sponsored by the major UK record companies. The knowledgeable British fans spent many hours with their ears pressed against the radio speaker, but the listeners had to put up with heavy interference, the sound level ebbing and flowing, in order to hear the new sounds emanating from America. There was enormous scope for British artists to 'steal the thunder' of their American counterparts. There was, however, still a predominance of American acts in the British charts and if an artist had charisma or if the record was unique in style then there was every chance that they would be successful.

Bye Bye Love was released in Britain at the beginning of June on the London American Label, a division of Decca Record Company which specialised in distributing the records of the small independent companies in America. The early advertisements for the record

started a trend that stays with Don and Phil today; by mis-spelling their surnames as Everley. Record reviewers favourably compared the Everlys to Elvis and generally liked the record. The public agreed and, on 10 July, the record entered the *New Musical Express* (*NME*) chart at Number Nineteen, moving slowly up the chart to Number Six and spending altogether sixteen weeks in the top thirty. Another music paper, *Disc*, actually had the record reaching Number One, although at that time the *NME* chart was regarded as being the most accurate.

It is interesting to look back at a particular time and see the spread of musical styles. As time goes by the remembrances of the period are that rock'n'roll completely took over the charts but in truth it was a gradual process and there was always plenty of room in the British charts for good records of any style. It may be that this accent on variety enabled the British music industry to accept rock'n'roll as a form of music in its own right much more readily than in America.

Attitudes towards rock'n'roll by the industry and media in the United States were totally different in that the music was looked down on and so were the performers. The tone of the *Variety* article reproduced earlier was the norm and that approach rankles with Don today. 'In the fifties it was very hard to get noticed when you were young. The world was very small to people of my age back then. The world belonged to the middle-aged and older people. I think rock'n'roll was the first acceptance of youth by adults. To be a rock'n'roll star in the fifties was to be low class. You were treated terribly, especially in the States. The people that ran the business hated it and made fun of it. You'd go to interviews and, especially being from the south, they would look and check if you had got your socks on. It used to be torture so that it got that I wouldn't go. Some people accused me of being bitter, but it is true. Everyone said the music ain't gonna last. I heard that a thousand times if I heard it once and I knew it was. I didn't know how but I knew it was going to last. The doors were opened by the early rock people. To get in television, to do the Perry Como show, to do the Ed Sullivan shows and those things. But people looked down their noses at rock'n'roll here in the States for an awfully long time. In England it wasn't that way.'

Phil's views on the subject are well documented: 'When we were eighteen, nineteen and some of us even younger, the establishment was ten, fifteen years older. They were into Frank Sinatra, and we were an abomination to the ear, and a blight to the eye. The older people in the industry were all hoping that rock'n'roll would go away. They were very reluctant to change and adapt ... and the TV hierarchy was the worst in terms of displaying negative attitudes. They were very condescending, associating the grease look with juvenile delinquency but there was no correlation, really. The thought process that we had to fight against was that "They're rock'n'rollers – they don't know what they're doing. This isn't going to last because they're not really performers."'

Irrespective of the attitudes of the people in the industry the young record buyers knew what they liked and when *Wake Up Little Susie* was released in Britain in November 1957 it was an immediate hit, reaching Number Two in a thirteen-week chart run. The success of the Everlys' first two singles sent the industry clamouring for more material. This represented a problem because there had not been enough time for a stockpile of recordings to grow. In fact, it was never to be the policy of the Everlys to stockpile, they were always concerned that their singles should sound fresh and up to the minute.

After the Autumn Show of Stars tour there was a short break before the Christmas shows at the Para-

mount. Don and Phil used the time to put down some tracks for their first album to supplement the four that made up the first two singles which were on the album. The choice of material reflects their influences as well as their problems in finding enough songs to record. Phil: 'We did a whole album in a week. We were running out of things we knew so that created a

Above left: *Signs of affluence as Don and Phil work on their cars in the Tennessee Countryside.* Above right: *The first advertisement in the* New Musical Express *got the name wrong!* Below: *The Everly Brothers created wonderful recordings given that conditions in the studios were primitive by today's standards.*

An important part of the Everly's appeal was their ability to convey the emotions of the teenager. As young men they pursued many of the same interests as their audience, and in the same spirit. The coffee bar was a favourite meeting place for friends and Phil's Nash-Healey was very much part of the young man's dream of speed and freedom. They enjoyed fishing and are seen here with Floyd 'Lightning' Chance. They were also happy on horseback, riding whenever they

got the opportunity to leave the studios behind for a while. But, inevitably, they found most of their entertainment confined to hotel rooms and fellow musicians, relaxing between shows and gruelling tours. Throughout their long career in the music business Don and Phil Everly never lost sight of their roots, and their music conveys much of the freshness of their early years.

little tension because it didn't look as if we'd be able to finish the album before going back on the road.' There were two Little Richard numbers, *Rip It Up* and *Keep a'Knockin'*; Gene Vincent's *Be Bop A Lula*; Ray Charles' *Leave My Woman Alone* and *This Little Girl of Mine*. The remaining three tracks were a Don Everly original, *Should We Tell Him*, a Bryant country song, *Brand New Heartache*, and an up-tempo country-style version of the Clovers', *Hey Doll Baby*.

The demand for a new single and the lack of time available to record tracks specifically to follow *Wake Up Little Susie* led Archie Bleyer to release two more of the album tracks. *This Little Girl Of Mine* was issued in America in January 1958, backed by *Should we Tell Him*. It was a strange choice for the A side as it is rather repetitious, but Don's song had a catchy chorus which accentuated the harmonies. The record was only in the Billboard top 100 for nine weeks getting no higher than Number Twenty-Eight which, compared with the success of the other records, meant it was a flop. This may account for the strange way the record was handled in the UK. It was released with the sides reversed. The record company played down the release. There were no advertising or reviews of the record so it is not surprising that it was the only Cadence single released in Britain that did not make the charts.

The relative failure of the record caused everybody to make an extra special effort for the next release and it was to prove worthwhile. Boudleaux Bryant said: 'It occurred to me that a change of pace might be in order. I really thought that, if they continued doing the same up tempo things with the same riff and everything, pretty soon people would get tired of that, so we decided to write a few ballads. Archie immediately liked *All I Have to Do Is Dream* and the boys liked it and so it was done and was an immediate hit.' Phil recalls: 'Finding hit songs is really a fun thing to do particularly when you find one that's really good. The first time I heard *Dream* I heard it sung by Boudleaux on an acetate and just knew. They could've put his out and it would've been a hit. It was just one of those songs. It was an important record for us because its success gave our career longevity and changed people's attitudes towards us so that when people think of the Everly Brothers they think of us harmonically.'

All I Have to Do is Dream was cut in only three takes, which is an amazing feat when one considers that it was cut live. Chet Atkins' opening chord sets the tone for the whole record which is, without doubt, the most outstanding ballad of the rock'n'roll era. The enormous sales of the record show that Boudleaux Bryant's lyrics struck a chord with young record buyers throughout the world. His ability to include a typically teenager phrase like 'gee whizz' is an indication of his awareness of the listening audience. 'I can't explain why I put it in the song. It was just a lucky rhyme fall. When Richard Chamberlain wanted to record the song his producer asked if I would take that part out and I said "No way!"' Archie Bleyer remembers that at this session Boudleaux was dying to buy a new Thunderbird car: 'When the session finished I said to him "Go

out and buy that Thunderbird – you can afford it. This record's going to be a big hit." It was and he did.'

All I Have to Do is Dream was backed by *Claudette*, a Roy Orbison song about his wife. Don and Phil were responsible for bringing Roy to Nashville and arranging a song-writing deal with Acuff Rose. While doing a show with him in Gary, Indiana, Ike, who had travelled with his sons, asked Roy if he had any songs. Roy played him *Claudette* and when Don and Phil came off stage Ike suggested that they listen to the song. They liked it and Roy wrote down the words on a cardboard box, the only surface available, so that they could record it straightaway.

The policy of putting the best up-tempo songs with the best ballad was to reap dividends with this release. The sides were listed separately in America. *All I Have to Do Is Dream* spent seventeen weeks on the chart and stayed at the top for four weeks. *Claudette* reached Number Thirty and stayed in the chart for ten weeks. After one week, the record was deemed a double A sider in Britain and the sales combined. The record was seven weeks at Number One on the *NME* chart while the *Record Mirror*'s top twenty had the Everlys at Number One for nine weeks and Number Two for three weeks in a twenty-week stay. The record was to be the Everlys' biggest seller in America and is regarded by many as the most distinctive of all their hits.

The Everlys were displaced from Number One in Britain by the Kalin Twins' *When*. The Kalins were the first Everly copyists to emerge but over the next year the growing status of Don and Phil was to produce a plethora of duos, particularly in Britain.

The pressure did not decrease for Don and Phil. Touring continued as did the TV and radio shows. A few days' vacation was grabbed when the itinerary allowed it. To relax the boys often went up to the Bryants' house on Old Hickory Lake outside Nashville. They might fish with the Crickets, or they might go horse riding. But there was always the publicity man to satisfy and the next promotion job to be done. The demands were tremendous and there seems little doubt that there were seeds sown during this period that were to lead to the eventual break-up of the brothers.

While *Dream* and *Claudette* were shooting up the charts, the Everlys' first album was released. The majority of tracks are up-tempo, with Don's acoustic rhythm guitar predominant, particularly in the driving version of *Keep a'Knockin'*. The album was titled simply *The Everly Brothers* although it is now usually referred to as *They're Off and Rolling*, due to the American LP's introduction by Archie Bleyer incorporating that phrase. The idea of an introduction was included on all the early Cadence albums. (The Andy Williams cover states 'He's all male and catnip to quail, says Archie!') It is perhaps striking that Archie Bleyer appears on all the covers. On the Everlys', he is seen riding a motor cycle next to Don and Phil!

Like all albums from rock'n'roll artists in the 1950s, the record did not sell in large quantities, the market being geared too much to singles at that time. Attention was, therefore, directed towards the next release and this time two Bryant songs were chosen: *Bird Dog* and *Devoted To You*. There is a story behind both songs. 'It's very difficult to explain the process of creativity,' explains Boudleaux. 'I think things just sort of fall into your head, out of the great upstairs. And in this particular case I was trying to get an idea for something really novel and unique for the boys, and I remember that my father had had an expression that he used when he saw somebody that was just a little bit pleasantly off. You know, a sort of a character. He would say "He's a bird" and I thought, let's see, he's a bird ... he's a bird ... and then it hit me, that the antithesis of that would be "He's a dog". He's a no-good. And then the two things fell together – he's a bird dog – and that was it. Using the two words together was as unexpected to me as it would be to anyone listening to the song for the first time. Once that happened, the rest of it was just a matter of mechanics.'

Phil recalls another element to the song: 'Archie was at the session for *Bird Dog* and wanted to use a dog puppet that was very popular here at the time to do the "He's a bird" bit. The puppet's whole claim to fame was to say "chocolate" and Archie wanted to get the guy in who did the puppet's voice to do those bits. Don and I looked down the line at each other and said "mmmmmmmm!". It just didn't fit and in the end Donald wound up doing it. I've often wondered what would've happened if we'd used that puppet. It would probably have been a disaster.'

Devoted to You was another sweeping ballad in the *Dream* mould except this time Boudleaux pushed Phil's harmonic abilities to the limit. 'Boudleaux worked out the harmony and taught me it. Although I had been using fifths I didn't know a fifth from a hole in the ground, but I would've spread the harmony out because I always look at harmony like water running down a mountain but the structure of the mountain determines which way the water runs and you have to flow like that. Boudleaux designed that piece for me to use more fifths to get that madrigal sound.'

Both sides made the American charts. *Bird Dog* reached Number Two and *Devoted to You* Number Ten, making the record the first of two double top ten hits the Everlys achieved. It was yet another immediate gold record. Both sides sustained a long chart run of eighteen weeks and fourteen weeks respectively. In Britain, *Bird Dog* was regarded as the A side, reaching Number Two on the *NME* chart, and was three weeks at Number One in the *Record Mirror*'s top twenty.

Throughout 1958 there had been growing pressure on Don and Phil to visit other countries where they had become big stars. After many false starts an unusual tour was finally arranged. Archie Bleyer saw value in promoting his three major acts – the Everly Brothers, Andy Williams and the Chordettes – on a whistle-stop tour of Europe concentrating on TV work and interviews. The tour was arranged for January 1959 and was to take in eight countries in ten days – a

Above: *Don and Phil with Andy Williams, during their first visit to Britain in January 1959.*

punishing schedule in anyone's book.

To coincide with the tour, the Everlys' next single release was delayed in Britain until 16 January 1959. *Problems* and *Love of my Life*, two more Boudleaux and Felice songs, were recorded in October and released in America while both sides of the previous single were still in the top 100. *Problems* repeated the success of *Bird Dog* in reaching Number Two in the Billboard chart and had a lengthy fifteen-week run. But although sales reached 989,000, it was the first of the big hit records not to go gold immediately. Boudleaux commented: 'Archie Bleyer, being an honourable man, wouldn't give a gold record for that but in a little while it did pass the million.' Phil's view was: 'When *Problems* didn't go a million in its initial impact everybody was surprised and I think we all had this sense of people looking at you with that open eye: "Maybe you're losing it". I always felt we failed someway in not making it a million seller but that's something you learn as you make more records. They don't all do the same.' Once again the flip side made the charts in its own right and peaked at Number Forty. In Britain amid the publicity surrounding the tour *Problems* reached Number Six.

The European tour ran into difficulties even before the artists left America. It was clear that the major interest was in Don and Phil. When the financial arrangements for their performance in the UK could not be agreed the TV company decided not screen *any* part of the show. Finally the British part of the tour was limited to thirty hours during which time Don and Phil appeared as guests on a TV pop programme called *Cool For Cats* in which they received some poll awards and were interviewed, but because of contractual difficulties they did not sing. They then undertook an

MY FRANK SINATRA STORY—By STEVE RACE

Melody Maker

Frankie Vaughan See Page 5

January 24, 1959   FOR THE BEST IN JAZZ   Every Friday 6d.

DON'T KNOCK THE POP!

Says U.S Record Chief ARCHIE BLEYER

ARCHIE BLEYER, boss of America's Cadence Records, arrived in London last weekend with The Everly Brothers, The Chordettes and Andy Williams.

His mission? A TV promotional tour that will take in eight European countries.

And this is what Bleyer had to say to the MM about the current music scene:

"Say what you like about pop singers, but I've studied them. I believe in what they are doing—and that's why they get their songs across.

"I get tired of these people who keep hitting out at pop music. What some people fail to realise is that, although the record buyers may be younger, the situation hasn't changed—fundamentally.

"Sophistication never was popular. People can only appreciate what they understand. They like simplicity and sincerity.

"All right, so many of the songs are simple. If I call pseudo-day pop songs and artists primitive, the term shouldn't be taken as derogatory. In that period, the sound is more important than the words. But there is nothing intrinsically unhealthy about them.

"Pop songs have become an international language. Young folk in Britain, Germany, Japan and other countries find a common meeting-ground with them.

"Some older people may find it offensive. Yet they numbers are decreasing all the time."

● Page Two, Col. 3

The Everly Brothers—Don and Phil

Andy Williams

Summer tour for Garner?

NEW YORK, Wednesday.—Erroll Garner, voted the world's top pianist in the MELODY MAKER Poll, is being lined up for British concerts in the summer.

Garner leaves for a tour of Europe on August 13 and his personal manager, Martha Glaser, told the MM the tour would include at least two concert dates in Britain.

The plans are subject to an exchange agreement being worked out with the Musicians' Union.

Said Martha Glaser: "We are hoping this can be done because we know Erroll has many, many friends in Britain."

Thanks!

SHIRLEY BASSEY TOPS NEW REVUE

SHIRLEY BASSEY is to star in a new glamour revue "Blue Magic," which opens at the Prince of Wales Theatre, W., on February 19.

Her co-stars will be two comedians—Tommy Cooper and America's Archie Robbins. The show will be presented

The Chordettes are known in Britain for their two records of "Lollipop" and "Born To Be With You." With the Everly Brothers and Andy Williams, they had their first in London last Saturday. It was put out on the disc spot on the Light Programme on Sunday (6.30-9 p.m.)

Humph to travel with Clara Ward

appearance on a live radio pop programme called *Saturday Club* and joined the other artists for a huge press conference at the Savoy Hotel.

The tour began in London. The timetable was in trouble straightaway because the flight from America had been delayed and it took a frantic dash to the TV studios for the Everlys to make their appearance. The package then jet-hopped its way through Belgium, Holland, Denmark, Sweden, Germany, Luxembourg and France. Archie Bleyer remembers the tour well. 'It was pretty hectic. What happened was that we put together a half-hour show and scripts were prepared in the language of each of the countries we were visiting. We had quite a lot of language problems and it could be difficult using the local people to carry out the production.' Don's view on the tour is more direct: 'It was so hectic it was just insane. I didn't know what was going on.' Phil has an additional reason for remembering that tour: 'I was dating Jackie at that time. I was having one of those romantic tours of Europe. It was really moving but it was pleasant. Don and I had accumulated some money by then so were able to enjoy the limited spare time we had. Jackie and I had an argument in Paris which was supposed to be the really romantic part of the trip. She seemed to want to spend her time hanging out with Andy Williams and his great art collection and I went off to the Crazy Horse Saloon and ran into an American from Chatanooga and we painted the town.'

During the tour, the Everlys' second LP was released in the States. Called *Songs Our Daddy Taught Us*, it was made up of twelve folk songs, the majority of which had been taught to them by their father. There were a few newer songs to set beside such songs as *Barbara Allen* and *Down in the Willow Garden* but they all worked well together in what can be regarded as an early attempt at a concept album. The songs are all slow and the lyrics on some are maudlin. Some people find the album depressing but it is classic Everly Brothers with the minimum of backing to detract from

the perfect harmonies. The only musicians in the studio were Don on acoustic guitar and Floyd 'Lightning' Chance on stand-up bass, who was heard to say at the session: 'Damn. You *would* put me on an album where you can hear every note I play.' Archie Bleyer says that it is this album about which he receives the most correspondence, twenty-five years after it was recorded, and Paul Simon has cited it as one of his favourites.

The twelve tracks were recorded in August 1958, some seventeen months after the Everlys signed for Cadence. Yet, Don's comments on the album show some disenchantment had already set in. 'I knew we would be leaving Cadence and I wanted the last album to be something musically that I loved but I didn't want them to have any possible singles which they would've kept releasing and interfered with our career. So I suggested *Songs Our Daddy Taught Us* and everyone went for it. It was easy to do. It touched what folk music ought to be – country folk music, songs people would sing sitting on the porch. It's still one of my favourite albums. It's got class and ages really well.'

Shortly after they returned from Europe Don and Phil suffered a great shock, along with the rest of the world, when Buddy Holly was killed in an air crash together with Richie Valens and the Big Bopper. Buddy had become a close friend to Don and Phil over the many tours they had done together. Don and Buddy had similar music interests, as Don remembers: 'Holly wrote *Not Fade Away* for us. I was taking some of my arrangements from Bo Diddley and Buddy knew it, and we talked about it and he decided to write the song for us using the Diddley style. I thought that it was too soon to go that close to Bo Diddley's sound. Besides we had just got *Dream* so we didn't need it then, but it was nice of Buddy to do that for us.' Holly was not going to give up that easily. He wrote two more songs for the Everlys and went to the trouble of making professional studio recordings of the songs rather than the usual quality demo. Buddy's versions of *Wishing* and *Love's Made a Fool of You* were hits after his death. Don Everly was not aware that the songs were specially written for the brothers so it is likely that they were rejected by Acuff Rose without the Everlys even hearing them. The Everlys were able to reciprocate Buddy's efforts to a certain degree. The Bryants wrote *Raining In My Heart* specifically for Don and Phil but they decided not to record it and offered it to Holly. On returning to Texas, Buddy told his parents: 'I'm going to record the prettiest song I've ever heard', which Boudleaux and Felice still regard as one of the greatest compliments they've ever received.

Buddy's friendship with Phil was a close

Above: Don and Phil relaxing with an old friend, Buddy Holly, who wrote Not Fade Away *for the brothers.*

camaraderie. They spent as much as possible of their limited spare time together. Phil heard most of Buddy's music in its early stages and had been with Buddy in New York just before that last fateful tour when Buddy played him all his new masters: 'They sounded sensational to me. He was so depressed at not getting hits and he was wondering if these new tapes would yield any.' Phil went down to Texas when Buddy died but, contrary to the stories at the time, he was not pall bearer. Neither he nor Jerry Allison went to the cemetery. 'I was really sad,' remembers Phil, 'but I was also mad because I knew why he was on the road and he wouldn't even have had to be out there had it not been for the predicament he found himself in. When I saw him in New York he said he wanted to stay off the road until he got back into the charts. The pressures applied to him at the time were just disgusting.'

During that New York trip Phil had collaborated with Buddy in recording Lou Gordiano. Two tracks were recorded, Buddy's *Stay Close To Me* and *Don'tcha Know* written by Phil (and not to be confused with the song recorded later by the Crickets). Both played on the session and even provided the background vocals in a falsetto which was described in reviews as 'very unusual female backing'. Phil explains: 'We were paying and we didn't want to pay any women. We sang falsetto because we were both signed to other companies.'

After the funeral Don and Phil went back into the studio to record the tracks to make up their next single. Again two Boudleaux and Felice Bryant songs were chosen – *Poor Jenny*, an up-beat light-hearted song telling the story of a teenage party raided by the police. It is interesting to note that there were two recordings of this song with slightly different words and backing. In one version the party broke up at one o'clock and in the other ten o'clock. It is not known whether the second version was made to allay Archie Bleyer's fears that the suggestions of an all-night party might get the record banned in some puritanical states, but it was the one o'clock version that was issued as a single. *Take a Message to Mary* is a song in the style of the *Songs Our Daddy Taught Us* LP and tells of an outlaw in prison. That side is famous as being the only Everly track featuring Boudleaux Bryant as a percussionist. The irregular clunking sound is made by Boudleaux hitting a Coca-Cola bottle with a screwdriver.

The single was issued in the Spring 1959 and it soon became clear that, while both songs were good, neither was up to the standard of the other hits. Neither song reached as high in the charts as had become expected of the Everlys. *Poor Jenny* reached Number Twenty-Two and Fourteen in the Billboard and *NME* charts, while *Take a Message to Mary* made Number Sixteen and Twenty respectively. *Take a Message to Mary* was probably not single material but, as was the case with all the Bryant songs, it suited perfectly the Everlys' style and thus achieved a higher chart placing than would normally have been the case. Its appeal was not lost on that great Everly Brothers admirer, Bob Dylan, who included it on his *Self Portrait* album. This was the last single to have a Bryant song as an A side.

On 16 April Don and Sue became parents of a daughter, Venetia Ember. Don didn't have much opportunity to settle down to fatherhood because he and Phil were booked for their first tour of Australia, where their records had sold well since 1957. As always, Lester Rose accompanied them as road man-

ager and remembers the tour for one particular reason: 'While we were in Sydney Don and Phil had had a disagreement about something and had gone into separate rooms and were tinkering on their guitars writing songs. Don was writing *'Til I Kissed You* in one room while Phil was writing *When Will I Be Loved* in the other.' The constant touring and recording had restricted Don and Phil's songwriting, but now this was changing. They were always anxious to find new sounds and perhaps they were beginning to feel that their music was getting into a rut.

Margaret recognised the change too. 'I can remember Don coming back from Australia and saying, "Listen to this song I've written," and he played *'Til I Kissed You*. It was a special time for me because I could see that he was maturing into a serious songwriter.' Felice on the other hand was trying to ease the doubts that Phil had about his song-writing abilities: 'Phil played me part of *When Will I Be Loved* and I told him I liked it and that he should finish it and he seemed surprised.'

It has been suggested that Don and Phil's songwriting talents owe a great deal to the influence of the Bryants but the Bryants disagree. 'Their style was very close to ours but as we were all writing for harmony then some similarity must creep in.' The Everlys were submitting their own songs for consideration as singles. 'We were always concerned about the quality of the songs that we did. We didn't record songs if we couldn't agree on them. Donald didn't care for one of my songs, *Gee, But it's Lonely*. I took his opinion and gave it to Pat Boone.' Boone was to have a Top Thirty US hit with the song.

Soon after their return from Australia, Don and Phil recorded *'Til I Kissed You*. Another Don song, the haunting *Oh, What a Feeling* was recorded for the flip. The backing personnel included Crickets Jerry Allison and Sonny Curtis this time. Don recalled: 'J.I. played tom toms on that session which was the first time tom toms had been in a Nashville recording studio.' Allison's special drum style is evident as is Floyd Cramer's piano playing. Recording the song had some technical problems as revealed by Bill Porter who had replaced Selby Coffeen as engineer. 'I had trouble with Archie Bleyer which nearly made me quit the record business for good. I had been with RCA less than two months during which time we had worked around the clock to instal a new console. Archie Bleyer had come to oversee the session and when Don and Phil started singing there was a terrible sound when they hit a particular high note. It happened again and I said I'd try to sort it out. I was under a great deal of pressure because all the musicians were waiting and Archie was standing over me and I couldn't find out what it was. After about twenty minutes I said, "I'm sorry there's nothing more I can do", which was the wrong thing to say. Archie just freaked out. He ranted and raved saying he'd come down from New York specially for the session but in the end he called it off. My boss rang me up and balled me out saying that if I ever said that to a producer again I would be fired. By that time I had realised

what was wrong and corrected the machinery. An engineer from New York had altered the equipment to the RCA standard without my knowledge and the settings just did not work with that console. Two weeks later Archie came down for another session to do the song with all the same people and when we came to the part that had caused the problem Archie smiled at me and said, "I see that you fixed it okay". From then on we got on okay and he must have liked my work because he used to ask for me.'

The record was released to rave reviews and became the Everlys' seventh million seller. In America the disc reached Number Four in the Billboard top 100 while in Britain it reached Number Two. For the last release of 1959 Don and Phil recorded a French ballad called *Let it Be Me* which Don had found on a Chet Atkins LP. Archie Bleyer liked the song as soon as he heard it and set about tracking down the English lyrics. Wesley Rose is reputed to have fought against the choice of songs in some cases; he preferred songs from the Acuff Rose catalogue. In this case the song was only the second of the Cadence singles not published by Acuff Rose. The session was the first to be held outside Nashville. The Everlys recorded the song at the Beel Sound Studios in New York and for the first time were backed with strings.

By now the Cadence contract was nearing its end and negotiations were already underway with other companies. There seemed little chance of the Everlys re-signing with Cadence. Success meant that big business became part of the equation that made up the Everlys/Acuff Rose/Cadence/Bryant team and this had soured people towards each other. Chet Atkins sums up the views of the musicians: 'At first the sessions were fun to do but then after all the success I think there got to be a lot of jealousy between Wesley Rose and Archie Bleyer. That happens sometimes; one of them feels that he should get more credit and that he is responsible for all their success and maybe the A & R man feels the same way and then they get into altercations about material. Like maybe Archie wouldn't always want to do Wesley's songs every time, but possibly Wesley felt that more Acuff Rose material could have been included. Whatever, it got to be that it was no fun to work anymore and this is infectious to the musicians. It was hard to play with all the fussing and quarrelling that was going on.'

The Bryants were concerned as to the effect the arguments were having on Don and Phil. Felice remembers: 'There was haranguing in the background over in the business side. That hurt the Everly Brothers. Not money-wise but it hurt their feelings.' Wesley Rose explained: 'We had decided, well actually the two boys had decided, they no longer wanted to be on Cadence about a year before the contract was over and I had transferred this information to Archie Bleyer. So it wasn't a thing of all of a sudden deciding to leave. It was sort of a personality conflict and it just wouldn't have worked any longer.' Don himself thought: 'It was a very painful period. There was so much bickering between Archie Bleyer and Wesley

Rose. I didn't feel anybody basically liked the way the Everly Brothers' music was going. We needed more than Archie Bleyer and Wesley Rose. Wesley was not a musician and Archie's idea of selling a record was not artistic at all. He'd get the weirdest ideas. He tried to get us to do *Standing on the Corner Watching all the Girls Go By* which was ridiculous. He was a musician but not into what we were doing. One day one would like one of the songs and on another the other one would. We had all that to contend with. It was a mess, to be perfectly honest.' These comments, made to me in an interview in the Autumn of 1982, shows the extent of Don's frustration.

It was unfortunate that such a successful relationship should end in such bitterness. Of the nine singles issued on Cadence during the 1950s seven sold over a million copies and earned gold records. In America those nine singles produced two Number Ones, three Number Twos, three more top ten records and four more sides that reached the top thirty. In Britain the roll of honour shows one record that reached Number One, three Number Two, two other top ten records and three more in the top twenty. From nobodys the Everlys had been catapulted to world stars, sought after for personal appearances and with many awards for top pop group. By the beginning of 1960 they were, with Elvis, the most prominent act of rock'n'roll.

An analysis of the strength of the Everlys shows that each part of the team had a part to play in the success. Wesley Rose was very important because, as head of Acuff Rose, he had influence and contacts. When he saw the potential of Don and Phil he was able to convince Archie Bleyer that they were worth signing. His company had some of the best songwriters assigned to it so that Don and Phil had the pick of that material. His preference for the Everlys to use Acuff Rose material clearly frustrated Don, but the statistics show that the songs that were recorded were what the public wanted. At the time, as Don admits, he and Phil had the final sanction as to what would be recorded. The limitations on using one publishing company became more obvious when Don and Phil split from Wesley. Wesley, therefore, was the catalyst which brought all the parts together.

Archie Bleyer's contribution was that he had a commercially tuned ear for the music. The Bryants are quick to praise his ability to look at a sheet of music and assess the potential of a song. Archie was always concerned that his artists should be happy with what they were doing and at the beginning probably brought Don and Phil into the discussions on material much more than an A & R man from a major company would have done. Although it must have been outside of his New York recording experience, he went along with the more relaxed way of recording in Nashville and probably achieved better, fresher recordings as a result. Don's comment that Archie was out of touch with what the Everlys were doing is understandable in view of Archie's background, but Archie was positive towards the music and was able to guide the sessions until he had a sound that he knew was commercial.

For all their differences, Wesley Rose still gives credit to Archie. 'He and I trusted each other and worked well together. I honestly believe that if we had put the Everlys on a major label we would not have had the success we did.' Phil's views also comment on Archie's 'hit sense': 'Archie was behind the production side of things. If you were to push it you'd have to say that Archie knew the intro of Don's was good and he also knew *Bye Bye Love* was good and he laid it on us. Nobody at that time did anything really to push us anywhere because they didn't know what we were doing. The real truth was that the bottom line was us and primarily Donald, because I was always a younger brother and basically followed pretty much what went down.'

The Everlys were to influence up-and-coming performers the world over but particularly in Britain. Bruce Welch of the Shadows was brought up on rock'n'roll and, with Hank Marvin, would sing all the Everly songs: 'When they started, Don and Phil were unique to pop music. Even by 1960 there were not many duos about and they were all straight copies of the Everlys. Dual harmony had to be done by brothers because there wasn't the technical equipment available then that there is today. When American acts came over to this country they were treated like gods because of the sound they got on their records. Very few of them lived up to expectations. Certainly not the one-hit wonders. Some of them were real thugs with no stage presence at all. The major acts like the Everlys enhanced their record image because they looked very good and were professional.' Phil comments on the harmonies: 'No two vocal chords are the same. Because we're brothers we were constructed physically the same way and our blend and our vibrato and our training had been under the same influences and that contributed a lot to the uniqueness of what we did. I imagine that if there were a bigger age difference it would be difficult because the timbre of the voices would be different.' Don identifies their success: 'I think we were successful because there were no duets in the pop field to speak of. That, and our guitar sound and Chet Atkins and the Nashville sound, all played a part of it. The music was good then and it is now.'

In Boudleaux and Felice Bryant the Everlys had writers with a remarkable ability to structure songs which perfectly fitted their style while at the same time writing lyrics which were aimed exclusively towards the young record buying public. Everyone is quick to highlight the importance of the Bryants. 'We ought to pay tribute to them,' Archie Bleyer remarks. 'It is unbelievable the way in which they were able to come up with song after song written specifically for the Everly Brothers.'

Don and Phil have recorded twenty-seven songs written by the Bryants. Of the eighteen sides issued as singles on Cadence up until the end of 1959 nine of them were Bryant compositions of which six sold more than a million records and all of them reached the Billboard Top 40. It was an amazing period for the

Above: *Boudleaux and Felice Bryant, photographed at the time that they were writing many of the Everly's big hits.*

Their unique relationship with Don and Phil is now legendary in the music business.

couple who were already regarded as being among the top writers in the country market before Don and Phil came along and they are still writing extensively today 36 years after they began writing together and with connected disc sales around the quarter of a billion mark. It is, however, the association with the Everlys that has made them famous around the world.

Boudleaux was born in Shellman, South Georgia, on 13 February 1920. His was a musical family who felt he was destined to be a concert violinist. It was not to be. He joined the symphony orchestra in Atlanta but quickly became a travelling musician with an assortment of bands and playing a variety of musical styles, most notably with Hank Penny and the Radio Cowboys, for whom he played fiddle in a jazz-influenced Western swing style. He met Felice, then twenty years old, in Milwaukee in 1945 and they were soon married. But it was another year before they started songwriting together. Felice had started writing lyrics out of boredom during Boudleaux's long absences on the road, and Boudleaux came across them by accident. Once they had completed eighty songs which they felt were of recording quality they began writing to publishers. They suffered a number of setbacks until Fred Rose (Wesley's father) heard *Country Boy* and signed them up. Little Jimmy Dickens had a big hit with the song in 1947, and went on to have twenty more hit

records with songs specifically written for him by the Bryants.

The Bryants moved to Nashville. During the early 1950s they had many hits, including a number of cross-over hits. *Hey Joe* was a country hit for Carl Smith and a pop hit for Frankie Laine, while *Having a Good Time* was a hit for Tony Bennett. When asked who'd written the song Bennett said, 'Well, Boudleaux Bryant and I think the other writer is his brother Felice'! When Fred Rose died, Wesley took over Acuff Rose. He had been more involved in the business side of the operation and knew little about publishing. Wesley wanted the Bryants to work full time and negotiated an unusual arrangement which had all the Bryants' songs published by Acuff Rose for ten years after which they were returned to the House of Bryant Publishing Company.

Bye Bye Love was written in 1956 while Boudleaux and Felice were driving down the highway one night. Boudleaux said: 'I always make sure that there is a pen and paper in the car just for these occasions. I got the first verse and the chorus down right there.' Despite the many refusals (Elvis Presley is reputed to have turned down the song) the Bryants never gave up pushing the song. They were disappointed when it wasn't taken because they believed in it, but they weren't despondent. Felice is a great believer in fate and feels that the song was made for the Everlys and had to wait until they came along.

Once the record had become a hit, the Bryants spent much but not all of their time writing for the Everlys. Boudleaux recalls: 'For quite a period we wrote song after song which was tailored directly for the Everlys' harmony. We had written a lot of harmony songs before so it came quite natural. I knew the song had to have certain ingredients like the harmonies, Don's guitar intro and of course the words of the song had to be aimed at the young record buyers. But a lot of our ballads the Everlys did later on were purely and simply vanilla love songs that had no age direction at all.'

There were many Bryant songs offered to the Everlys which they did not accept. *Raining In My Heart* was recorded by Buddy Holly. *Love Hurts* was made into a hit by Roy Orbison, who was a good friend of the Bryants. However, the Everlys did record the song twice for albums, a slow version on *A Date with the Everly Brothers*, which was how the song was written, and a raunchier version on *Rock'n'Soul* in 1965. In Felice's mind it is still an Everly song and she feels that the success the song has had is due to the Everlys' original version. The song has become one of the Bryants' most successful, with big hits for Nazareth and Jim Capaldi as well as marvellous album cuts by Jim Webb, Cher and Gram Parsons. Occasionally problems arose being associated with only one act. Felice believes: 'A few people would think we were only offering the Everly rejects although people who really knew us knew that we wouldn't offer Everly songs to other people. We would write for soloists and groups and occasionally another duet would come out and ask if we had anything the Everlys didn't want.'

The Bryants were continuing to produce hits for other acts while writing so much for Don and Phil: Jim Reeves' *Blue Boy*, Kitty Wells' *A Change of Heart*, Johnny and Jack's *That's Why I'm Leaving*, Sue Thompson's *Willie Can* (Alma Cogan in Britain), Bob Moore's *Mexico* and Bob Luman's *Let's Think about Living*. (Don and Phil brought Luman to Nashville and played on the session.) During that period, the couple faced a great deal of pressure as Boudleaux remembers: 'It was a lot of fun but we really humped it. We got up and would write about six to eight hours every day and we wrote a tremendous amount of all kinds of material. We worked hard.' In those early days of the Everlys' success the Bryants were regarded as *the* songwriters and had to maintain that high standard. The pressure was so intense that Felice was physically ill.

There are many classic Bryant songs: on the early Warner Brothers albums *Love Hurts, Sleeping Nights, Nashville Blues, Just in Case, So How Come*. Many were strong enough to be singles and were to make classics of the albums on which they are included. Above all, the songs show a maturity in the lyrics that was essential if rock'n'roll were to survive. Boudleaux thought ahead and worked on the natural progression of the music. It is these songs, performed by Don and Phil, which were to influence Gram Parsons and forge a positive link between Don and Phil's music and the contemporary rock and country music of the 1970s and 1980s.

In the late 1960s, the Bryants wrote *Rocky Top* which was an enormous hit and has become the state song of Tennessee. Although the Everlys did not cut the song originally, they included their version on the album *Pass the Chicken and Listen*. Don and Phil's version could well be regarded as the definitive version, because it shows that Boudleaux and Felice had lost none of their ability for writing songs which were perfect for the harmonies of the Everly Brothers.

Phil Everly sums up the special magic of the Bryants: 'It was an education working with them. Boudleaux's one of the great writers of the century. He's extremely brilliant, honest and talented, and you can't say more than that about anybody. He was one of the mentors of my life. I've talked to him about a thousand things. He says everything with a light hand and Felice is all heart. They're just good people. Two of the finest people I've ever met.'

A unique sound, together with a perfect run of songs, probably sums up the reasons for the tremendous success the Everlys achieved during their time with Cadence. 1960 was to see the first change of direction in the Everlys' career. In America they were never to repeat the consistency they achieved on Cadence, but in Britain and the rest of the world they were to reach a higher level of success which was to keep them at the top as recording artists and performers for over a decade.

Below: Don and Phil top the bill in Alan Freed's Christmas Jamboree at the Paramount Theatre in New York, 1958.

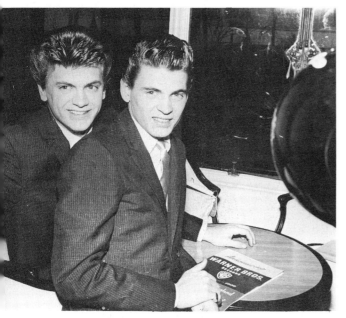

5

The Move to Warner Brothers

When the Everlys' recording contract came up for grabs they must have been the most bankable product in the whole entertainment industry. Elvis was tied into a long-term contract; Haley was on the decline; Lewis was in the doldrums; while Vincent had never truly fulfilled the promise of *Be-Bop-A-Lula* although he was to remain a committed rock'n'roller. In 1960 black performers such as Chuck Berry, Little Richard and Fats Domino were still not regarded as commercial propositions.

Don and Phil's career had been nurtured carefully. Their songs were aimed at youth but their ballads appealed to parents and children alike. No scandal surrounded them. They looked good and were quiet, polite and professional; as a result they were well liked by the media. Records were released at regular four-monthly intervals and the steady sales meant that it was rare for there not to be an Everly Brothers record somewhere in the charts.

Wesley Rose began negotiating with several companies and clearly felt that it was time for the Everlys to cash in on all the hard work undertaken since 1957. He looked for a guaranteed income for them.

The suggestion of a guarantee was totally abhorrent to Archie Bleyer. 'A performer makes no guarantee that he's going to make hits. A hit record is a difficult combination of a performance and a song and when that comes together and sparks fly you have a hit.' Even if the Everlys had wanted to re-sign, Cadence had neither the money or the long-term plans to satisfy Wesley Rose's stipulations.

Wesley was able to negotiate the best deal with the company in the most need of success. Warner Brothers had been formed, with a great fanfare, a couple of years before but had traded disastrously. The company was desperate to attract a major name. The terms finally agreed between Rose and Jim Conklin, head of Warner Brothers Records, were unique and a stepping stone for rock'n'roll. The contract was the first ever $1m contract. The Everlys were guaranteed $100,000 a year for ten years. Included in the terms were the provision of a movie test for Don and Phil, the artists' approval of all art work, and approval of releases to rest with the Everlys and Wesley Rose.

The financial benefits of the contract were considered the most important. Don and Phil were, by

Opposite: *Don and Phil in Melbourne, May 1960.* Above centre: *A London press conference, March 1960.*

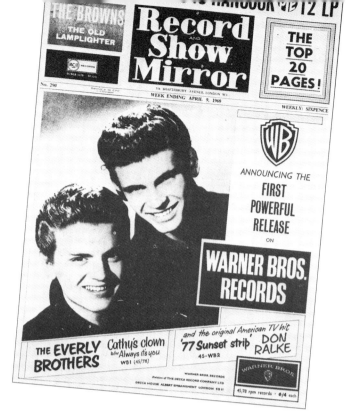

this time, affected by the fear that oblivion was just around the corner so the contract provided some financial security. Wesley Rose saw other benefits: 'I knew both the President and Vice-President of Warner Brothers from previous jobs they'd had and I knew we could work together. Apart from the financial benefits, we had total freedom and control without having anybody thinking against us.'

The decision to move labels was not regarded as a good move by everyone, not least by Felice Bryant. 'The time came to deal again and Wesley wanted a bigger royalty rate but Archie wouldn't go for it so Wesley put them on Warner Brothers for a million dollars. I think that was a mistake because Archie contributed as much as anyone.'

Completion of the deal put pressure on Don and Phil. They now had to justify what was regarded as the ridiculously high amount of money that Warner Brothers had invested in them. The label switch was to bring about some fundamental changes in the Everlys' work. Their recording was aimed much more towards the LP market to the extent that immediately they were free of the Cadence contract they began recording their first album. Secondly, the production of the records was directly in the hands of the Everly Brothers; primarily Don, but Phil also contributed. Thirdly, Warner Brothers were much more marketing-oriented and the demands on Don and Phil in this area increased enormously.

The first Warner session took place at the RCA studio B in Nashville on 8 March 1960 when three tracks were laid down for an album. The first songs recorded were the Bryants' *Sleepless Nights* and *Nashville Blues*, and Ray Charles' *What Kind of Girl are You* (although the Everlys' version is far removed from the original). They then undertook a short tour but went back into the studio immediately on their return to Nashville. They were scheduled for their first extensive tour of Britain in April, to be followed by a tour of Australia.

At the same time Warner Brothers were anxious to put out a single, but Phil was waiting for the right song. 'We had just come in off the road. Don called me and said he'd started writing a song and could I come over. He'd written the chorus of *Cathy's Clown* and had the melody for the verses. I just put together the verses and it was finished. We went into the studio and cut in maybe two days and we knew it was a hit.'

The song was primarily Don's as had been most of the songs put out under their joint names. The copyright situation was resolved in 1980 when Phil signed away his rights to the songs. 'Some of the things were inaccurate. I worked on *Cathy's Clown* but not on those other early ones. At the time I did the work on it I said to Wesley, "Give the song to Donald to make up for the others", knowing that it was going to be a big hit.'

Cathy's Clown was about an old high school girlfriend of Don's: 'I knew we had to have a strong record to come out on Warner Brothers. Archie Bleyer had obviously really helped to make us successful. Like a lot of people he felt his own importance and had often wanted to assert that importance on different occasions. I knew that if we didn't have a hit the first time out with Warner Brothers everybody would say, "Ah, it was Archie Bleyer that was the secret", and I was determined that that wasn't going to happen. The Grand Canyon Suite was my inspiration for the melody. The record had that walking thing with the drums which hadn't been used in pop music before. That came from the old Philip Morris commercial here in the States and I always liked it.'

Cathy's Clown was first released in Britain to coincide with Don and Phil's visit. Prior to the release Warner Brothers had tied up a distribution deal with Decca so that the record was issued with the distinctive bright red Warner label with the number WB 1. Around the world the release of *Cathy's Clown* was backed by a massive advertising campaign. The record was like nothing the Everlys had recorded before, with a heavy echo and a strident drum beat behind a crescendo of sweeping harmonies on the chorus. It was Don and Phil's best-selling record around the world topping the British charts for eight weeks which, by 1960, was unusually long and made it top record of the year. On the flip side was a Boudleaux and Felice ballad, *Always it's You*. The disc reached Number One in America (with the flip getting to fifty-six) and sales exceeded two and a half million.

The sound was to be repeated on all the sides recorded in Nashville over the next two years. Bill Porter, who engineered all the sessions, gives a clue as to why they were different from the Cadence recordings: 'They were recorded in the same studio as the Cadence ones. The sound is different because Archie Bleyer wanted things a certain way. As a result the tracks all had a similar sound. With Warners I had much more freedom. Don and Phil were also more involved in the music. They spent a lot of time developing the sound of the guitars, Don got quite heavily into it. The trouble was that primarily the sound was too early for the people so unfortunately the records weren't as successful as they should have been. The arrangements took away the melody which was uncommon at the time. It was much later that people went more into production and caused the drastic change in recording technique.'

The drummer on the session was Buddy Harman. 'Few people would let me express myself. Don and Phil wanted me to play more and so I worked on it. They were looking for something different but didn't know how to tell me what they wanted me to do. They would explain what they were looking for and I would adapt it and develop the idea. They probably got more out of me than anyone else in those days.'

'Donald and I stayed with the basic principle of rock'n'roll,' confirms Phil, 'which was that the music should develop so we were always looking for something new. That's why good Bryant songs appeared on albums rather than singles.' Don agrees: 'I like all the early Warner things. I think they're the best things we ever did. There's a sound that we captured that is hard to duplicate today. The things that we did that were experimental in those days are really fantastic today if people sit down and listen to what we were doing.'

But there were problems in the studio. 'Although there were many good records made at the studio and people talk about the freshness of the sound produced on those records, the studio wasn't that good really,' remembers Bill Porter. 'It was made the wrong way around and the sound was difficult to get right. It was set up in a way that different sized units could be recorded and the positions where there was the best sound were marked with X's on the floor. In fact the sound was so bad that we made up various fibreglass pyramids which were fitted in the studio. They were all different heights and sizes and made a drastic difference to the sound. They were known jokingly around Nashville as ''Porter's Pyramids'' but I didn't mind because they did the job.'

The Everlys' first tour of Britain was a resounding success with sell-outs at each venue. There was a surprise for the audiences when Don introduced their backing trio: Jerry Allison, Joe B. Mauldin and Sonny Curtis. In fact, the Crickets' career was in limbo at that particular time so it probably made sense for them to undertake the tour, although their name did not appear on the bill nor did they·do their own set.

Having their own backing group was a new departure for the Everlys. On their American package tours they had either used the tour band or a group of local musicians, while for occasional dates, Don and Phil used members of the Nashville Sound. However, the session men travelled with Don and Phil for one particular show, a huge package playing before thousands in the Gator Bowl in Jacksonville, Florida. There was a chain link fence between the stage and audience and a line of police to keep back the fans. The Everlys were at the height of their success and, when they came on stage, the crowd surged towards the fence, as Buddy Harman remembers: 'The police made

to push the fans back who retaliated by throwing hot dogs which were being given away free. There we were singing and playing having to dodge hot dogs all the time.' Eventually the weight of the fans pushed over the fence and posts and the Everlys and the musicians had to race to the dressing rooms in the near riot. Phil now says: 'Since that time I've made it a policy not to go anywhere where they give away stuff because people have a tendency to throw things they got for free. They started throwing things about three acts before the end when Jerry Lee Lewis was on stage. We closed the show and we dodged and dodged. There was a hot dog got stuck on the cymbal. Some of the cokes were like ice balls because they had ice in them and they were dangerous. They were throwing hot dogs everywhere and we were slipping on them and everybody had to duck. If you put that in a movie no one would believe it.'

The record-buying world was bombarded with Everly Brothers material during 1960. This was due to Cadence issuing singles from the small amount of unreleased material in their vaults and linking the records with the Warner releases. During that year five singles were issued, three Cadence and two Warner Brothers, with three albums in the States and two in Britain. The public didn't mind the sudden glut of material. In fact they lapped it up, particularly in Britain where in the singles chart from the time *Let it Be Me* first entered the Top Thirty on 12 February there were to be only two weeks when there wasn't an Everly Brothers record in the charts. Very often there were two as the Cadence and Warner Brothers releases overlapped.

Cadence issued the first post-contract single *When Will I Be Loved/Be Bop A Lula* only a few weeks after *Cathy's Clown*. The A side was the first Phil Everly composition recorded by the brothers. It has all the ingredients of the Cadence hits but with a much stronger backing. The song was recorded some three weeks before they started working for Warner

Brothers. In retrospect, it is hard to understand why such a strong track was given to Cadence so near the end of the contract. 'I don't think that anybody thought it was very special except me,' said Phil. Neither record suffered from the competition offered by *Cathy's Clown* hitting top spot and *When Will I Be Loved* reaching Number Eight in May. There was later interest in *Be Bop A Lula*, a track recorded in 1957 which reached Number Seventy-four in July.

When Will I Be Loved was issued in Britain in July by which time *Cathy's Clown* was beginning to slip down the charts. This was a logical decision because Decca were distributing both records so it was counter-productive for the singles to 'compete'. *When Will I Be Loved* had a sustained chart run, reaching Number Four. Phil Everly said of it: 'I was very proud. The song came out of personal experience. I was learning the art of being real to myself in my songs.' The song was to become the most successful in terms of sales of any Everly composition. It has been recorded by many different artists, most notably Linda Ronstadt, who had a massive hit with it in 1975. Surprisingly, the song never figured in the brothers' stage act until the Reunion Concert, although Don has performed a brilliant rock'n'roll version over the past couple of years.

Carol Drakely—her mother wants a showdown. | Pop singer Phil Everly—"I don't remember her."

Pop star hides from girl fan

AN angry mother drove 60 miles with her pretty 16-year-old daughter yesterday for a showdown with American pop singer Phil ("Bye - bye, Love") Everly.

But 21-year-old Phil would not come out of his room to see them at the Midland Hotel, Manchester.

He said he could not remember the girl, Carol Drakely, who arrived with her mother

By
JOHN AUSTIN

from Rossington, near Doncaster.

Dark - haired Mrs. Elizabeth Drakely, aged 50, said: "That's not true. It is making Carol look such a fool.

"She has even lost her job in the gown shop because of all the publicity.

"All I really want is for him to admit he knows Carol."

Everly's manager, Lester Rose, stood in the

doorway of Room 207 and told me: "I won't have my boy humiliated by being confronted with this girl.

"My lawyer, Harold Orensten, said we mustn't talk to anybody about this.

"If this girl's got any complaints, I suggest she sees a lawyer herself."

Carol said: "My friends think I've been shooting a line."

WARMER
Bright periods, warm. TOMORROW: Little change, colder.

When Don and Phil returned to America they found two albums had been issued simultaneously (competition again). Warner Brothers issued *It's Everly Time*, which included six Bryant songs as well as one by Ray Charles, a Fats Domino song, *I Want You to Know*, and *Memories Are Made of This*. Neither *Cathy's Clown* nor its flip were included. The album was unique for its time because it did not follow the normal formula of filling the album with songs already known to the prospective buyer. It was usually felt by record companies that unless most of the songs were well known, people wouldn't gamble the price of the album. The Everlys, once again breaking with tradition, included nine original songs out of twelve and gave their own distinctive style to the other three so that they sounded fresh and new. In such a strong album it was agreed that the best song was Don Everly's *So Sad (To Watch Good Love Go Bad)*. It was in pole position on the album – Side 1 Track 1 – and was chosen as the Everlys' next single release.

In competition Cadence issued a strong compilation album, a 'hits' LP titled *The Fabulous Style of the Everly Brothers*, and the second of its kind issued by Cadence. In March of the previous year Cadence had released *The Everly Brothers Best*, comprising both sides of the first six singles. For *Fabulous Style*, Cadence included both sides of the singles from *Take a Message to Mary* onwards, the one remaining unreleased track *Like Strangers*, and three tracks issued on the first album.

In Britain the albums came out to rave reviews, their release staggered to reduce competition. Both sold heavily. *It's Everly Time* was issued in June and reached Number Two in the LP charts. *Fabulous Style* was delayed until October and reached Number Four. For some reason London had not released *The Everly Brothers Best* so the opportunity was used to alter some of the tracks so that there would be no duplication with the first album. The result was that the album was made up of both sides of the singles from *Dream* to *'Til I Kissed You* with the addition of *When Will I Be Loved* (still in the singles chart at the time) and *Like Strangers*. This was the only occasion when the make-up of albums fundamentally differed between America and Britain.

Don and Phil did not rest on their laurels. The response to both the first single and album had been so good that Warner's wanted another album out as soon as possible. The Everlys went back into the studios during July, and put down enough tracks to make this possible. One of the tracks, *Lucille*, caused so much excitement when it was recorded that Warner's linked it with *So Sad* and put them out as a double A side. *So Sad* reached Number Seven and *Lucille* was Number Twenty-One in the Billboard chart while in Britain, where the sales of two sides were combined, the disc reached Number Four. Both songs were to become irreplaceable ingredients of the Everlys' stage act.

Lucille was a reworking of the Little Richard hit of three years before. The record has a long guitar introduction, which has a heavier sound than had ever been heard on record before. When Don and Phil added their searing harmonies the song became, indelibly, an Everly Brothers classic. 'We cut live with eight of the main session guitarists in Nashville all playing the same riff,' explains Phil. 'We had no multiple recording then. That large guitar approach was Donald's idea and it was a good idea which has never really been explored. It made the sound so big and I think that was probably the reason the song was able to come back so soon. We made an effort to be a little more innovative.'

The last legitimate Cadence release was a Bryant song, *Like Strangers*, which was issued in America backed by *Brand New Heartache*; while in Britain it was released with *Leave My Woman Alone* as the flip. The record, although considered not sufficiently strong for release when Don and Phil were with Cadence, was good enough to make Number Twenty-Two in the Billboard Top 100 and Eleven in *NME* chart in Britain.

In October Warner Brothers issued the Everlys' second album, *A Date With The Everly Brothers*, which repeated the formula of *It's Everly Time* by including a collection of mainly original songs. There were six Bryant songs including *Love Hurts* and *A Change Of Heart* which had been hits for other artists, and *Always it's You*, the flip of *Cathy's Clown* which was also on the album. Rock'n'roll was served by *Lucille*, and rhythm and blues by Jimmy Reed's *Baby What you Want me to Do*. There were two new Everly compositions – Don's *That's Just Too Much* and Phil's *Made to Love* which opened the album and became a big hit for another Cadence recording artist, Eddie Hodges.

Before the album was released the Everlys had embarked on the next important stage of their career. The connection with Warner Brothers held obvious possibilities for Don and Phil to break into movies. There had been lucrative offers while they had been with Cadence, but they had rejected them as being low-budget rock films where the Everlys were expected to appear as themselves. Don and Phil were setting their sights higher. If they were to appear in movies they would do it as actors, not as pop stars, and, with their usual dedication and professionalism, they turned their backs on valuable live work (reputed at that time as being in excess of £100,000). They moved to Hollywood for six months and enrolled in Warner Brothers' acting school under the direction of Peyton Price. Apart from a few short visits to Nashville for recording sessions and for Don to visit Sue and Venetia, the brothers shut themselves off from the public.

The Everlys would no longer use Nashville as a base from which to work. Phil remembers: 'Spend six months in California and you'll never leave.' Initially they concentrated on their acting studies. The music press told frequent stories of their progress and in January of 1961 it was suggested that a movie script had been chosen which would see Don and Phil as brothers graduating from military academy. The film never did get started and the only time the Everlys were to work in front of the film cameras was in a screen test which Wesley Rose had arranged. 'Wesley somehow managed to get a screen test through an

agency which cost about twenty-five thousand dollars, which was a lot of money in those days,' remembers Phil. 'They strapped guns on Don and I, and Donald was dressed as Black Bart and I was Kind Charlie, in brown. They had us in a real cabin and it was the director from *Bonanza*, somebody like that. When things are going bad on a set it gets real quiet and things got so quiet there that you could hear everything like squeaking shoes and so on. Donald is supposed to be a stranger and he comes by the cabin window. I'm sitting in the cabin and I'm saying, "These are the words of a frontier lad, who lost his love when he turned bad" and then we sing *Take A Message To Mary* together and he says, "Howdy stranger" and I say "Howdy stranger" and we just sung this duet together! There was a particular line Donald couldn't remember and everything became very tense – the line is, "And bravely dare the danger that nature shrinks from". Good line, uh? How do you like that one? They finally wound up writing it down on the table on a piece of paper and about the eleventh take and Donald's last line is "Well, I'll be seeing you" and I said, "Not in the movies" and that's the way it worked out. We weren't that interested in a movie career anyway.'

The six months at acting school could be regarded as wasteful, particularly as it interrupted Don and Phil's musical career. It appears that the motivation towards the movies emanated from Wesley Rose, but Don Everly feels their time was not totally unproductive. Wesley says of his decision: 'Well, I had negotiated a motion picture deal for the boys and I wanted to make sure they had at least the fundamentals of acting. The picture we had would've been a very big picture but they changed their minds about doing it.' 'I never really wanted to be in the movies,' disagrees Don. 'Because you're a great recording artist doesn't make you a great movie actor. It's not where my abilities lie but they kept pushing it as a natural progression. It was a lesson-learning experience which can't be bad. I remember applying some of that teaching to the recitation on *Ebony Eyes*. It all had a value.'

Ebony Eyes, a morbid tale of a love lost in an aircrash, was written by John D. Loudermilk. With *Walk Right Back* it became the Everlys' next single, their second double Top Ten hit in America, and their tenth million seller. In Britain the record was released with *Ebony Eyes* as the A side but, as interest in the other song

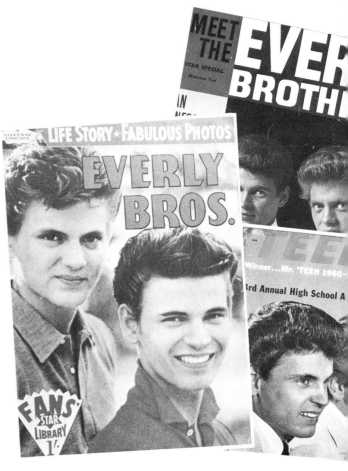

Above: *Don and Phil settle down to prepare for acting school at Warner Brothers.*

increased, the record received double A side status. The Everlys had another massive world-wide hit on their hands. In America *Ebony Eyes* charted first and was to reach Number Eight but *Walk Right Back* was not far behind, reaching Number Seven in the Billboard Hot Hundred. In Britain, with sales combined, the record reached Number One staying there for three weeks in a lengthy chart run.

Both songs have become synonymous with the Everly Brothers, but it is *Walk Right Back* which has been more frequently recorded by other artists. It contains only one verse which the Everlys repeat in full. The reason for this is that their old friend Sonny Curtis had shown them the song as he was writing it. They had immediately wanted to record it and they had asked Sonny to finish it. At that time Sonny was being drafted into the army and, because Don and Phil were short of time, they recorded the song as far as it went (at that time titled *I'm So Lonesome Everyday*). By the time Sonny got the second verse to them they were in acting school.

Despite its morbid lyrics *Ebony Eyes* is a huge favourite. 'They bought the song in and it was almost like walking along a beach and finding a billfold and its got money in it. It was such a temptation that we did it. It is the most requested song that we never did live.' Phil thinks, 'It was just a kind of a downer and I'm so scared of flying. Don never wanted to do the recitation anyway. It was too depressing.'

For all its success, *Ebony Eyes* was to be a significant record because it was a prime factor in the Everlys'

acrimonious split from Wesley Rose. The arguments started with the Everlys' recording of the standard *Temptation*. The brothers were committed to the song. *Temptation* was Don's idea. 'I dreamed it in my sleep. I woke up one day and said, "I'm going to record it just like that" and got the session together. I was very proud of it. Wesley was a real drag at the sessions. I think he did everything he could to keep it from happening. When the Warner contract was signed, Wesley had the choice of singles which meant that he could veto anything he wanted. He did that to me with *Ebony Eyes*. That was an Acuff Rose song and was released in preference to *Temptation* and I didn't know anything about it. That was the end as far as I was con-

cerned. I wasn't about to stay in a business where people picked what I was going to sing.'

Phil adds another dimension: '*Temptation* brought on the argument and the changes in our music after that are based on that problem. The reason we broke from Wesley wasn't just from the music. I believe that, had that whole thing been allowed to continue and there had been some more co-operation, not necessarily from Don and I but some of the outside influences, it could've been more interesting than it was. It was inevitable that we would leave Wesley Rose though, because we were doing Acuff Rose songs almost exclusively. We needed more freedom.'

Wesley Rose has his own views on the split. 'Somewhere along the way, being separated from them led to this break. It is not right to say that the split occurred because Don and Phil insisted on releasing *Temptation* as opposed to Acuff Rose material. *Let it Be Me* was not an Acuff Rose song but we recorded it and had a big hit with it. The split occurred after we recorded *Temptation*. In my own mind I didn't feel it was a great song but one hundred per cent pop and the harmony didn't come through to me but for some reason the boys took to it. It was a total surprise to me when Phil came in one day and said that they felt they wanted to go their way alone because we didn't have one single thing go wrong. Now, I hadn't talked to Don at all, but Phil told me he and Don were agreeable and it was a mistake not talking to Don because Don didn't know why I didn't go out to the coast. So he actually thought that I broke it up. It was a very disappointing period because I felt they were like my sons and there was nothing personal in it, it was just the end of an era with me.'

It would appear from Don's comments that he was, in fact, in agreement with the split and that the difficulties arose because the Everlys' musical development had extended beyond the boundaries of country music and Acuff Rose. Wesley Rose had followed a path that was common within the evolving rock'n'roll industry. He, like Colonel Tom Parker with Elvis and Norman Petty with Buddy Holly, had seen the potential of a highly talented act and had guided the Everlys' career to success. In the early days, although Don and Phil were highly professional performers, they had little commercial experience; it was logical for Wesley and Archie Bleyer to have a big say in their career. Once the recording restrictions imposed by Archie Bleyer were removed, Don and Phil showed that they had an immense musical awareness and were producing sounds that were artistically satisfying to them as well as maintaining their level of success. It is probably true to say that Wesley misjudged their feelings towards *Temptation* and as a result alienated them by pushing *Ebony Eyes*. His commercial judgement on the latter cannot be questioned because it was a very successful record but Don and Phil had now reached a stage where they felt able to gauge the market and it was only to be expected that they should consider that their decision should prevail. However, it is worth highlighting that, unlike so many of their contemporaries, there has been no suggestion from either

Above: *This EP cover, issued in France, shows Don and Phil on the Warner Brothers lot in Hollywood.*

Don or Phil of financial mismanagement.

The Everlys immediately severed all managerial links with Wesley Rose and issued instructions that he was not to receive any fees. This led to Wesley Rose suing them for loss of earnings on his management contract which had a further year to run. The film plans were shelved and the Everlys entered a period of uncertainty. Wesley Rose said of that period: 'At the time the biggest problem I had was to sort the business side out. I had to protect myself. I no longer wanted the responsibility and took my name out of the Warner contract. It was purely a business decision and did not affect our personal relationship.' Although the legal action was aimed at removing Wesley Rose as manager, the music publishing arrangements were not included. The Warner contract had also committed Don and Phil to Acuff Rose as songwriters and it was this aspect that today colours Don's views. 'That contract was no gift to us. It ended up with us being tied to Acuff Rose for ten years for which we weren't compensated at all. I like Warner Brothers, I think it's a tremendous company, but the tie-up we had with Warner Brothers *and* Acuff Rose was no good at all. It really was a bad deal for the Everly Brothers.'

Temptation is notable for being the most innovative (and the biggest production number) the Everlys were to record. It opens with Buddy Harman's distinctive drums before moving into a heavy guitar refrain achieved, like *Lucille*, by filling the studio with every available session guitarist in Nashville. The strident female chorus complements Don and Phil's soaring harmonies. Both Don and Phil regard *Temptation* as one of their best records. 'I'm very proud of it,' says Don. 'It was the first standard to be recorded and put into a rock sound.' And Phil: 'I was well pleased with it. We were trying to find another way of expressing our music.' Don is also quick to praise the work of Buddy Harman on their sessions. 'We got an awful lot

Everlys' hit written before they were born!

says KEITH GOODWIN

FRESH as this morning's milk and just as tasty, a 27-year-old song—dressed in modern finery and tailored to the requirements of 1961's beat-conscious pop music fans—comes bounding back into the hit parade with a mighty bang!

The song? The Arthur Freed-Nacio Herb Brown composition "Temptation." And the people responsible for the facelift that has given it a new lease of life? None other than the world's top vocal team, the Everly Brothers, who weren't born when the song was written! Originally made famous by Bing Crosby in the film "Going Hollywood" back in 1934, "Temptation" now takes on new dimensions in the hands of the Everly boys, whose driving, punchy performance has resulted in one of their best records yet.

Aided by a female chorus and the sparkling percussion work of drummer Buddy Harman, Don and Phil hit peak form on this disc which, incidentally, marks the first occasion they have notched a hit with a standard. Their previous hits have all been original compositions.

"Temptation" is one of the most recorded songs around today.

There have been vocal versions by such international stars as Billy Daniels, the Platters, Perry Como, Billy Eckstine, Caterina Valente, Sammy Davis Jr. and the late Mario Lanza; instrumental versions (including discs by Stan Kenton, Morton Gould, Bill Snyder, Carmen Cavallaro and Martin Denny) and even comedy versions (notably by Red Ingle's Natural Seven with Jo Stafford).

Last year, the song was revived instrumentally by American pianist star Roger Williams, whose excellent disc enjoyed a good degree of success in the States.

But the Everly Brothers' interpretation looks like eclipsing all the others in terms of popularity, phase in the Everlys' career—at a time when they are preparing—and could so easily hit the No. 1 spot within the next few weeks.

The success of "Temptation" comes at a particularly exciting time when they are preparing to widen their scope via two entertainment mediums which are entirely new to them, namely films and night club engagements.

Until now, the pair's appearances have been confined to TV dates and concerts.

But their new manager, Jack Rael, Patti Page's manager for the past 15 years, has great things in store for them in the near future. Rael has tremendous faith in the boys—in fact, apart from Patti, they're the only artists he's ever handled.

Their guide

The man who will guide the Everlys on their film and night club ventures will be the same man who guided Elvis Presley in several of his films—director Charles O'Curran, who is Patti Page's husband.

O'Curran's first task is to devise a crisp, showmanly, colourful cabaret act for the boys.

He will concern himself solely with the visual aspects of the act and will show them the finer points of presentation.

After that, he will settle down to work on some ideas he has in mind for Don and Phil with regard to movies. He believes they have great potential as movie actors — not, surprisingly, as a team but more as individuals.

O'Curran feels that because of differences in temperament and looks, the Everlys needn't necessarily have to portray brothers when they finally get around to making films. He plans to feature them in the same picture—but playing totally different, unrelated characters.

Now living in Hollywood, Don (who recently bought himself a £28,000 yacht) and Phil recently went into business on their own—forming a disc company to be known as Calliope Records.

Their aim is to develop and record new talent which they have discovered during their various Stateside concert tours.

Whenever possible, the brothers will supervise the recording sessions for Calliope, and they are also enlisting the aid of their father, Ike, a prominent country-and-western artist in bygone years. Ike's extensive knowledge of country and folk music will be put to use in the repertoire department, and he will also handle the bulk of the arranging.

The formation of Calliope Records, however, doesn't mean that Don and Phil will be leaving Warner Brothers, with whom they signed a 10-year contract last year.

The Everlys will remain with the Warner label, who will distribute material from the Calliope catalogue in Britain in the future.

The rapid rise to prominence of "Temptation" tends to suggest that the disc will top the million mark in no time at all. But Warner Brothers are aiming even higher. They want it to top two million, so that they can award TWO Gold Discs—one to each of the brothers!

ANTHONY SHAW writes from Burnley : I can't think why "Juke Box Jury" voted Duane Eddy's her record company has made the mistake of plugging the wrong side. It is a dull, uninteresting ballad.

---

out of him. He has contributed more to the music coming out of Nashville than almost anybody else.' 'He is the original main man,' agrees Phil. 'Everybody who plays drums has picked up some inspiration from him.'

The record was to be a huge international hit, reaching Number One for four weeks in Britain and selling well in France and other European countries. In the United States, however, the success of the record did not match previous releases, although both sides did make the Billboard charts. *Temptation* reached Number Twenty-Seven and *Stick With Me Baby* Number Forty-One. It is hard to comprehend this relative lack of sales. It has been suggested that *Temptation* was so pop-orientated that it was not played by the country music radio stations which concentrated instead on the B side.

Their professional career may have been in a state of limbo in the Spring of 1961 but it did not stop Don and Phil developing in different areas of music. Their progressive ideas were bound to lead them into production work and they decided to start a label which would not only enable them to produce their own acts and have their songs recorded by other artists, but give them the opportunity to record outside the Everly Brothers.

They formed Calliope Records, a name conceived by Don, with the agreement of Warner Brothers who were to handle distribution. The company was very much Don's baby as was reflected by the records that were ultimately released, the first of which was a rock version of *Pomp and Circumstance* by Adrian Kimberley. 'I started Calliope because I wanted to do things with horns and big bands and I couldn't fit it into what the Everly Brothers were doing. I did *Pomp and Circumstance* under the pseudonym of Adrian Kimberley. It was a real rocking instrumental version with lots of brass and a girl vocal group. It was recorded in Los Angeles with Neil Hefti who is still one of the world's finest arrangers. It really moves along. The joke is that *Pomp and Circumstance* is the graduation theme in the States and my idea was to release it at graduation time starting (like cheer leaders), "No more pencils, no more books, no more teachers' dirty looks" and then into the song.' The record sold well and reached Number Thirty-Four in the Billboard charts but was banned in Britain. 'I didn't realise at the time that it

was a national monument in Britain or we might've had a hit with it there.'

Throughout 1961 the Everlys were active in Calliope. Don released two more singles under the name of Adrian Kimberley. The tracks included *When You Wish Upon a Star*, *Draggin', Draggin'* and a rock'n'roll version of *God Bless America* but they were not so successful and did not reach the charts. Don also produced an artist called Jack Pegasus who had been introduced to him by Chet Atkins. Pegasus recorded a song of Don's called *Time to Spare* but, because of the dispute with Wesley Rose, the songwriting was acknowledged to Jack Pegasus so that the copyright was not owned by Acuff Rose.

Phil's input appears to have been limited but he had a hand in one record which will be of interest to all record collectors. 'We did a song called *Melodrama* under the name of the Keystone Family Singers. Don had left the session and there was Carole King, Glen Campbell, myself and the session drummer. We put the song together in twenty minutes.'

The build-up of career and domestic pressures during this period began to affect Don's creativity so that the life of the label was short-lived. It could have been a different story if the original ideas for the label had come to fruition. When Don and Phil first went to Hollywood they already had a number of friends resident there: the Crickets, Dorsey and Johnny Burnett and Eddie Cochran; Lou Adler and Tommy 'Snuff' Garrett were friends who were involved in the publishing and production side of the industry. The group became inseparable. 'We got to be very, very good friends. We hung out together all the time. We had a lot of laughs and a lot of good times,' remembers Garrett.

Garrett, one of the leading producers, was signed to Liberty Records at that time and was particularly close to Don during the disputes with Wesley Rose. 'We talked about setting up a label together. We talked about most things when we were together twenty-four hours a day. Originally, it was the intention that the company would be owned jointly by Don, Phil and me, but Al Bennett of Liberty Records wouldn't let me be a part-owner of the label so it didn't materialise.'

While the lawsuits with Wesley Rose were taking place, Don was also involved in an acrimonious divorce from Sue. There had been growing unhappiness between them and Don is reputed to have told Sue, 'Babe, you just ain't Hollywood.' It was clearly a painful experience for both of them and one that Sue still does not feel able to talk about. It is not really surprising that the marriage faltered. They had faced long periods of separation during their marriage, especially when Don and Phil went to acting school. Don and Phil's success had outgrown Nashville and, although their parents still lived there, with the split from Wesley Rose and the divorce, they had all but severed their links with the city. Don and Phil were now residents of California.

The Everlys returned to Nashville at the end of May to record their next album, *Both Sides of an Evening*. In view of the circumstances it is not surprising that there was no Acuff Rose material on the album. The songs were a selection of standards, one side up-tempo for dancing, the other slow for dreaming, given the Everly treatment backed by the best of the Nashville sound. 'Lightning' Chance feels that the sessions were not as spontaneous as before. 'We lost a lot of personal input when they went to Hollywood. After that, someone from Warner Brothers would come to the session with them and it was more or less cut and dried.'

The album was well received, although there were some doubts expressed at the change of direction in the material. The change wasn't altogether as a result of the split from Wesley Rose. 'We had no contact with any other writers but Acuff Rose, and that was specifically cut off,' Don explains. 'There was our own material but we hadn't been pushing our own writing because we'd been pushing the act. That was one of the sad parts of the situation at Cadence and Acuff Rose. We had no contacts at all. We were completely on our own. So we did resort to recording a lot of old standards. I felt that we had to develop away from country music. We couldn't just keep singing about teenagers and school and all that. I wasn't that crazy about myself, anyway. I felt all the songs were done with enthusiasm and vim and vigour but that wasn't going to be enough to survive.' Phil, however, feels the enforced change in musical direction affected the Everlys' career. 'Leaving Wesley was no problem for us but missing the Bryant songs was a tremendous

Above: *In Hollywood, 1961.* Below: *The break from Wesley Rose becomes public knowledge.*

problem for us. We were writing our own songs but if you were to write a hundred songs and have two that are sensationally great, you're doing very, very well, at least at my level of writing, but Boudleaux Bryant writes at a higher level. I would imagine he'd have ten, maybe fifteen, that would be great and all would be of very good quality. It's like a Rolls-Royce compared to a Chevy. Now, you might have a great Chevy but a Rolls-Royce is something else, and Boudleaux's songs will be mostly Rolls-Royce songs.'

Boudleaux was frustrated at not having access to Don and Phil. 'We never wanted to stop writing for them but once they split from Wesley Rose we were never allowed to give them our songs. In fact, I went to Wesley once with eight songs that I had written for the Everlys and he just refused to let me show them to Don and Phil. They wanted the songs but Acuff Rose just wouldn't license them.' Wesley's version is different. 'Felice and Boudleaux Bryant were signed exclusively to Acuff Rose and when the split came it was a case of we had other acts we were managing and our writers' songs at the time were used for the artists we had. I don't recall Don and Phil asking for any songs. For one and a half years after the split I didn't hear from them. I wanted to protect my name from my own end and they wanted to do something else.'

The standard of their recorded material was not the only move towards the establishment that Don and Phil made at that time. They followed Elvis into the nightclub circuit of Las Vegas, playing there for the first time in the Summer of 1961. Their new manager, Jack Rael probably influenced the change in direction. Rael, who has been Patti Paige's personal manager since 1946, looked after Don and Phil until 1971 and in

fact has only ever managed those two acts.

'Don and Phil approached me when they had already split from Wesley Rose. They were inactive – retired, so to speak – driving their Cadillacs. They weren't talking to one another too much. They were getting along. They came to me and said they wanted to get back into the business. I thought about it and finally said, "Okay". I made most of the decisions but I would never take anything without first discussing it with Don and Phil. Most of the time they seemed to agree but if they didn't I had to convince them to take certain dates. I spoke to Patti Paige's husband, Charlie O'Curran, about putting together a cabaret act for the Everlys. At that time, Charlie was doing a couple of movies for Elvis. The boys wanted no part of it and they were right. He didn't think the way they did. When they finally put their act together I'd listen to it and make suggestions. I know there was one special

material thing they did that was comedic in nature and that was fun.' Rael, however, denies any influence in the Everly recordings. 'The reason their albums of 1961 and 1962 included a high proportion of standards was because they wanted to go in a different direction and they weren't writing much at the time and this was their decision. They basically called their own shots when it came to recording.'

It was time for a new single for the Autumn market and Don and Phil chose two tracks from the new album. Following the established procedure, an up-tempo number *Muscrat* (a song partly written by Merle Travis) was backed by *Don't Blame Me*. At that particular time the volume of sales for singles in America was causing the record companies concern. Warner Brothers introduced a unique concept with the single by adding shortened versions of two former Everly hits, *Walk Right Back* and *Lucille*. *Don't Blame Me* proved

Opposite and above left and right: *Relaxed shots during a break from acting school, grabbing snacks at the Warner Brothers studios.* Below: *Robert Crabbe of Decca Records presents an award to Don and Phil in 1960. Their career was full of such presentations.*

to be the more successful, reaching Number Twenty in the charts while *Muscrat* only reached eighty-two. The record was issued in Britain with *Muscrat* as the A side. This was the first of many occasions when Decca promoted the wrong side. *Muscrat* was not good single material and only made the lower reaches of the top twenty.

While the *Both Sides* album was being released in America, Don and Phil were back in the studio recording their next album. The choice of songs indicates the problems Don and Phil were having at that time. The selection included established standards like *Bye Bye Blackbird*, *Autumn Leaves*, *The Party's Over*; a comic song *When it's Night Time in Italy (It's Wednesday over Here)*; *Trouble in Mind*, a Bertha 'Chippe' Hill blues song; two traditional songs adapted by Ike Everly, *Ground Hawg* and *Long Lost John*; and reasonably modern songs like *True Love*, *Jezebel* and *O Mein Papa*. The songs arranged

by Ike have a bright accompaniment but the most outstanding is *Jezebel* which really captures the excitement the Everlys were able to inject into their recordings.

Immediately the session was over Don and Phil left on an extensive and highly successful tour of Australia and Asia. It was to be their only major tour of the year. On their return to the States in November they went back into the studio to record material suitable for singles. In two days they recorded eight songs which were much more in the accepted Everly style. Among the tracks were two written by 'Jimmy Howard', another Don Everly pseudonym to avoid the Acuff Rose publishing contract: 'I was so mad and upset with Wesley.' These were the first of their own compositions recorded by Don and Phil for over sixteen months. There was a degree of urgency because Don and Phil were shortly to be out of circulation again – in the United States Marine Corps.

69

6
The Marines

Don and Phil faced a pause in their career when they became eligible to be drafted into the armed forces for two years' National Service despite the record company's efforts to minimise the service requirements. Don and Phil had managed to postpone the duty for some time because they had contractual commitments to fulfil but it became clear that, unless they volunteered, they could be drafted without any control as to the unit they were assigned to or the period of duty. Through Jim Conklin it was arranged for Don and Phil to enlist in the Marine Corps which only required a six-month enlistment period although one or both of them would be subject to a month's reserve training each year for eight years. This was felt to be less damaging on the Everlys' career than two years out of the public eye. In addition, the Marines agreed that Don and Phil could do their service together which was contrary to the normal arrangements.

The Everlys were happy to join the Marines. There was a family tradition to uphold; one of their uncles had been a Marine. Phil suggests, jokingly, that there was another reason: 'To this day I blame Donald's choice because Donald said that the Marines had the best-looking uniforms and I said: "Donald, that's a rough outfit!"' Once the terms were agreed, Don and Phil quickly arranged a break in their appearances and recording schedule to enable them to complete their service time.

They reported at the Marine Corps Recruit Depot in San Diego early on 25 November 1961. After preliminary instruction, they toured the base before being sworn in by Captain Kalis. They then obtained their kit and were subjected to the traditional Marine Corps haircut. With them was Joey Paige who was to become the bass player in their backing group for a couple of years and is still a close friend of Phil's, and Marshall Lieb, a member of the Teddy Bears.

As one would expect there was great interest from the entertainment press so the Marines agreed that Don and Phil could be photographed on their first day. 'That was no joke in there. To see these pictures is even

Above: Captain Kalis swears in two new Marines – Don and Phil Everly and below: the next step is the regulation haircut, a procedure the style-conscious boys must have dreaded. Opposite: Don and Phil line up with the other Marine trainees at the San Diego Marine Corps Recruit Depot.

70

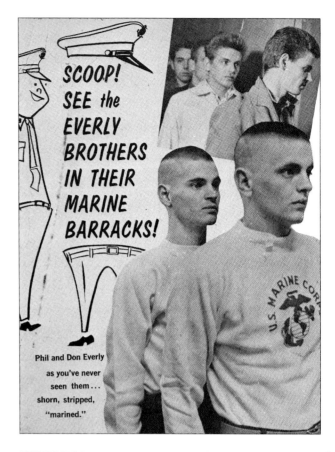

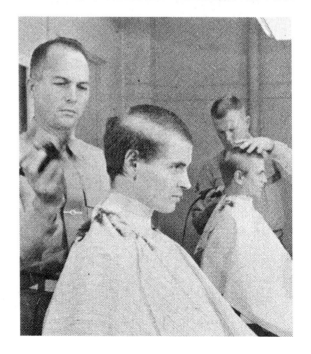

more staggering than I thought,' said Don. Phil also said of the shots taken in the canteen: 'The reason we were eating like that was because a sign says, "Take all you want but eat all you take." The first day I read the sign as I came through the door. I didn't feel like eating, it wasn't the most pleasant thing I've faced, so I took a little salad, kinda Hollywood, and there's a Lieutenant watching you as you come through the line and I didn't have enough on my plate and he said, "Hey" and sent me back and loaded up my tray and I had to eat it all. I didn't feel like eating – I did in a day or two because by then I was so hungry I could've eaten a horse.'

After that first day Don and Phil were treated like any other recruits, perhaps worse, and were not allowed any contact with the outside world. Their basic six-week period of training was to be the most vigorously demanding of their lives. They were woken at 4.30 a.m. and undertook a regular routine of exercises, fatigues, drill, hikes, classes, learning to handle weapons and protect themselves. They were obliged to run between activities and were once punished for 'slacking' when they stopped briefly to listen to the military band. It must have been a harsh life for two men used to sleeping most of the day and working at night. Perhaps the greatest strain was being limited to three cigarettes a day!

Once the basic training was complete, Don and Phil were transferred to the 8th 105 MM Battalion for a further six weeks' training after which they were fully-fledged Marines. 'Looking back on it,'' says Phil of his training period, 'I wouldn't go into a boot camp again for a million dollars. We didn't get any special treatment except that they kept a close eye on us to make sure we weren't killed. They didn't have us replacing the targets on the rifle range. Licking and sticking we used to call it. It did happen that people got wounded or killed down there. In fact I did it for about half an hour one day before they realised and pulled me off.' Don and Phil referred to their time in the Marines on a Merv Griffin TV Show in 1968. Asked if they ever fought each other, Don replied: 'We were in the Marine Corps together and I think they got all the fight out of us,' to which Phil added: 'Don was a platoon leader which meant that he got to wear a wrist watch which during boot campus was a big deal. I was a flunky, sweeping up and things.'

While Don and Phil were suffering the rigours of the Marines, Warner Brothers kept their name to the fore with a number of record releases. First *Crying in the Rain* backed by *I'm Not Angry*. The A side emanated from the Brill Building songwriters, and is unique in being the only collaboration between Howie Greenfield and Carole King. It is a sweeping ballad with Greenfield's lyrics a classic example of troubled young love. The B side was an up tempo song written by Don. It is an unusually constructed song and maintained the Everlys' practice of releasing two strong sides on a single.

The comparative drop in sales of the previous two singles in the States had worried Warner Brothers.

They had recruited an established disc jockey, Joe Smith, as head of national promotion, later to become A & R man, responsible for the Everlys among others. Smith has remained with Warner Brothers despite all its many corporate changes over the years, and is now head of Elektra/Asylum/Nonsuch Records: 'One of our first records was *Crying in the Rain*. Warner Brothers Records was not one of your great hit factories at the time and to have a record that sounded like a hit was a major thing for us. I got our very small promotional crew together and I said: "We've got to try to do something with this record." We told our distributors it was a do-or-die record for us which in fact it might have been. Had that record not happened it would have been another blow for Warner Brothers. The picture company was planning on closing the record company anyhow, but the record started to come alive and it was a top ten hit in the States.'

The promotion obviously paid off. The record reaching Number Six in a thirteen-week run in the Billboard Top 100. There was no need for special promotion in Britain. In fact, the Everlys' enlistment in the Marines had increased the normal level of publicity and the record quickly entered the charts and similarly reached Number Six.

The single was quickly followed by the new album, *Instant Party*, made up of the tracks recorded the previous Autumn. In America the record was attractively packaged in a gatefold sleeve with pictures of Don and Phil in matching tuxedos. The sleeve also printed various party tips such as the 'Ice breaker' and recipes for the 'Demon Don Sandwich' and the 'Purple Phil Punch'. The concept of a party album was good, but the material did not work well together. Six slow, slow ballads out of twelve songs did not augur well for a swinging party! When the album was released in Britain one of the ballads, *Love Makes the World go Round* (theme from *Carnival*) was replaced by *Temptation* to bolster the set. Despite less than ecstatic reviews the name Everly was still enough to guarantee strong sales.

On 13 February Don and Phil graduated as Marines and, on the same day, Don was married for the second time. His bride was British-born actress, Venetia Stevenson, whom he had met in Hollywood. They were married by the Everlys' platoon chaplain, Lt. Commander R. L. Crabtree, at the chapel of the San Diego Naval Training Center, with Phil as best man. Snuff Garrett and Lou Adler flew down to San Diego for the wedding.

Their graduation entitled Don and Phil to three days' leave and Jack Rael was able to arrange a booking on the Ed Sullivan Show on 16 February which also covered as a honeymoon for Don and Venetia: 'Ed Sullivan did the show out of Miami. I had a friend at

Opposite page: Scenes from the Marine life, from the viewpoint of the Everly Brothers and the press. After receiving their first taste of Marine food, Don, Phil and Joey Paige await orders with their possessions piled up around them.

ARMY LIFE SUITS'
THE EVERLYS

REPORT BY
BRUCE CHARLTON

Just back from his Middle East tour—
RUSS CONWAY WINS NEW HONOUR

BY MIKE HELLICAR

Get a Beat

the
making
of TWO
MARINES

☐ Into each and every life a little sunshine—and a little rain
—must fall. The Everly Brothers, Phil and Don, seem to have
a monopoly on both these days; only Don has cornered the
rain-market and Phil the sunshine. Don, whose Bye Bye Love
was one of his biggest songhits, has bid love goodbye in a
court, (after less than four years of marriage) and his tragic
bottle with wife Mary Sue for custody of their three-year-old
daughter, Venetia, was one of the less pleasant headlines of
recent months. Faced with the loss of his child, Don has
declared that he will never give her up in a thousand years.

And even Don's romance with another Venetia—or
Venetia Stevenson, seems to have reached an impasse,
on the other hand, is in the throes of what many of his
mates consider a new romance. She's a pretty young st
named Jackie Shannon, and Phil, with characteristic in
ishness, has been doing everything in his power to help a
her career, furthering her contacts and rending advice
contracts, costuming and what not. At this date it's a t
point whether Phil will sub for Don as a married man,
sibly the spectacle of Don's current marital unhappiness
put him off—and besides first things first. And the first t
in Phil's life is the new career that's facing both he and
for a long time to come: as a member of the United St
Marine Corps. Phil is now 22, Don is 25, and rather t
waiting to be called into service.
Perhaps the time away from show business enlisted in the M
of pull to avoid Army duty—both boys trying to use some
needed breather to straighten out his
Neither boy is concerned he wants t
for as Phil is worried
get out." Both
acting ca

Above: *Don is married to Venetia Stevenson by Platoon Chaplain Lieutenant Commander Crabtree.* Below: *Snuff Garrett, Phil, Lou Adler and Don in a line-up at Don's wedding reception.* Opposite: *Don and Phil smartly turned out at their passing out parade on the completion of their basic training.*

Miami Beach and I called him to get us some accommodation down on the beach. Don and Venetia had a bungalow to themselves and Phil and I hung out together and we had a good time. They both loved warm weather, they always have.'

On their return from leave, Don had to separate from Venetia and return to the Marines with Phil. For the second part of their services they were at Camp Matthews at Pendleton between San Diego and Los Angeles. The training was just as hard as before but the discipline was not so strict. Don and Phil were

given the opportunity to work for a weekend pass as Snuff Garrett reveals: 'We put on a show at the Marine Training Center. Lou Adler and I did comedy bits. Don and Phil sang. We brought down a bunch of friends like Dorsey Burnette and Johnny Burnette, the Paris Sisters and whoever we could round up together for the weekend. We went down and played for thousands of Marines and had a really great time. The show was so successful that they let Don and Phil off for a long weekend and they were thrilled to death.'

They used the weekend leave to go into the recording studios. Another single was required as it was felt that the stockpiled material did not contain two tracks of sufficient quality for a single release. *How Can I Meet Her* was recorded, coupled with *That's Old Fashioned* which had been recorded in Nashville the previous November on the same day as *Crying in the Rain*. Reports at the time said that the Everlys had flown to

Nashville for this session, but the noticeable difference in the sound from that on their other records (and with Don's bride in Los Angeles) it is probable the sessions took place in Hollywood. It is a fast up tempo number with a busy arrangement including a harmonica which was very unusual on pop records at that time. *That's Old Fashioned*, on the other hand, has all the hallmarks of a classic Everly record with an introduction of horns and steel guitar attracting the attention. In America both sides made the charts. *How Can I Meet Her* reached Number Seventy-five while *That's Old Fashioned* was the last of Don and Phil's top ten entries, reaching Number Nine. In Britain, the former song was, for some peculiar reason, designated the A side, and consequently reached only Number Eleven.

Marine service was not detrimental to Don and Phil's career. By careful timing of their releases and the strength of the sales those records achieved, the name of Everly was only absent from the charts for a short period. The singles were more successful than the releases prior and subsequent to their time in the Marines, which suggests that their military commitment had a positive affect on sales. In Jack Rael's words: 'They were never really out of show business. We always managed to keep them in front of the public eye.'

Don and Phil obtained honourable discharges towards the end of May and were free to resume their careers. They had endured six months with one of the world's toughest fighting units. 'It takes you out of what you're doing,' recalls Don. 'It will change you. Even the six months we did will change you. You'll come back a little bit different.' Phil agrees: 'They certainly straightened us out. They don't allow you to do anything but right'. Don didn't regret it at all. 'It saved my life in the long run.'

The newspaper clipping on the left:

NEW MUSICAL EXPRESS ●

brother Don 'disappears' in America—

L EVERLY WILL
MPLETE TOUR

ur continues. **Phil, younger of the brothers, is determined to finish the** one. **Don, after collapsing three times last weekend, is now in his doctor's** , but his whereabouts, reports Nat Hentoff, from New York, is unknown.

nformation if
or not.
t never have
erly had been
some time.
advised him to
re and rest.
he had an obli-
ns to meet his

d visit for him
missed the plane
ondon alone last

ours later, Don
s wife, actress
again missed the
to get another
ter.
rived on Friday
, they went with
rince Of Wales
h their act with
ad brought over
c and Joey Page

and drummer Chas. Blackwell.
   Singing " Crying In The Rain,"
Don broke down. Phil immedi-
ately stopped the rehearsal and the
Everlys went back to their hotel to
rest.
   Soon after midnight, Don was
taken more seriously ill and was
sent to Charing Cross Hospital. He
discharged himself after six hours,
but on Sunday afternoon he was
rushed to Middlesex Hospital.
   Phil went to East Ham Granada
for the first concert hoping that Don

could join him. Instead he went on
stage alone.
   The elder Everly left hospital on
Monday morning and was taken
direct to London Airport, where he
caught the noon flight to New York.
   Phil told promoter Arthur Howes
he would either continue or with-
draw from the tour as requested.
Pleased with the reception given Phil
on Sunday, Howes asked him to
continue—with Frank Ifield and
Ketty Lester.
   Although concerts are going ahead
as arranged, Phil will not be appearing in ATV's " Sunday Night At
The London Palladium " this weekend. The Everlys' place will be
filled by the Kaye Sisters.
   It is not yet known whether or not
Phil Everly will appear in ABC's
" Thank Your Lucky Stars " and on
the Light Programme's " Saturday
Club " and " Parade Of The Pops "
as planned.

7
Don's Illness

On their discharge, Jack Rael quickly arranged a countrywide tour for Don and Phil covering fifty cities to run from 4 July until 20 August. It was a 'getting to know you' tour and Don and Phil travelled everywhere by coach. The tour was a resounding success with attendance records broken at many of the venues, and TV and other promotional dates fitted into the schedule to make up for lost time.

To coincide with the tour, Warner Brothers also took the opportunity to release a new album. As Don and Phil had not had time to record new material, Warner's put out a compilation of twelve sides of the brothers' first seven Warner singles and titled the set *The Golden Hits of the Everly Brothers*. This attractively packaged album is one of the Everlys' biggest selling albums and is still available as a regular release.

There was no relaxation when the tour finished because Don and Phil were back in the studio recording new material for much of September. The difficulty of finding good songs was particularly evident at this time. Instead of recording an outstanding album in three days as in 1960 they managed only a total of eight tracks of which only two were to receive a release at the time. One of the songs recorded but not released was the Goffin and King song *Chains*, which two months later entered the Billboard charts by the Cookies and later was recorded by the Beatles for their *Please Please Me* album. Although their tight schedule meant Don and Phil had little time to pick good quality songs or write their own material, the cause of the problem was more deep seated. According to Don: 'Being into drugs made for indecision. I really blame it on that because there was an inability to get anything done after that.'

It is not clear exactly when it began but sometime before the Marine service, Don and Phil became involved with a couple of New York 'speed' doctors. One, Max Jacobson, numbered among his patients Archie Bleyer and his stepdaughter Jackie Ertel. A lot of people blamed Phil because he brought Donald to Jacobson. 'It was Archie Bleyer that started it. I locked in because I was staying at his house in New York and I was hysterical one night and I wound up there. The doctor was very famous at the time, treating all of these famous people you wouldn't believe. His theory was that our society had become accustomed to all

Opposite: Phil in London, 1962, warming up for another series of concerts.

77

kinds of instant things: ''Quick, I'm not feeling good, I want to feel better.'' So he would change the metabolism of your chemical make-up, but it wasn't good for you because you had no permanent control of it and you were depending on some outside influence. You were supposed to note psychologically how it kept you and strive to be like that when you weren't involved with it. With me, the idea was just to use it as a guide to make myself more stable, better able to handle my own pressures. I don't know if it worked for me but I could see from what it was doing to Donald that it was dangerous to mess with. At the time we went there it was better than the other options. It seemed right at the time. There were other avenues but it wasn't really seedy.'

'It was very fashionable to go to a ''speed'' doctor. He was a real Doctor Feelgood.' At the beginning Don didn't realise what was happening. 'In those days people didn't realise that amphetamines were drugs and that they were addictive. Unbeknown to me I got involved. I saw Eddie Fisher in his office loads of times. I saw pictures of the doctor with John F. Kennedy, and I figured, ''Hell, this fella can't be wrong'' but he was. It didn't seem to be an unusual thing to do either. I had the drug on prescription and injected myself. At the beginning you don't realise what's happening but finally you catch on that you're awake for three days on B12. I got to a point where I couldn't go on stage without it. If you'd go searching for him he'd be there'.

In the early 1960s the term 'drug addiction' was something that could finish a career in the pop music industry. Even now Jack Rael becomes defensive when the subject is raised: 'Dr. Jacobson was their doctor when I inherited the act. He was a strange doctor but I didn't care for him. I remember once he had to leave quickly because he said, ''Eddie Fisher will not go on without me being there'' which I felt was ridiculous but this is what the guy did. I think that whoever sent Don and Phil to this guy did not do them any favours. Don reacted terribly to it. I don't know what the drug was, but it was not heroin. They were never involved with any high drugs so they didn't have a problem as such. It was on prescription and the police never bothered them because it was all legitimate.'

By the Autumn of 1962 Don's health was reaching crisis point. After the recording sessions in September Don and Phil went to Nebraska to record an album of Christmas Carols with the Boystown Choir. It is notable for containing the first solo recordings of Don and Phil to be released. Don sings *What Child is This* while Phil performs *O Little Town of Bethlehem*. Shortly afterwards they flew to Britain to begin a third European tour. To coincide with the tour Warner Brothers released a new single with two of the tracks chosen from those recorded in September, *Don't Ask Me to be Friends* and *No One Can Make my Sunshine Smile*. The latter song was the A side in Britain but the sides were reversed for American release.

They arrived in London separately, Phil on 9

October, Don and Venetia (who was expecting their first child) a day later. Reasons given for Don's delay was that his car had broken down on the way to the airport. The Everlys stayed in The Savoy Hotel and on the Saturday they went to the Prince of Wales Theatre near Leicester Square for a runthrough of their act with their back-up band, Don Peek – guitar, Chris Blackwell – drums, and Joey Paige (their friend from the Marines) – bass guitar.

Main support to the Everlys on the tour was Frank Ifield who had just had his first colossal hit *I Remember You* while his second *Lovesick blues* had just been released. 'On the Saturday they were due to rehearse after me but when I finished and before the Everlys did their runthrough the whole show was cleared out. We weren't allowed in while they were rehearsing so I could not even watch them from the wings. I went to my dressing room so I don't know what happened but there was a bit of a fracas and that was the last we saw of Don.'

Don had broken down and Phil had immediately called a halt and they went back to the Savoy. Don was later taken to Charing Cross Hospital but he discharged himself after six hours. On the Sunday the day the tour was due to start at the East Ham Granada, Don was taken ill again and this time went to the Middlesex Hospital where he stayed overnight before flying back to America with Venetia. To protect their image it was reported that he was suffering from a nervous breakdown or food poisoning. In truth, at the age of twenty-five Don had twice tried to commit suicide by taking an overdose of drugs. 'I was so high it didn't matter whether I went on living or not.'

The first show at East Ham was planned for 6.30 and Phil went to the theatre thinking that Don would join him there. Frank Ifield explains the situation on that first night. 'The talk that was going round was that Don's trouble was drugs but there was a very tight net around them so no one knew exactly what was going on, even to the extent that the fans who had come to see the first show didn't hear about it until the very last minute. Everything was so sudden. I was asked to extend my act there and then to give Phil a bit of breathing space. I had hardly any notice at all. Fortunately I had worked with the band before so it wasn't

78

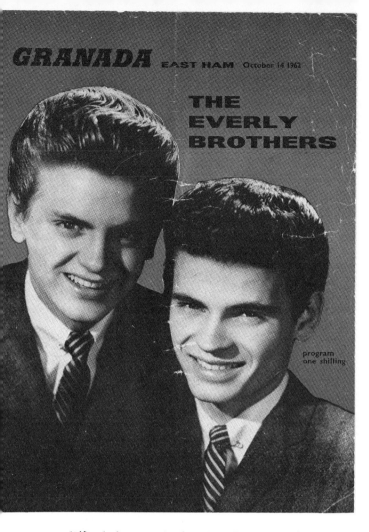

GRANADA EAST HAM October 14 1962

THE EVERLY BROTHERS

program one shilling

Left: The cover of the programme of the fateful tour, in which Frank Ifield (right) was main support for Phil.

too difficult for me. At that time I was very big which was fortunate because my extending didn't make much difference from an audience point of view and as second top I was able to give strong support to Phil who rightly topped the bill.'

Just as the Everlys were due to appear an announcement was made to the audience that Don had been taken ill and that Phil would do the show alone. The Everly Brothers Trio then went into an extended instrumental before Phil went on stage looking extremely nervous. His act lasted about fifteen minutes beginning with *Lucille* and finishing with *Bye Bye Love* with which he got everyone to join. At the end he said: 'I really do appreciate this. Would you please give a big hand to my brother? He's not here to enjoy it.' In the circumstances it took courage for Phil to undertake the show. Frank Ifield agrees: 'I think Phil did a very brave job going on alone. It was a hell of a thing to do. Half the time Phil was singing the harmony but it worked. Nobody asked for their money back. Obviously they were disappointed like I was, but they were happy that Phil had the guts to get up and do it on his own.'

The extent of Phil's courage can be seen when it is appreciated that when he went on stage he didn't know whether or not Don was alive. 'I was in the hotel room with him at the time but deep down inside I just refused to believe that he was really trying to kill himself. Donald had not been well for a while and we were semi-cognisant of his situation. It was just the most dreadful period I could ever imagine. There were

like eight thousand different things causing it. It was just terrible. Joey Paige got me through the 1962 tour, particularly the first night at East Ham. That was my first solo on stage. I had done solos on radio but not in years. I just had to switch over to Donald's part which I found very difficult. I sang the harmony part of *Lucille* all the way through. But there was nothing else I could do – it was like "the show must go on" kinda silliness or put everybody out of work, but also too I didn't know whether it was the end totally, I had no real idea of knowing what the situation was. I knew we'd best continue and bring the funds in.'

Jack Rael was in the States when Don became ill. 'We had to bring Don back and we had an ambulance meet him at the airport and we put him in a hospital. Phil called me and asked me to go back over to England and continue the tour with him which I did. Everywhere was sold out and Phil would go out and say, "My brother said to tell you he's so happy you're here – he's coming along fine." Phil handled it beautifully. He and the group did tremendous business; naturally Don was missed because he was very important but they didn't have to give back any money.'

As the tour progressed tension built up within the package. Frank Ifield recalls the problems. 'There was no connection by Phil with the rest of the acts on the tour because there were a lot of people protecting him very strongly from not only the press and public but also from us. I had no protection at all because there was so much around Phil, and consequently when the press couldn't get in to see him I got hounded to death and had to get someone to look after me. The bill was falling apart because nobody was able to get together

79

Extraordinary exit of the Brother Everly

EXPRESS
PHOTO 🄽 NEWS

by
LOGAN GOURLAY

DON EVERLY—one half of the Everly brothers pop singing act—was flown out of London Airport yesterday, "Sobbing," according to reports, "in the arms of his wife.

And so Tony Newley's peremptory — and somewhat immature—demand, "Stop The World, I Want To Get Off," is echoed again in the frenetically-spinning world of hit records.

A name appears in the Top Ten. The owner has no equipment to cope with the almost vampiric adulation of the teenage record-buyers.

★ ★ ★

He has a vocal gimmick. Plus perhaps an electric guitar, which has as much relation to music as a fuse box.

The result is predictable. Nervous exhaustion. Collapse. Sometimes barbiturates. And always the statement: "The strain at the top is too much."

Within the previous 12 hours Don Everly had been taken to hospital twice for emergency treatment. "Nervous exhaustion . . . he may have taken some drugs to quieten himself down," said one of his staff. "He's worn out." All Mr. Everly said was: "I don't feel good. I wanna go home."

★ ★ ★

Bunny Lewis, impresario and record expert, told me: "The teenage audience is the most fickle in the world, constantly demanding new names, new idols. They have no loyalty. . . ."

Mike Sullivan, who guided Shirley Bassey to stardom, said: "It's tough to make the transition from one-hit record star to all-round performer. Nine out of 10 fail—tragically."

The story spins on as harsh and trite as the lyrics on the records.

PICTURE BY MICHAEL STROUD
A drug overdose. Now pop singer Don Everly drives with his wife to the airport. To fly out, sobbing, in her arms

---

with anybody. So I decided to move out of my chauffeured car and travel on the coach with the rest of the gang. I wanted to see Phil to suggest that he move into the coach as well and asked Wally Stewart, who was looking after Phil, if I could see him but he would not let me so I just barged past him and I asked Phil, "How's about coming on the coach?" and Phil was delighted and said, "Yes". He got on the coach with us and we had a ball, but the funniest thing to me was to see the two chauffeur-driven cars travelling behind with the two managers travelling in style while we were in the coach having a ball of fun. Phil was obviously very tense at the time but relaxed a lot more when he mixed with everybody and understood everybody was right behind him. He was great company.'

Phil completed the British tour, even managing to increase his act over that first night performance. Everywhere he went he received a good audience response. Self-confessed Everly fanatic, Albert Lee, saw the show and gives an indication of the atmosphere: 'The Everlys were so big at that time and everybody wanted Phil to do well and that probably made it easier for him.' Billy Kinsley of the Merseybeats goes along with that comment: 'When I saw Phil with just a trio, I wanted to get up and harmonise with him. I think nearly everyone in the audience did.'

Despite the success of the shows all the remaining dates were cancelled as Phil wanted to get home and see how Don was progressing. He left Britain in the

knowledge that the tour had not affected the Everlys' standing with their British fans. *No One Can Make my Sunshine Smile* sold well, reaching Number Eleven in the charts while in America, presumably due to the lack of promotion, the other side only reached Number Forty-Eight in the Billboard chart.

Don was still convalescing at the end of 1962. He was visited in hospital by, among others, Felice Bryant. 'He looked terrible. He suffered from all the pressures on him and it took a lot of rest to pull him round. I still feel that all the troubles at that time were caused by him sub-consciously trying to get away from the terrible demands that touring put on him. They had such an excessive schedule that it's not surprising that one of them cracked.' Snuff Garrett also lays a lot of blame on the pressures Don was facing. 'The Everlys were basically producing their own records and Don at that time was pretty much taking the helm on everything. He was constantly trying to prove himself and he did have a terrible bout of problems at that time.'

Don and Phil spent Christmas with their parents in Nashville discussing their future plans. They could not realise it at the time but they were at the watershed of their career. From being automatic top ten hits their records were from now on only to hit the charts sporadically and even then mainly in the lower reaches. It was a remarkable turnaround for an act that for so long had been able to do little wrong. Don has few doubts as to the reasons. 'When I look back on it there's no way it could've lasted much longer. Things developed too fast. There were too many things happening at the same time. The mainspring was the law suits with Wesley and my wife, the Marines and the drug addiction we wound up with.' From September 1960 when they went to Warner Brothers' acting school until 1964, the Everlys were, to a large extent, out of the public eye especially in America which is notorious for discarding yesterday's heroes for new stars and sounds. When they were able to work consistently again they were regarded as 'cold'.

For six years the Everlys were unstoppable. They were the number one group throughout the world as was evidenced by the numerous awards they won: world's outstanding Vocal Group in the *New Musical Express* (England) each year from 1958 to 1962; similar awards from *Muziek Press* (Holland), *Muziek Parade* (Holland); *Cashbox* and *Billboard* polls as well as *Record Mirror. Disc* and *Melody Maker* in Britain, and music papers in Australia and Europe, had Don and Phil as top group for the period 1958/1963. Don and Phil were also voted top country and western group for 1957, 1958 and 1959. It is a mark of their status and their professionalism that Don and Phil were able to effect a resurgence in their career, although never to the dizzy heights that they had known.

Below: *Don signs an autograph for Vera Lynn's teenage daughter.*

8
Resurgence

Don's crisis with drugs may well have reached a peak in London in October 1962 but it did not simply take a short convalescence to resolve the difficulty. 'It's a habit that catches and there was no treatment for it. It was administered by a doctor of medicine supposedly curing me but it was giving me the psychosis. It took two or three years to get it out of my system. I spent quite a bit of time in two or three hospitals but they didn't do anything. They treated me for being crazy rather than for drug addiction and just locked me up but when I got out I just went back to the doctor again. I wound up really having to just pick myself up and start again, plus I had to cure myself of the addiction. I did get off it finally. I realised it was killing me.'

The year started on a high note for Phil when on 12 January he married his long-standing girlfriend Jackie Ertel, Archie Bleyer's stepdaughter and the daughter of Janet Ertel Bleyer, a member of the Chordettes. They had been close for five years although the romance was an off-on affair. They married at the Episcopalian Little Church Around the Corner in New York, and Don was well enough to be best man. After the wedding, Phil and Jackie spent a two-week honeymoon in Nashville before moving into Phil's apartment in Hollywood.

The Everlys' career did little more than mark time during the first half of 1963. Once again a new single release was a priority and Don and Phil went into the studios in Hollywood immediately Phil and Jackie finished their honeymoon. Five songs were recorded of which two, (So it Was, so it Is) So it Always Will Be and Nancy's Minuet, were released. The A side is a slow ballad notable for the remarkable short final bars. The B side is a strong beat ballad written by Don which Phil feels 'should have been another Cathy's Clown and would've been had it been released when created'. The Everlys believed in the song and recorded it three times, each with a different arrangement. The song, however, was relegated to the flip side and received no exposure. The record failed to reach the top 100 in America but achieved some slight success in Britain where it reached Number Twenty in an eleven-week run in the charts.

A short tour of the West Coast followed the recording session and work continued on a similar basis throughout the Spring. In April, further sessions took

Above left: Jackie, Phil, Don, baby Stacey and Venetia arrive in London in September 1963.

82

THE EVERLY BROTHERS
and BO DIDDLEY

83

Phil Everly weds —Don best man!

By Nat Hentoff & Georgia Winters

NEW YORK.—Don Everly, fit again, was best man when his brother Phil married 22-year-old Jackie Ertel in Manhattan last Saturday!

This was Don's first important appearance in public since the illness which cut short his British tour in the autumn. His wife, Venetia, was also present.

Phil and his bride, daughter of Janet Ertel, lead singer with the Chordettes vocal group, were married in the Little Church Around The Corner, Manhattan. It was a formal affair, with the men in morning clothes.

PARENTS MISSING

The Everlys' parents did not attend the event, because notice was too short, and because their mother does not like to fly.

After the wedding—forecast by the Alley Cat on August 24—there was a reception for 100 guests at the Sherry Netherland Hotel. Among show business friends invited were singer-songwriters Barry Mann and Carole King.

Jackie is the stepdaughter of Archie Bleyer, chief of Cadence Records, the Everlys' former U.S. label.

The couple are now on a two-week honeymoon. Soon after this, Phil and Don will undertake a U.S. concert tour.

place but none of the four songs recorded was considered suitable for a single, so Warner Brothers released a two-year-old track, *It's Been Nice*. It is a light-hearted piece and a good contrast to the run of ballads that Don and Phil had been releasing as singles. In America the song failed to reach the top 100 but in Britain Don and Phil's status was such that the record reached Number Twenty-six. The B side was *I'm Afraid*, written by Jim Gordon, who was then sixteen and had been in a college band that was supporting the Everlys. Don and Phil were so impressed with him that they signed him up as drummer for their touring band. He was to stay with them for about three years before going on to become one of the leading session men on the West Coast.

The record was issued in May and coincided with the birth of Don and Venetia's first child, Stacey Dawn on 5 May. Don did not see much of his daughter because soon after her birth he was touring again. Recording sessions and the Marines reserve period both followed which put such a strain on the marriage that Venetia filed papers for divorce. However, the difficulties were soon resolved and Don and Venetia, together with Stacey, travelled to Europe where Don and Phil undertook a long tour in the Autumn.

By the time Don and Phil went into the studio in June concern was growing at the sudden fall-off in sales. 'No one wants the hits to stop,' remembers Phil. 'It doesn't happen to you suddenly. You don't panic inside yourself right away. It is only in retrospect that you can see the pattern. You're a hot act for five years, then there's a cooling off period and then it's hard to have hits. Every time you put out a record you're shooting dice but when you're used to the top five rush, anything less just doesn't provide the same get-off.'.

Phil felt that the decrease in sales occurred when they were deserted by the country music disc jockeys. 'You have people that like to hear you, but the only way they know you have a record out is if the disc jockey plays it. After we left Acuff Rose it was hard to get plays in the country market and I've always resented that because it was part of our heritage. I find it amazing that country stations were reluctant to play our records. We're so country it's silly. I have my CMA Card Number Five or Six. Don and I were, and are, country at all times, but it seemed we were always carrying a banner just by the nature of our music, I guess.' In an attempt to reach the country market it was decided that the Everlys would record an album of

country songs. They were all fairly recent and included Johnny Cash's *I Walk the Line* and Don Gibson's *Oh, Lonesome Me, Just One Time* and *Sweet Dreams*. It is a fine album of country rock music and was probably some years ahead of its time. It would be five years before the Byrds and Gram Parsons produced music which followed the concept of *The Everly Brothers Sing Great Country Hits* album of linking true country songs with rock'n'roll arrangements: Unfortunately, it was felt that none of the tracks could be released as singles – probably because in most cases the original version was still fresh in people's minds.

Immediately their Marine service was over, Don and Phil spent a day in the studio and recorded three songs for a single to coincide with their European tour. The session had been arranged for Don and Phil to record two songs by husband-and-wife team Barry Mann and Cynthia Weill. At the last minute Don and Phil asked if the song writers had any further material. The song that was offered became the A side of the new single. *The Girl Sang the Blues* was another up-tempo number which was thought to have more chance of success than the beautiful ballad *Love Her* which was on the flip. Once again the fans thought Warner Brothers got it wrong, a view exonerated when the Walker Brothers had a big hit with the song in 1967. That does not mean that the A side was not a good record. It sold well enough to reach Number Twenty-Five in the British charts but in America it was to be the third record in a row not to reach the top 100. It might have done better if Don and Phil had promoted it on the tour dates but they hadn't had time to learn the song before they left for Europe.

The Everlys returned to Britain to headline a country-wide tour promoted by Don Arden. They were joined by Bo Diddley and the Rolling Stones. 'I always thought that the Everlys were an extremely talented act with an exceptional touch of class.' Even though Don Arden had great respect for them, he detected at the time of the contract being signed that 'they would have to have pretty big support and we got together a pretty powerful bill. It was the first ever tour of the Rolling Stones, and it was just at the time when they were getting a name. Everybody was talking about them and I was lucky enough to get them for the ridiculous fee of £40 a night. However, when we opened the bookings for the tour, the advance sales were disappointing and I wanted to bolster the show with another star name and the artist who first came to mind was Little Richard.' Don and Phil had wanted to

undertake the tour after the disappointment of the previous year and the tour was enthusiastically received by the fans. Little Richard joined at Watford about a week after the start but even the improvement in sales that his presence achieved did not put the tour in profit.

Playing guitar with the Flintstones was Terry Slater who became good friends with the Everlys, particularly Phil, and they remain close today. 'It was a very diverse programme. Don Arden pulled such a wide range of people when you think of Bo Diddley, Little Richard through to the Everly Brothers. The people under Don and Phil quite accepted they were top of the bill. The trouble usually came between Bo Diddley and Little Richard as to who would go on first.' (That may be so but Jack Rael remembers 'Don and Phil complaining bitterly that Little Richard did too much damned time that when they got on time was short and they didn't like that'.)

The tour was typical of many undertaken through Britain during the early and mid 1960s. They were modelled on the American tours but with fewer acts so that everyone had a chance to put over their music. Terry Slater misses those tours. 'They brought people together. You became good friends but more important was the interchange of musical ideas like American guitarists would've shown us certain little passages to play and we'd show them things and it was a very good breeding ground for music that doesn't exist today. Because the tours were so long we learned good stagecraft, how to work audiences but most of all was the interchange.'

Perhaps the tour's lack of commercial success was due to the rapid change that had come over the British music scene. When Phil was touring Britain the previous year a record was released called *Love Me Do*, by the Beatles. By the time Don and Phil started the 1963 tour the Beatles had already achieved two Number One records and were receiving massive exposure in the media. Don said: 'When I arrived at the airport, all the press wanted to know was what I thought of the Beatles and I had to say that I hadn't heard anything.' The charts were dominated by British acts. Don and Phil used to watch the Rolling Stones from the side of the stage and were impressed by them. Even at that stage the charisma was evident. Phil recalls: 'They were just bringing in that not dressing for the stage and they looked quite peculiar but they did a good job. They stood out. They were an easy bunch of guys to be around but they kept to themselves as well.'

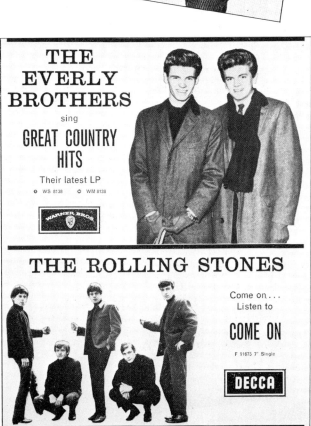

THE Everly Brothers have slipped. I'm not knocking them, I'm not saying they're finished, but whether their fans like it or not they have slipped from the uppermost bracket of the charts in which they were such regular residents. They're still such world's undoubted top vocal gro and they're still regular hi visitors, but lately they've to meet the high...

earlier in th...

In f...

Clown", the brothers' first recording for Warner Bros. and Warner's fir disc in this country. It reach... stayed there for... months in th... nate t...

The Everly Brothers hold their own . . .

THE Everly Brothers are at this moment fighting the biggest battle of their careers in Britain —and they are winning with colours...

...'s unfortunate illness ...here, which...

Phil, the Everlys have emerged triumphant.

Wooing their audiences with magnetic singing skill, whether balladeering or rocking, and the great showmanship which they have acquired after 11 starry years in the pop world, the boys have left the fans yelling for more.

Their melodious vocal technique has won through, and the clamour and ...tion of r-and-b has been somewhat ...shadowed.

...herefore it is rather surprising that, ...sidering their reception in this ...ntry, the boys haven't already got a ...on their hands with their latest ...xing "The Girl Sang The Blues."

...Although it has been selling well it ...s not yet achieved chart status. It ...ould be just a slow starter, but some ...ritics are inclined to think that the ...ipside " Love Her " would have been ...more suitable for British ears. " Love Her " is already big in the States.

In fact "The Girl Sang The Blues"...

was a last-minute choice, for ...ing session was initially ...waxing of " Love Her." ...number complete with a 23...tra, which included strin...horns.

When Don and Phil ...posers of " Love Her." ...Cynthia Weil, if the...numbers, they cam...and it was recorded...session before th...Angeles for Britai...

Anyway, this...Everly song still...of chart honours.

If this happens it should...complete the boys' desires, for wi...now completely fit, and their wor...about the British tour over, both Don and Phil are laughing now.

DISC October 26, 1963

Everlys have a hit with 'Girl' —but it was a real last-minute effort!

"IN the Thirty". That's great'" chorus... Brothers at 1 when...

Throughout the tour Don and Phil saw the way things were going. One night in the North East, Phil went with Mickie Most to a club where the Animals were playing. Most signed them up and was to produce all their big hits. Don and Phil went back to America full of what they had seen in Britain. Joe Smith remembers: 'They came back from this tour and told me about this group they'd seen. Don said: "Well, these guys have long hair and they dress funny." Now at the time he had long hair by our standards and was dressed in a leather jacket and I said: "They look funny – what are you talking about?" But they were both so hip about what was happening in music yet it couldn't happen for them.' The changes that were occurring in Britain in 1963 were to cross the Atlantic in 1964.

Don and Phil began 1964 once again in the recording studios looking for suitable material. Of the five songs recorded, four were Don Everly compositions which indicates that he had undergone his most productive bout of songwriting for a long time. This was probably due to the comparative lack of success achieved by the songs provided by the Brill Building writers. As it was, the fifth song, Jimmy Reed's *Ain't that Lovin' you Baby* was chosen as the next A side, coupled with Don's song *Hello Amy*. The single was released in March, a good six months after their previous record. It was popular in Britain where the rhythm and blues feel to the record was more in keeping with the music at that time. But, although the record sold consistently, the name Everly was no longer enough to ensure a chart entry. In America it sank without trace, becoming the first Everly disc to fail to make the charts both sides of the Atlantic.

Warner Brothers were now looking down every avenue to try to get Don and Phil in the American charts again. It was decided that the Everlys should return to Nashville for recording purposes in an attempt to recreate the hit formula. In fact, Lou Adler suggested that Don and Phil record some of their old Cadence material for a Warner hit album. Joe Smith explains: 'We tried to make a deal to buy the original masters from Cadence. Andy Williams was at that time renegotiating his contract with CBS and insisted that they buy the whole Cadence catalogue so that his earlier material couldn't be released. When we couldn't get the originals we put the Everlys in the studio to record the big ones again.' It was arranged that Don and Phil would go to Nashville and record under the guidance of Wesley Rose.

It seems amazing that after the acrimony of three years before they were all prepared to work together again. 'Warner Brothers and Acuff Rose got together and somehow we managed to patch things up for a while so that we could record in Nashville again. There were no songs there by then. Boudleaux had gone dry and Wesley had nothing much.' Don regards *Ring around my Rosie* as one of the worst things they ever recorded. Jack Rael reveals that Don and Phil had some say in the matter. 'I think they were just going home to Nashville to visit family and friends. They kinda made up with Wesley and finally agreed that

really he was not a manager but a good publisher and a pretty good A and R man. They were very professional and wanted hit records. They knew they couldn't do it themselves – they tried with different people at Warner Brothers. I was very proud of them and very proud of Wesley because there was ill feeling between them and they made up. I thought it was big and gracious of all of them.'

Don and Phil went to Nashville in May and in two sessions recorded fifteen tracks, eleven of them on one day. Ray Edenton exclaims: 'Eleven cuts in one day was not unusual,' while Don reminisces: 'Most of the stuff we did was pretty fresh. Sometimes I don't like doing that unless you've got it figured out ahead of time or you're familiar with the people your working with. That's what we had with the people in Nashville. They had it figured out like we did.' Six of the Cadence hits were recorded and the remaining songs were recorded as potential singles. Four of the new songs were Boudleaux and Felice Bryant songs. 'That only happened because somehow Wesley made up with them. When Wesley was satisfied with them then they could have some of our material so they did a few things. By that time they were going downhill and we were trying to recapture something that had gone down the drain really.' Felice was unhappy: 'What upset me was that they wanted to do things "the way they were being done today". The poor babies didn't realise what they were doing but they were imitating their imitators. Don thought that this was what was happening so that this was the way it had to be done.' Don's reaction is concise: 'Sure, we were producing different sounds, we were being affected by what we were hearing. Lord knows we were on the road enough.'

Wesley Rose was pleased with the results: 'Those things we recorded were very good indeed. I didn't understand why they didn't sell well although I understand they were quite successful in Britain.'

Enough good material was recorded to provide three more singles during 1964. The first was released ten days after it was recorded. *The Ferris Wheel* was backed by a simple Bryant ballad *Don't Forget to Cry*. Perhaps it was the move back to their country roots that gave Don and Phil a minor hit in the American charts. The record has a prominent Buddy Harman drum beat running through it and the Everlys begin the vocal in unison (then unique for them) before changing into the searing harmonies which nobody before or since has been able to produce. In Britain the record sold well and in the Record Retailer Chart, which since the early 1960s had been regarded as the most accurate, the record peaked at Number Twenty-two as against Seventy-Two in America. Neither Don nor Phil liked the song, Don saying: 'I wasn't real crazy about it,' and Phil joining in: 'We were searching around for songs and it was the best that we found at that period of time. It is not one of my favourite songs. That's more a piece of business than when you find a *Dream* or *Let it Be Me*. I was surprised at its success in Britain, I really was.'

The year was spent touring the North American continent and spending the required month in the Marines. Jack Rael put them on dates in Canada but mostly in the United States so that they could earn some money. They were as busy as they really wanted to be. Don didn't always agree with the policy but it was necessary. 'It was a case of having to keep doing things what with the divorce and law suits and all.'

The improvement in the Everlys' disc fortunes in America led Warner Brothers to release simultaneously their next single and album in August. The A side of the single was *You're the One I Love* written by the Bryants (backed by the dreaded *Ring Around my Rosie*). It was a up-beat number which, as one would expect from the Bryants, concentrated on the Everlys' harmony. The song does not have the instant appeal of the earlier Bryant material and is only saved by the vocals of Don and Phil. But it was another record that failed to register in the charts.

The album, *The Very Best of the Everly Brothers* consisted of the six re-recordings of the Cadence hits, plus the six biggest Warner hits. The views of the brothers to the re-recordings differed, Don liking the originals best. 'Warner's wouldn't like me saying that, but it's true. If you've ever done anything for the first time it's never quite the same after.' Phil said: 'We were trying to figure out what to cut and we didn't have any songs again. I don't have the problems about old stuff that everybody does. I'm very proud of the lasting ability of the music. So I was never concerned that we were doing old stock.'

It was an extremely successful release, still available today. The publicity photographs, pre and post Marines, show that from looking filled out and comfortable in their matching check jackets on the front, the brothers had become gaunt, with harsh haircuts on the back.

The third single to come out of the Nashville sessions was Don and Phil's song *Gone Gone Gone* backed by *Torture*, a John D. Loudermilk composition. Warner's, perhaps realising their mistake about *You're*

Opposite: This photograph was used on the 1966 album In Our Image, *but Phil's haircut had changed by then.*

the One I Love released *Gone Gone Gone* six weeks later. It was another fast number with a driving guitar introduction from Don. 'I started playing electric guitar on the sessions about that time and did a lot on that particular track.' It was the Everlys' most successful record in the States from 1962 up to the present day reaching Number Thirty-One in the Billboard charts. In Britain the record did not sell as well as some of their immediately preceding releases and only reached Number Thirty-Six. It is strange that, with the appeal of the record, it was only the third choice single. Phil reveals that not everybody liked the record: 'I really pushed that song on the recording session. I knew it would be a hit but not everyone agreed.' It was to be their last entry on the American charts for two and a half years.

Don and Phil went back into the studio early in December while *Gone Gone Gone* was still in the charts. They were in buoyant mood. Don was well on the way to recovery and enthusiasm showed in their work. Relations between Don and Phil were good and they were writing songs together more than at any other time. Their recording output was comparable with the period when they first joined Warner Brothers in 1960.

The tracks recorded at the Warner studios in Hollywood in December were for a new album although there were some earmarked for singles. The concept of the album was for Don and Phil to record twelve rock'n'roll standards and give them brand-new arrangements. Backing them was an élite group of musicians: Glen Campbell, James Burton, Sonny Curtis and Don on electric guitars, Jim Gordon on drums, Larry Knetchel on keyboards and Terry Slater was on bass: 'When I first went out there Don said that he wished me to play on their album and I went to the studio on the first session, I sat down between James Burton and Glen Campbell who were the two foremost session guitarists and to me were like gods and that scared the hell out of me. But they're great guys and put me at my ease.'

After the 1963 British tour, Terry had kept in touch with Phil. His ambition was to progress from the group he was with and he saw the United States as the place to be. 'My desire was to go to America and Phil sponsored me over. I had no idea what I was going to do. In fact the first thing that Don and Phil did for me was to get me a job at Warner Brothers. I never did start the job because by accident I became the boys' bass player. Their regular bass player went off on an expedition down the Amazon and disappeared and I took over very quickly. Sonny Curtis and Jerry Allison of the Crickets had just come off a tour backing Don and Phil and were rehearsing a new band. I was jamming around in the grounds of Phil's house one day and Sonny said to Phil: "Hey, Terry could do it, he can play bass." I literally sat up two days and nights learning all the parts of their whole programme on bass and took a plane to Detroit where they were playing and went through all that I had learned in one night. I was so excited and nervous to get on to a stage with them. You could get near enough their sound with a three piece. They didn't use much more in the studio. One thing I will always give the Everlys credit for is that they always had a great trio and they always demanded the best of every musician they took out. They really rehearsed us hard and never took second best which is right. Some great musicians came out of that band.''

The resurgence in Don and Phil's career was to give their fans a bumper year for record releases. In 1965 six singles were released in both America and Britain and there were three albums put out in the States while Britain had four (*The Very Best of the Everly Brothers* was not released until January). In one month in Britain two singles and two albums were released. This occurred because Warner Brothers were transferring their distribution from Decca to Pye Records and Decca wanted as much material issued before the transfer was effected.

The first single of the year was made up of two of Don and Phil's compositions recorded the previous month. *You're my Girl*, with a beat heavier and raunchier than anything on an Everly record before, was backed by *Don't Let the Whole World Know* but failed to sell either in Britain or America. A follow-up was quickly released. The A side was Buddy Holly's *That'll be the Day* coupled with another Loudermilk song *Give me a Sweetheart*. The arrangements are less cluttered than on the previous record, and Don and Phil's harmonies sound as clear as ever. Not everyone compared the record favourably with Buddy Holly's original but it sold well, particularly in Britain where it reached Number Thirty and would probably have gone higher had it not been that the Everlys' next release was issued the day *That'll be the Day* entered the charts. As Don and Phil were in Britain to promote the newer single all attention centred on that release.

Don and Phil recorded four Everly compositions in April, three by Don and Phil, and the other a collaboration between Don and Boudleaux Bryant. The song Don and Phil felt strongly about was *The Price of Love* which was backed by *It only Costs a Dime*. The record was released in Europe to coincide with a promotional and recording tour in May. *The Price of Love* was in tune with the times, with a harmonica, over-dubbed by Don, high above the pounding guitars on the instrumental introduction. The British public had such exposure to pop music by 1965 that personal promotion was essential and the results of the Everlys' heavy schedule paid off when the record stormed up the charts and reached Number Two in a three-month run.

With the Everlys high in the singles charts the release of two albums almost simultaneously cashed in on the fresh interest. The first album was titled *Gone Gone Gone* and contained much of the material recorded in Nashville the previous May, although some of the tracks had been recorded some years before. Apart from the title track there were *The Ferris Wheel* and *Ain't that Lovin you Baby* which had both been singles, and *Donna Donna* which was on the *Date with* album but had been re-released as a single in

America early in 1964. From the vaults came two Bryant compositions, *Lonely Island* and *Radio and TV*, recorded in 1960 but presumably locked in because of the Everly/Acuff Rose law suits. Finally there were two fine Don Everly songs, *The Drop Out* and *The Facts of Life*.

The second album was a collection of rock'n'roll songs issued under the title of *Rock'n'Soul*. Added to *That'll be the Day* were versions of classics like *Hound Dog, Maybelline, Dancing in the Street* and *Kansas City*, while James Burton reproduced his guitar work on *Susie Q*. The reaction to the album from critics and public alike was enthusiastic.

The Everlys were still big stars throughout Europe but they seemed unable to make a real impression in their own country which was by now dominated by British acts. The 'invasion' had begun early in 1964 spearheaded by the Beatles, with the Dave Clark Five and Herman and the Hermits close second and third. It was as if you had to be British to sell records in America.

The different attitudes of record buyers either side of the Atlantic is analysed by Phil: 'When I first heard the Beatles, I didn't say "My God! they're doing something I'm not doing". Everybody was doing basically what

we had been doing. What had happened was that the industry in the States had gotten into teenage idols. They pumped up a lot of acts based more on the fan appeal than the music. The British just picked up the music and brought it back over to us. It's American music cut and dried. So I never felt like that we had to emulate anything because I always thought it was from this side anyhow. What we had to do was get back to what we'd done successfully before and do it again instead of all that silly stuff trying to be innovative. *The Price of Love* was successful in Britain and not in America because the English people are more honest about their music than Americans. In America you can jive turkey them. That's why we had the teenage idols here and they didn't have them much over there. To make it in England you have to be able to stand and deliver. People were saying, ''Well the music's right. They're doing it right again, and we'll buy it.'' We were still busy so it didn't really mean anything to us. We weren't in financial need. If we hadn't had any money and couldn't work then we might have become resentful but it wasn't like that so I never felt that way. When the English came, specially the Beatles, they made rock'n'roll an art form and commercially acceptable to the press. I remember reading that President Johnson's daughters were trying very hard to see the Beatles. That meant that rock'n'roll had reached the very epitome of American culture and that's an important turning point. It was no longer negative to be involved in the music where with Presley and the other early acts it was a rebellion, a juvenile delinquent kind of activity.' Don feels equally strongly: 'I think the stuff we did on the *Rock'n'Soul* and *Beat and Soul* albums was some of our best. That was our best period, I like those albums right through to *Two Yanks in England*. Phil and I were writing together. We wrote *Gone Gone Gone* and then had quite a run of songs that were worthwhile but no hits. *The Price of Love* was a good record but was not a hit in the States. We were just out of vogue here. People just didn't want to hear American acts. That was frustrating.'

Although the period of massive hits was at an end, and future releases would only occasionally reach the charts, Don and Phil's many years of performing had given them a highly professional stage act which ensured that they had sufficient work to keep them busy even if it meant that there was an even greater emphasis on touring.

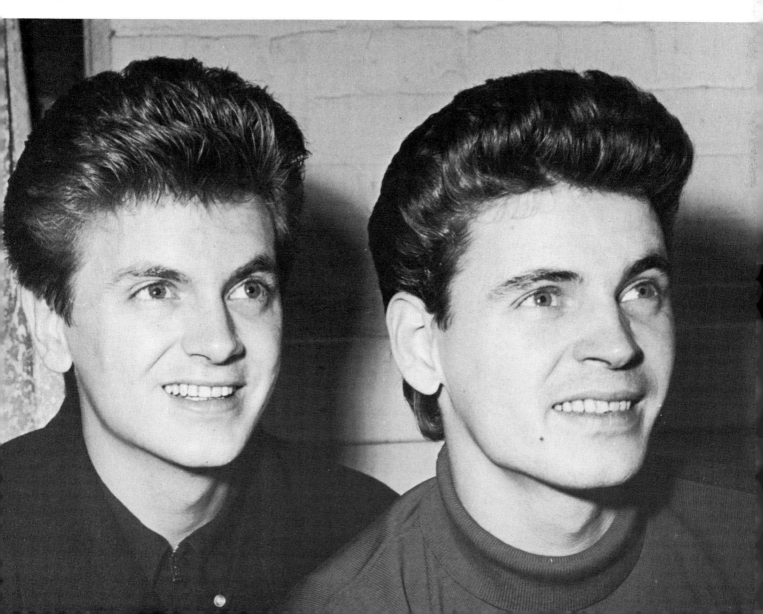

9
Out On the Road

On returning from the promotional tour of Europe, Don and Phil undertook a tour of the mid west and Canada which Jack Rael indicates was typical of the road work the Everlys engaged in during the latter part of the 1960s. Don and Phil were particularly popular in that part of North America; initially they played auditoriums but, as their audience aged with them, they moved into the lucrative nightclub circuit.

The Everlys toured with Ral Donner, a singer in the Elvis Presley mould who had had success with *You Don't Know What You've Got* in 1961, and a group called the Zebras. Earl Hensley was a member of the group and, unlike so many of his contemporaries, he retained many of the photographs and papers he collected on tour and has kindly lent them to me for inclusion in this book. He has many fond memories of touring with Don and Phil. 'We were contacted by a booking agency in Minnesota that wanted to book Ral Donner. The band we had was dubbed the Zebras by the booking agency because all groups had animal names at the time. We signed the contracts and went to Duluth, Minn., where we found out that we would also be touring with the Everly Brothers. Everybody was excited to be working with them. It was a strange tour because we worked in Duluth, Minn., and the next night or two nights later we had to be in Spokane, Wash., one thousand six hundred miles away and it was just a bunch of travelling. Mostly everybody travelled on a Greyhound bus going back and forth from date to date. We had a super time. Don and Phil travelled with us and we'd play cards and the like. The first time we met them we were backstage at the first show. They came over and introduced themselves. The guys off-stage were always very humble-type people. They would do their thing but they were fantastic both on and off stage. They were very hospitable and very gentlemanly-like. One show in Spokane, Washington, was in a gigantic auditorium and our group carried its own P.A. and our own sound system. The house P.A. system which Don and Phil were to

Opposite: Scenes from the tour of Canada and the Mid-West during June 1965. In the main picture Sonny Curtis, Don, Jim Gordon, Phil and Dale Halcombe pose outside their tour bus. Conditions were often less than ideal and sleep had to be grabbed whenever possible on the bus. Card games helped to pass the time. Top right: Don and Phil with Ral Donner (centre) and the Zebras. Below: On stage in Fargo, North Dakota.

use had one speaker which was forty or fifty feet directly above the stage which was funny because you would say something and it would be like three or four seconds or more before you'd hear your sound come back to you and it threw the whole sound system out. So we hooked up our own equipment and told Don and Phil it was just as easy for them to use it and it worked out real good for the rest of the tour.'

Although the tour was hectic there were always opportunities to relax. 'If we didn't have to be in another town one thousand miles away the next night, we'd sit down and have a little party. Just joking around and singing and the like, relaxing after the show.'

There is one subject on which Earl is adamant. 'I've heard people who do not know the Everly Brothers and did not travel with them, who say they were into drugs and I can honestly say that the time I spent with the Everlys, there was absolutely no drugs and I mean no drugs came up of any kind. No uppers, downers, grass – whatever.' This suggests that Don was now fully recovered from the drug addiction.

This particular tour was a happy and successful one, of which fond memories remain, both for Phil: 'The Zebras were some of the nicest guys we ever hung out with,' and for Earl: 'I know the times I spent with the Everlys are something I'll never forget and I'll always be grateful to have had the opportunity to work with them. I think they're the greatest and I consider them to be good friends.'

Don and Phil had time to go into the studio again to record a new album before Phil was due to go back to the Marines for his reserve training. The album was a follow-up to the *Rock'n'Soul* concept but this time the material moved much more towards black music, including *Walking the Dog, The Girl Can't Help it, People Get Ready* and *Money*.

While the album was being recorded Don and Phil had a new single issued, their own composition, *I'll Never Get Over You*, backed by the Don/Boudleaux

Bryant collaboration *Follow Me*. Both tracks were closer to the accepted Everly style than *The Price of Love* and appealed more to the disc critics. However, the public were not so impressed and the record only reached Number Thirty-five in the UK in a short chart run while, once again, the disc failed to register in the U.S.

Following the success of *The Price of Love* in Britain, interest in the Everlys was renewed and Brian Epstein, manager of the Beatles, saw the commercial possibilities of putting Don and Phil on a UK tour. He gave the Everlys good support by drawing from his NEMS stable Cilla Black, Billy J. Kramer and the Dakotas, and Paddy, Klaus and Gibson. Don and Phil were reported to be receiving £7,000 a week ($14,000) for the tour which at the time was regarded as 'phenomenal'. Brian Epstein's commercial judgement was exonerated when the tour sold out. Phil remembers the tour fondly. 'It was a grand tour to do. It was one of the best times we ever had on the road. I have always held Cilla Black in high esteem. I have great respect for her. There was a time in Birmingham, when we sang *Dream*. When we finished the song we just knew that we had sung it so well and you know when you have that feeling inside. Everybody did everything just right. The audience felt it and I looked at Donald and he looked at me. The reaction was great and we did another ballad immediately after which was very rare for us and that got the same feeling. I remember that extremely well. That's an important time in my life.''

For the first time since *Bye Bye Love* Don and Phil did not look identical on their tour, Phil had received his regulation hair cut in the Marines and it had not grown sufficiently to be swept back in the well-known bouffant style. He combed it forward and the reaction to the new style was so enthusiastic that he kept it. About a year later Don followed suit.

To coincide with the tour Warner Brothers issued a single, an EP made up of recent hit singles, and an LP. The single was made up of two tracks from the LP. The A side was *Love is Strange*, the old Mickey and Sylvia hit backed by Don and Phil's own composition *Man with Money* which Phil in retrospect regards as a peculiar song. *Love is Strange* is an Everly classic with a strident guitar introduction. It is memorable for the spoken dialogue between Don and Phil in the middle of the song:

'Donald?'

'What, Phil?'

'How would you call your baby home?'

'Well, if I needed her real bad, I'd call her like this.'

The record was just right for the times and was justifiably a hit; the Everlys' last Top Twenty hit in Britain, reaching Number Eleven.

The album titled *Beat'n'Soul* proved a big seller in Britain. Apart from the greater black influences the whole sound is fuller than that of its predecessor. This was achieved by expanding the number of session musicians; added to the regulars was Billy Preston who played keyboards and organ. The album contained two Don solos: *Hi Heel Sneekers* and *The Girl Can't Help it* which have the heaviest beat of all the tracks on the album. Neither song suited harmony and so it is understandable why Don sang them alone. It was to mark the beginning of a trend which saw solo tracks become common on the brothers' albums.

When Don and Phil returned to America they had a short break, during which time Don and Venetia's second daughter, Erin Invicta, was born (on 8 November). Don and Phil used the break to reappraise their career.

They knew that they had retained a solid following of fans in Britain and Europe but were still striving to recapture the success they had achieved in their own country. They went back into the studio again almost immediately and started laying down tracks for a new album. They started looking in new directions as well as returning to established Brill Building writers to make up the next album, *In Our Image*. It is a varied selection of songs which together make up a fine album and must rate as one of Don and Phil's best. There are four of their own compositions on the album including *The Price of Love* and *I'll Never Get Over You*. Also included is Don's *It's all Over* which is notable because Phil sings the main part and the solo, while Don sings a lower harmony. Cliff Richard had a Top Ten hit with it in Britain a year later.

In the Spring of 1966 the Everlys undertook one of the most prestigious dates of their career during an Asian tour. They were booked to play five days at the Araneta Coliseum in Quezon, in the Phillipines, which was then the largest covered auditorium in the world, seating over 25,000 people. Each of the scheduled shows was sold out well in advance and the demand for seats was so great that the show was extended for three more days and those shows too were sold out. In the eight-day booking more than 200,000 people paid to see Don and Phil perform. Terry Slater remembered it as 'one of the highlights of my life and, I'm certain, theirs. It was just a thrill to go out every night and see that amount of people and the response was just beautiful. I just felt so proud of them.'

Don and Phil visited Vietnam and performed for troops at Tan Son Nhut Air Base. They donated all the show proceeds to the Go-Vat Orphanage which cared for many children left homeless by the war. While on the same tour they had also performed at the hospital at the Clark Air Force Base in Hong Kong to which many American servicemen injured in Vietnam were taken. Jack Rael plays down the visit to Vietnam. 'There was nothing to it. It was just a stop-over and they did maybe one or two dates for the troops. We weren't looking for any publicity.' On the other hand Joe Smith suggests that there was a move among the show business fraternity to support the troops. The Everlys answered it. 'There was, all of a sudden, this rush of boys going to the Far East and there was a desire to re-create the things that had gone down in World War II. Bob Hope was taking out tours and trying to make it a big happy party again. Unfortunately it was not that kind of war, it was not popular in the States and didn't affect everybody, and there was

SEEN OR UNSEEN

Everly Brothers Thrill Shrieking Manila Fans

There's something spec-... By Ma. Paz I. Munson ... tune of "Wake Up Little Susie" and "Bye Bye Love..."

very little desire to go over there and do shows. You weren't going to England to play in an Air Force base and going to London afterwards, you were going to Vietnam which wasn't very pleasant and there were Viet Cong around the corner who could lob a few shells into the show too. But the boys were very patriotic, they had a great love of the country flag and great respect for the military, and they were among the very few people who volunteered to do shows again.'

The concerts left their mark on Phil. 'Politics didn't come into it at all. We got to Vietnam and they came and they stood there and it was about one hundred and twenty degrees on the stage and in the room it was jam to jam. The floor was wringing wet from sweat and we all sat there and we sang everything we knew. All I got out of it was the view that no war is worth one leg. No place, nothing.' Terry Slater recalled: 'It was very scarey for all of us because it was a very dramatic experience to be there, very frightening, really it made you grow up very quickly. When you saw what went on there.' Don dispels any suggestion of patriotism with a joke: 'I had a manager who would book me into any toilet between here and Hong Kong and I found out I was playing there.'

Immediately they returned to the States Don and Phil flew over to London to record their next album. By mid 1966 the American music industry had decided that anything that was going to be successful was going to come out of England, so Warner Brothers arranged for some of their artists to record in London. Dick Glasser who had first produced the Everlys on the *Beat'n'Soul* album said at the time: 'The Everlys are tremendously popular in Europe, perhaps more popular than in the States and the album title *Two Yanks in England* seems a pretty good idea. We intend to include as many English songs as possible.' This suggests that there had been no material prepared for recording prior to Don and Phil's visit, and in the final analysis, eight out of the twelve songs on the album were written by the Hollies who were great fans of

95

Don and Phil. Of the remainder there is a beautiful song called *The Collector* which is credited to Sonny Curtis but which he insists is really Don's song; Don and Phil's own *Kiss your Man Goodbye* and two songs high in the British charts at the time; *Somebody Help Me* and *Pretty Flamingo*. Don still regards the album highly: 'England was so alive and vital then and I was enthusiastic about what we were doing. I felt that going over to England and joining forces with the Hollies was one way of getting the music heard.' The single taken from the album (*Somebody Help Me* in the USA and *I've Been Wrong Before* in Britain) failed to register and was to be the last single in those countries for some seven and a half months although in some European countries the two solo tracks on the album, Don's *Fifi the Flee* and Phil's *Like Everytime Before*, were issued on a single and sold quite well.

In retrospect, the L.P., like all the Everlys' albums, contains top quality performances from Don and Phil but somehow lacks the overall strength of previous albums. Perhaps the fault lies with the arrangements which on occasions are not sympathetic to the Everlys' harmonies or maybe there were too many Hollies' songs. The group had not been writing for very long and were fortunate to have come into contact with the Everlys when they were facing such a dearth of suit-able material to record.

From mid 1966 until their eventual break-up Don and Phil became primarily a 'live' band while still experimenting with their recording to try to find the elusive hit formula. Extensive touring was a strain on the Everlys and their families. 'We toured all over the States, UK, Ireland, Germany, France, Phillipines, Hong Kong, Australia, Canada,' remembers Terry Sla-ter. 'We'd go out from Los Angeles across to Australia then work our way right round. We'd do that twice a year. It put a strain on our lives. We all suffered our divorces.'

Don and Phil were divorced from Venetia and Jackie in 1970. By that time Don had a son, Edan Donald, born on 25 August 1968 as well as three daughters. Phil and Jackie had a son Philip Jason, born on 9 September 1966. Phil's divorce was particularly traumatic. He and his wife parted in 1968 and there followed two years of negotiation before settlement was reached. 'It's a price you pay but that's the way it is', said Terry Slater. 'They weren't unhappy marriages but at the end of the day the wife assumes that she takes second place, which to a certain degree she does, but on the other

spectrum I was doing it for my own satisfaction but also for the pride of my family and to support my family. But they never see it like that. They just think you're out having a good time, which you are, but our wives were always very important to us but I don't think they realised it so we all suffered there.'

Six-week tours were the minimum for business reasons as Jack Rael explains. 'When you went out you had the salary of the musicians and the road manager and in order to amortise the cost of the transportation you had to stay out for four to six weeks. They enjoyed it – it was hard work, naturally. They didn't work many night clubs to begin with, mostly one-nighters. They started to work night clubs in 1967 when one nighters were getting more difficult.' Jack Rael remembered that 'The older people were accepting the Everlys and I started to put them where they could sit down but they were making very good money in the night clubs getting their ten to twelve thousand dollars a week sitting down, which was awfully good money.'

Their working pattern settled down to roughly six months on the road and six months at home, recording and Marine reserve training. Terry Slater felt this was a reasonable arrangement. 'Besides working, because you're artists, etc., you also do it for the money. Because of their upbringing and the way they were, Don and Phil tended to work when they needed the money. They had to pay taxes, a band, and for their homes. They always lived very well. They always bought a new Cadillac every year. They also had ex-wives and children to support. So they earned a lot of money and spent a lot of money. Don would like not to have to work. He's a live-for-today kind of person and he'd say, "Oh, I've got enough to last me for a bit, maybe we won't work so much this year." Phil was always the more businesslike who'd say, "Don, let's go out for the next six months and earn ourselves another quarter of a million and give us a bit more security". But they didn't overwork. Our trips were never more than two months – that would be a really long one – and then we'd be back for anything up to four and six weeks off. We toured a lot, but not exces-sively.'

Phil regarded touring as an acceptable evil but the constant travelling leaves him with few specific memories: 'We stayed on the road throughout. In fact it got progressively longer as things went on. The last year of my first marriage we toured eight months and that was a hard year but we weren't doing one nighters

SOMETIMES IT'S HARD to imagine a time when the Everly Brothers weren't making records. There they were singing 'Bye Bye Love' and 'Wake Up Little Susie,' when many of us were at school. In fact it's hard to think of life without them. And it looks as though we won't have to. For the Everlys flew into London last week and calmly announced that they were well into fully expected to be singing when they were Phil, and I feel the same way about singing. Of course we couldn't do anything else after all these years. We've been singing for ten years. of more than people might say: 'just of this to be 'has been' at 30. to laugh when we

– we were doing mostly a week or a two-week stand. A lot of places are foggy, and you get into life styles and things and life just gets complicated. There were some good places but you only remember strange things. Like I remember early on, we had had quite a few hits and our picture had been everywhere. We were playing Australia and there was a mob scene at the airport. In those days you used to try and keep your travel plans quiet. But our booker was trying to create business and he had a big mob scene as we got off the plane. I grabbed Joey Paige's arm and said, "Let him by let him by" like he was me. Joey and I look alike and they beat me to death trying to get at him. And when I got through I just said, "That shows you the whole crux of the matter. People don't really know you. They think they do. It's just a matter of how you get it up." But places are just places. They are all different. But most of the time you're just in a hotel. The bigger you get the more isolated you become.'

Don had always had an antipathy towards touring so that his views are somewhat stronger. 'It was just a matter of hawking. Someone would pick up the phone and say, "Do you want the Everly Brothers?" and they'd say, "How much?" and off we'd go. That was the extent of management. There were no goals or anything. Others would disagree but that's how I saw it. In the late sixties we did a lot of hard work. We worked everywhere and spent a lot of time in clubs and touring. Ten years of really heavy road work. I wouldn't want to do it again. I loved tours of England and Ireland but the road's the road. You ain't at home.'

The strains caused by the constant travelling were heightened by the lack of record success which in turn soured the relationship between Don and Phil. Joe Smith suggests that the constant search for hit records was a relevant factor: 'They had the goods, they had the vocal sound, that was not the problem. It was a case of just trying to find some songs for them and to update the way they made records. We cannot underestimate the impact that the British invasion had. The playlists were so full of the Searchers and every other group that came out of England it was damaging the Everly Brothers. We went through a three- or four-year period of just awful searching, trying to rediscover an identity for themselves. They went through so many changes in their approach to repertoire and as the music changed even more radically with hard rock bands, they found it terribly difficult to contend with. American music was making a comeback but it was

singer/songwriter or something else than what the Everlys were, and they made an attempt to go middle of the road, to sing standards, to sing Playboy club dates and night clubs and try to find an identity there. And you'd hear the same cry from producers and writers, "Boy! if I could do a record with the Everly Brothers I could get them back". Well, in fact they couldn't, we tried a number of producers, we tried a number of writers and the boys with each blow regressed even more. As each record comes out and doesn't make it, you say, "Oh my God, now we've got to go three more months for another one" and after a series of zeros it's a question of self-doubt that maybe they would never happen again. They were having enormous internal difficulties between the two of them and they were constantly bickering. You could understand it. These boys had made it very young and been rather unsophisticated, unworldly, attained enormous success and now while still at a relatively young age, in their middle-late twenties, people weren't wanting what they did.'

The Warner sessions from 1967 until they left the label in 1970 appear haphazard. Don explains: 'All the albums had to be fitted in. We didn't have the time. We never took time off from touring to record.' 'The period was so mixed up, we were running back and forth and in the confusion and the problems of the situation it was most difficult to get something done,' says Phil. 'What we should've been doing was writing our own songs and singing them but you can't do that unless you can function together and I had reached a maturity where I no longer was willing to ruin our career. It's interesting – I didn't know this until I read a discography recently – that we'd done nineteen of Donald's songs and two of mine. The two of mine were *When will I be loved*, which was a hit by Donald and I and a number one in the country by Linda Ronstadt, and Eddie Hodges' *Made to Love*, which was also a hit. I tried to get Donald to record *Sweet Grass Country* which is a sort of a *Bowling Green*. He didn't like it. He didn't like those sort of things and you can't do anything with that. I had to say, "Hey, I think this is good" and "I think we could do this" but you can't sing by yourself when you're with someone and get it done. I pushed *Bowling Green* on the recording date against a wall, like I had with *Gone Gone Gone*, and as they came out and were well received I still feel that we should've done that kind of material.'

They worked with top-level producers, among

97

them Dick Glasser, Lenny Waronker, Wes Farrell and Lou Adler. 'We went all around with whoever we could to produce them because he had to be an outsider,' explains Jack Rael, 'Don tried to produce, Phil tried to produce and, you know, they didn't get on, so one wouldn't listen to the other. Boy, when they both agreed on something nothing would top these guys but they, in essence, produced their own albums most of the time.'

Very often, according to Terry Slater, the choice of material was decided at the recording session. 'Everybody approaches their recording in a different way. The time would come to make an album, and you'd pick your songs according to the mood you were in at that time. Someone might say *"Trains and Boats and Planes"* and someone says, "Yea, that's good" and you do it. Three or four weeks later you might have regretted it. Everything was born at the moment. You just say, "Grab this song, grab that song", get excited about it and it was done, and in many cases, weeks or months later, some of the things they did they'd say, "That wasn't such a good idea", but it's all hindsight.

'A lot of things we did for feel. We'd just sit there and someone would say, "This is how it goes", and Don and Phil would pick it up and sing along and we'd just jam until we got a real good feel to it. Others, though, the boys knew the song and knew that it called for an arrangement. The guy who did the arrangements for them was Leon Russell. Some, very few I must add, were done that way but mostly we went into the session and it would be created there and then until each musician was playing something that Don and Phil really liked the feel of and then we'd record it. Ninety per cent of the time Don and Phil would record their vocals live but if ever there was a part that was either difficult or Phil might, because he sang the high harmony part, have strained his voice, he would say, "I'll sleep on it and put my part on tomorrow" but in most cases they would try to do it together.

'Obviously we didn't pick the best material because we stopped having hits but there were a lot of reasons. The Beatles did change an enormous amount for a lot of people. There was a great emergence of self-contained groups writing their own material. For me perhaps we should've gone to the better writers of the day but everybody wanted to write for the Everlys because they were respected. So where do you draw the line? You get so many people pouring material at you. Don and Phil were fine writers so they were very, not touchy, but they'd look at everything and think "Can I write better?" So, whoever outside wrote a song he really had to write something special to knock these two out in the first place. Now, their judgement was obviously wrong on occasions but you can't tell why any act stops selling records. There are so many reasons beyond the actual songs.'

Don and Phil's search for a musical direction that would satisfy both of them and rekindle the public's interest in their music can be seen in the varied nature of the Everlys' record releases in the late 1960s. Three albums were released, two of them in 1967. The first, *The Hit Sound of the Everly Brothers*, was mainly an album of old rock standards together with two newer ballads. The album as a whole is strong, with *Good Golly Miss Molly* and the first recorded Jim Webb song, *She Never Smiles Anymore* the outstanding tracks. One or two songs sound as though they would have benefited if more time had been spent on them, particularly *Let's Go Get Stoned*, where Phil is overstretched on harmony. Next came *The Everly Brothers Sing* which ranks as the weakest of all Everly albums. Although the Everlys' last American Top Forty record, *Bowling Green* is included, the remainder is a strange mix of psychedelia and soul. Big Band arranger, Billy Strange, is credited on the album and is no doubt responsible for some of the excessive brass arrangements which on occasions drown the vocals.

There was a long delay before the third album was released but the wait was worthwhile. *Roots*, issued early in 1969, was a classic collection of contemporary country songs interwoven with one or two traditional tunes and recordings from an Everly Family radio show dating from 1952. Included is a reworking of *I Wonder if I Care as Much* which shows the extent of the Everlys' musical development. 'We thought it would be a good idea to do something like *Songs our Daddy Taught us. Roots* was more of an artistic success than

Below left: *Terry Slater (left) and Jay Lacey rehearsing with Phil in 1967.* Right: *An interview with Warren Neilson on KMTV, Shenandoah, 1967.*

financially. I believe it will eventually do something.' Don agreed with his brother: 'I thought *Roots* was a good album, one of our best, but it didn't sell as well as some of the others.'

Joe Smith explains that Warner Brothers had high hopes for the album. 'We decided to do one all-out assault. Lenny Waronker and Andy Wickham had an idea to do a definitive country pop album. It was brilliant but unfortunately it was the kind of album that seems, in retrospect, maybe four or five years ahead of its time.'

The move towards contemporary country music continued. Four songs were released as singles in the USA but not in Britain. The first was made up of tracks recorded with members of the Byrds, Clarence White and Gene Parsons. 'People had ideas as to ways to get people to notice what we were doing. We'd have probably worked it out better for ourselves,' said Phil.

Both singles were commercial country rock records and should have sold well. They are among the best of the Everlys' later work for Warners and it is hard to understand why they were not released in Britain. It was not that there was alternative material to release. The only single issued in Britain between August 1968 and the end of 1969 was *Cathy's Clown/Walk Right Back*.

The Everlys recorded a substantial amount of country rock style music which no doubt would have been issued had either *Roots* or either of the singles been commercially successful. As it is, the material remains in Warner's vaults with little likelihood of being made available to the fans. Songs such as *Deep Water, Meet me in the Bottom, Eden to Caiman, Casey's Last Ride, Glory Road, Mr. Soul* and Scott Mackenzie's Vietnam protest song *Stained Glass Morning* are there to show that Don and Phil have a legitimate place as innovators in the development of contemporary music. They were prepared to develop their sound away from their basic two-part harmony, although Phil indicates that he was not in agreement with the way the music was developing: 'I didn't like those things – I never agreed with the experimenting with double and triple tracking we did. I did that under duress. *Stained Glass Morning* was a solo. The harmony was put on as an afterthought and it should've stayed

a solo – but you can't be the Everly Brothers and sing solo – it just can't be done.'

The Everlys were always looking for commercial songs to issue as singles and they found some strong material. *It's my Time* is a powerful Loudermilk song more in the style of Don and Phil's early hits with prominent harmonies. The record was a minor hit in Britain, reaching Number Thirty-nine in the charts. Conversely *Love of the Common People* and *Milk Train* failed to sell, due mainly to their lacklustre and gimmicky productions. Don didn't want to record *Milk Train*: 'I tried to get the producer to cut *Aquarius* with us and couldn't get him interested at all. I really regret not having put my foot down. The show had just opened on Broadway and no one had recorded it.' It is one of many 'what would've happened?' situations the Everlys have faced, the most celebrated being when Bob Dylan offered them *Lay Lady Lay* which they rejected. Relegating *Lord of the Manor* to the B side of *Milk Train* was regarded as the final crime of Warner Brothers.

By far the most impressive single of the period was *Bowling Green* which reached the American Top forty and was a big hit in many parts of the world. It was to be the first of numerous Terry Slater compositions that Don and Phil were to record and as a bright up tempo number was to become the standard opener of the Everlys' live show. Its writer recalled 'I had never been a writer really, but being around Don and Phil, I gained inspiration from them to make me write. Phil's help and influence developed me, bringing out talent within myself which I didn't know, at the time, I possessed. Once I started getting involved we really started writing collectively between Don and Phil and myself. Looking back now we wrote a lot of songs between us, and no one above anyone else takes any credit, there's feelings which came from all of us at that time. Now there is confusion as to who wrote the songs between us. We all participated. The three of us were probably closer than anybody else. Their Mum and Dad used to say that I was their third son. I'm older and more businesslike to think, "Oh those things should've been cleared up" but when you're younger you're just writing. We didn't really worry,

Below left: *Don and Phil on German TV in 1965. Note the unusual angle of Don's guitar, to avoid hitting Phil's.* Right: *Don in the studio, late 1960s.*

Above: *Don and Phil on the Lulu TV Show in 1968, playing the famous Gibson Everly Brothers guitars.*

there was no one ego bigger than another.'

This has led to some confusion on *Lord of the Manor*. The record labels state Terry Slater as writer but he maintains: 'It really comes from Don and that's really all I can say on that.' Don did not know 'where that song came from lyrically; whether it was Phil or what', but Phil is adamant. 'That's Donald's. Maybe his name is on that by now. Because I won't admit to writing it my name's not on it. All I'll say is that if I'd written a song called *Lord of the Manor* it would sound like that.'

Apart from the collective nature of the writing there were commercial reasons for Terry's name appearing as sole songwriter. At that time Don and Phil were still signed to Acuff Rose as songwriters under a contract which was clearly unattractive by 1967. Don explains:

'We had some songs that we put Terry's name on to avoid Acuff Rose although I was still giving songs to Wesley.' However, on the subject of his songwriting during the time of the Everly Brothers, Phil said: 'We recorded only two of my songs. I can't speak for the quality of the songs I was writing but the fact was that they were not of such a quality that Donald wanted to record them or we could not agree on them. There are some songs I've never put my name on and there are songs I've put other people's name on. There were lots of reasons, sometimes personal reasons.'

The dissension between Don and Phil was not limited to the direction of their music; by this time they were no longer in agreement as to the type of bookings they wanted to do. 'They had never played Las Vegas and they always asked me about it,' remembers Jack Rael. 'They wanted to sit down on certain dates where they didn't have to work and I finally got them booked in May 1969 at the Riviera Hotel in Las Vegas and after that I got them quite a few dates in Las Vegas. Although they maybe played ten weeks a year in Las Vegas, they still had to do a lot of touring and their Marine Corps time. We started to get a little hot and they were doing good business and by playing Vegas they were witnessed by people from advertising agencies and by people in broadcasting and television, producers, writers. Instead of playing Wausau, Wisconsin and Peoria, Illinois they were now playing for their peers.'

Terry Slater adored playing Las Vegas because 'it was clean, it was showbiz, conditions were great, forty minutes a night, beautiful dressing-rooms with showers and good food and a couple of times a year it wasn't a bad way to go. It was a rest in a way. When you're touring all the time it's a demand on you. Phil and I saw it as in a way making it. You didn't necessarily have to keep having hit records to play Vegas. You had to be able to pull the audiences and we did.

'We played capacity crowds for the casinos and clubs and in turn we were paid very well. Don didn't like playing Vegas but Phil and the rest of us did. Don wanted to play the Fillmore East and the Fillmore West. There were a lot of events outside his affections at that time. He got into that jeans and T-shirt brigade, as I call it, which is okay, it's his view and you must respect him for it. At the time Phil liked the tuxedo and the bright light appearance and the cleanliness of Vegas which is his opinion and what's wrong with that? They just so happened to be brothers that performed together so that was the problem.'

Don clearly disliked Vegas and all it represented. In 1971 in a concert broadcast by Australian television he said: 'If you happen to be in Vegas in three weeks time do drop in at the Landmark. Oh, I do hate it there.' His feelings culminated in a song he wrote for the 1972 album *Stories we Could Tell* called *I'm Tired of Singing my Song in Las Vegas*.

Jack Rael tried to arrange bookings to suit both brothers but it is clear which ones he thought more useful. 'They played both Vegas and progressive clubs. I know when I put them in the Bitter End they had never done anything like that before, that was a big turnaround for us, where the people of New York discovered them. They could've played the intimate little clubs any time they wanted to but I think the Vegas thing helped us along with their television performances.'

The Everlys were always welcome in the clubs. In 1970 Paul Colby, co-owner of the Bitter End, said, 'Terms don't mean too much. It's what you do that counts. Every time we have the Everlys here the place is filled and everybody in the business who's in town will come over and catch them. The Everlys are professional, always prepared, on time, always a good job. They don't play games with the audience.'

Switching from clubs to Las Vegas could be difficult to adapt to. Phil highlighted the contrast in a 1972 interview: 'We've closed at the Kinetic Playground in Chicago, an underground place with light shows and

all, and opened up in the Main Room, Las Vegas two days later. So we've done it all pretty much. I don't think there are any categories left that we haven't been put in during the last fifteen years.'

1970 was to see a re-awakening of interest in the Everly Brothers. Their contract with Warner Brothers was nearing its end and was unlikely to be renewed. Don particularly was opposed to the big business element that had crept into the record industry. 'I don't like business of any kind – how we're going to make money and who's going to divide this up and percentages – it just doesn't interest me. The record business is turning into a lawyer's business.' Warner's was clearly going to be unacceptable as by now it was part of a major conglomerate, the Kinney Corporation which, in Don's words, were more involved in car parks than the record industry.

The Everlys were committed to producing two more albums for Warner's and they decided to fulfil that obligation with a double 'live' album. They recorded their 6 February show at the Grand Hotel Anaheim in California, a disappointing end to the Everlys' ten years with Warner Brothers. Neither Don nor Phil were entirely happy with it. Don never listens to the album. 'That's just a record of our night club act at the time.' 'Our show was interesting', thought Phil, 'but that wasn't a good recording. We weren't able to control the master so it had to be that way.'

The slower songs come across the best – *Kentucky, Lord of the Manor* and *I Wonder if I Care as Much* are outstanding – but it is the hits, some performed at breakneck speed, *Wake up Little Susie* (1.44), *Cathy's Clown* (1.24), *Bird Dog* (1.59) including applause! that obtain the best audience reaction. This is typical of the frustrations that the Everlys faced. 'People paid to see the Everly Brothers,' said Terry Slater, 'because of what they created which was very restricting to them because they had to do their hits. It had a frustrating effect because it was the same show all the time but that was put upon them by what they became.'

To maintain a freshness in the songs they made changes to the words and timing. 'Changes occur nightly,' explained Don. 'It gets a bit like chanting after a while – when you've been singing a particular song for fifteen years, the identity of it changes, and it becomes something else. What you see is not exact recreation, but a stage presentation of what was done in the studio. If you really want to sing properly and correctly, you have to re-evaluate yourself constantly, so we just take it apart, put it back together, and come up with something that sounds fresh again.'

Phil has always been motivated by the work. 'You get a reward for it. I think even if I wasn't getting paid for it I'd still do it.' In 1981 he explained why he felt he never tired of the music to the extent that Don did: 'By singing harmony, and singing the way I sing it, I had to listen to every little variable that Donald did and each time he sang *Bye Bye Love*, he may have felt he was singing it the same way but he never did, because you can't say a word the same way twice and to harmonise with someone is rather like talking in unison. To do it is a fine art and I guess I was always busy on stage and I never had the feeling, ''I'm tired of doing this''. There are times when I didn't enjoy performing – it depended. But I was so busy trying to blend or hold a note for the same time or get the same vibrato or keep on pitch or whatever, that was the difference – it didn't bore me.'

Despite the frustrations the audience never suffered. Terry Slater said: 'There was never a single night when I didn't stand behind those guys and think they were absolutely fantastic; so professional and their rapport with the audience was unique.'

All the hard work of the late 1960s had not been wasted. In 1970 Don and Phil still looked much younger than their thirty-three and thirty-one years. They had appeared on so many television shows that the medium held no fears for them and they had a stage presence which put the majority of their contemporaries in the shadows. Those qualities were not lost on producer Hal Cohen when he saw them perform in Las Vegas and on Johnny Cash's TV show. He signed them up for a ten-week networked series to be the summer replacement for Johnny Cash. Jack Rael thought they did a commendable job. 'The show was just fantastic. It was the epitome of the years I spent with them – that I was able to get them to the top of the heap without a big, big record. Everyone we had on that show was hand-picked, every guest artist was hand-picked, and I just thought it was a thrilling, thrilling show. It made the world know the Everly Brothers were back and they were in charge which was great.'

The show offered great variety, with comic sketches involving Don and Phil and an experienced character actor by the name of Joe Higgins, and well-chosen guest artists like Stevie Wonder, Johnny Cash, Neil Diamond, Melanie, the Carter Family, Arlo Guthrie, Rick Nelson, Brenda Lee, and Ike Everly who had come out of retirement to perform with Don and Phil. Phil has a video of one of the shows his father did with them when he sang a song he'd written *Sure Looking Good to Me*. 'That was very special to me.'

Don and Phil performed many songs during the series. Of course most of the hits get an airing, but so do numerous songs not associated with the Everlys. The Beatles songs are particularly to the fore and there is almost enough of their material to make up an 'Everly Brothers sing the Beatles' album. Exceptional performances are *Lady Madonna*, *Take a Letter Maria* and *Proud Mary* together, *If I Were a Carpenter* and *Hard Days Night* by Don and *Something* and *The Last Thing on my Mind* by Phil.

Don felt that 'The way television works we didn't have as much time to choose our songs as we wanted. We would have a weekly meeting and we would give them song titles. They would then search the songs out and we'd go down to a little trailer on the backlot and rehearse them during the day. The music went out on that show live which was a little bit difficult in the

Above: *In 1970 Don and Phil appeared on American TV in the show 'Johnny Cash Presents The Everly Brothers'. The show was highly rated and indicated a resurgence in the fortunes of the Everly Brothers and their careers.*

time available but we accomplished it. They don't give you much time to do a summer replacement series.'

Phil remembered that: 'The material was picked mostly because of the speed with which we had to produce the shows. We did two shows a week. They were done very fast and there was a tremendous amount of music and we had never varied our act much, or we had but we'd always had to do the hits because that's what people really wanted. So it was difficult and quite pressured really. But the music always came out pretty good I think. It was hectic to do – but there's nothing as powerful as television. It was important for us.' The series was screened across America throughout the summer of 1970 and the response was good enough for suggestions of another series the following year.

Numerous albums were issued to coincide with the series. Warner Brothers released the *Everly Brothers Show* double album while Barnaby (Andy Williams' label) issued a double album of twenty Cadence tracks under the title *The Everly Brothers Original Greatest Hits* which became a top seller on both sides of the Atlantic and heralded the beginning of a constant repackaging of the Cadence tracks which has continued to this day.

10
The Split

On sale Friday, week ending October 9, 1971

ALBERT HALL, TUESDAY

THE Everly Brothers never thought they'd fill the Albert Hall for their two shows there next Tuesday (12). A sometime pessimist, sometime realist, Phil Everly pictured acres of empty seats facing them as they sang in the echoing wilderness of a half-empty hall. "It is," he said the day they arrived in London, "kinda big. It'd sure be awful..."

He needn't have worried. Standing room apart, the concerts sold out after 48 hours, and eventhen it's a safe bet they could have gone quicker if it hadn't been for some earlier chaos in finalising the date. In passing, the way these...

THE EV
BRO
SELL
OUT AT
ALBERT
HALL

different back in the late fifties and early sixties. Remember that the Everlys...

During the Summer of 1970 Don recorded an album for Lou Adler's Ode label, which included country standards *Tumbling Tumbleweeds, When I Stop Dreaming* and *Sweet Dreams* along with a number of Don's own compositions. Don's songs are those of a troubled mind and give the album a dark, brooding feel. 'They were songs I'd written over a period of time on my travels which really Phil and I couldn't do at all. The album served its purpose at the time. I was frustrated musically. We weren't getting anywhere with our records at all. It was done apart as an experiment only, it really was.'

It was suggested that Don was looking for a sympathetic label to work with but there were also rumours circulating that Don and Phil had split which Phil won't confirm or deny. 'I felt tremendously let down by Lou Adler, who was a friend of mine too. It was something Donald was doing and the private gossip between various women we knew at the time was "That was it! the end of the Everly Brothers". I don't really know what prompted Donald to do it. I never did understand it and I never understood Louis doing it because I considered him one of my closest friends and we've never had any kind of relationship since.' The way the album was contracted and recorded clearly upset Phil and was probably the beginning of the end of Don and Phil's working relationship.

There were also changes afoot in the running of the Everly Brothers business. Jack Rael remembers it well: 'At that time they changed accountants. They blamed the fact that they both weren't wealthy on their accountants but they spent money like it was going out of style. It was about this time that Donald got involved with Lou Adler and I have no axes to grind with Lou but maybe Lou didn't think I was a bright enough manager. I thought I was. I think I still am. To be with these guys for so many years and keep them apart and keep them together. I wasn't cocky but I didn't know anyone who could do it better than I because I was like, to a point, a father to them but not a father. I was pretty strict and when there was a problem then I would be out there and I would go and straighten it out. The poor guy on the road had his

Above left: *News articles on the Albert Hall concert and the split in 1973.* Above right: *Don and Phil with their parents in London.* Below: *Ike Everly on stage with his sons at the Albert Hall in October 1971.*

Left and right: *An RCA publicity shot and an article showing the musical frustrations of the Everlys.* Opposite: *On stage at the Albert Hall, 1971.*

it's put across as being nostalgic. For me it's not that nostalgic. It's still rock music and we do produce the Everly Brothers sound but as individuals we also have other directions in music other than the Everly Brothers. That just happens to be a period of time that we can still do.'

In 1971 Don and Phil undertook their first major European tour in six years, a special tour because their parents accompanied them and Ike did a short set of his own within their act as he had last done successfully in Las Vegas. Phil was very excited about it. 'One of the greatest pleasures I have is to see Dad wowing the audiences and he always does.' The venues were a mixture of major auditoriums and nightclubs. The most important concert, however, was at the Royal Albert Hall in London where, despite six years having passed since their last big record, they produced a sell-out in two days. Just as Phil predicted, Ike almost stole the show with his warmth, humour and simple country style. Don and Phil were in superb form and received a standing ovation. For an encore they performed *Kentucky* with a simple acoustic guitar accompaniment which moved the complete audience to silence. They followed it with *Lucille*, which had the audience literally jiving in the aisles, a sight unknown to the Royal Albert Hall at the time, and led to the subsequent banning of the Everly Brothers from performing there again.

Don and Phil had extended their backing band to include a pianist, Warren Zevon, now an accomplished performer in his own right, who was also band leader. 'I was introduced to Phil and he expressed the desire to get a new band going, and kind of refresh themselves. I toured with them for about a year and a half. That was my first experience as a musician on the road and it was a pretty comprehensive education. I'd written a song called *Frank and Jessie James* that was inspired by them, and they invited me to do it in their shows. So, towards the latter part of my work with them, I found myself singing before concert audiences with Don and Phil and Waddy Wachtel singing harmony. That was a very major breakthrough for me. Which I thank them for.'

Waddy Wachtel, now known for his work with Linda Ronstadt and Zevon, joined the band as lead guitarist. 'We rehearsed for a fortnight without Don and Phil. They were finishing their album. At that time Don and Phil didn't get on at all and Bob Knigge (the established bass player) said "Don't try to get them together" but that was my dream to sit with them and sing and play with them. Finally, one night in England

hands full. Sometime in the middle of 1971 I got a wire from Don saying "You no longer represent us". I went to Phil and said, "I've got this wire from Don and don't know what to do. I love you and I love Don but I can't handle one brother." I didn't have a contract with them but they paid me everything they owed.'

Jack Daley became their personal manager. In 1971, Don felt 'the management was responsible for the last six years of work which I didn't feel suited our personality any more. Jack Daley turned out to be more to our way of thinking. He negotiated the RCA contract and brought Paul Rothschild in as producer of our album.'

The contract took many months to negotiate. The terms finally agreed were a three-year contract with a two-year option, and it called for three albums a year, one joint album and one solo album each. Knowing Don's antipathy to big business it is surprising that they signed for one of the major labels, but his brother said: 'They paid a lot of money which enabled us to judge their enthusiasm.'

'Phil and I don't discuss what each other are doing because we have so much to discuss on our own work. I try to keep things separate so as not to interfere with or dilute the Everly Brothers sound. Solo records have to happen because it's not good for mental health. It's not good trying to be creative and then only having half the decision to be made. I think it's important for psychic growth for everyone to have their individuality. People associate the Everly Brothers with the sound. The record companies want that sound. They wouldn't try even when the Everly Brothers changed their sound. Even less with one Everly Brother. It locks you into a saleable thing. If the record company had its way it would say, "Let's have the nostalgic trip" which would be wrong. They'd say everybody wants to hear the Everly Brothers and remember how they were in the fifties. Well, I don't want to. I want to live in the seventies, not in the past. When we go out on the road

we all got together in my room. Prior to that night you'd have Phil hanging out with you or Don hanging out with you. You'd never have both of them. Then one night they both came in and sang and it was just the most beautiful thing you ever heard. Just those pure gorgeous voices and from then on it just developed musically to a point a month later where all we ever did on the road was all get into a room, Don, Phil, Warren, Knigge and me and sing at each other and it became this beautiful relationship. They were really friendly towards each other. I was with them about a year and then had a bad fall-out with Don and had to leave. We resolved it a year later and became friends again.'

The beginning of 1972 saw the release of the first RCA album, *Stories we Could Tell*. It is a good collection of songs from contemporary writers: *Breakdown, Mandolin Wind, Ridin' High, The Brand New Tennessee Waltz*, and *Stories We could Tell* with three offerings from the Everlys which are outstanding. Don and Phil together wrote *Green River*, a song about Kentucky which has a superb choral and slide guitar fade-out while *Up in Mabel's Room* was written by Phil and Terry Slater to be performed by Phil alone, a soft, uncluttered simple track. Don recalls: 'The album took over nine months to get done. I think that sometimes people have to justify their existence. It became agony and painful during that period.' Phil agrees: 'It was a bloody war. I mean, it was just a war with people leaving the studio and all that. It was one of the worst periods of my life. The tension was so much that when I woke up in the morning I was so tense my body was in cramps and I couldn't straighten my leg out. That's how bad it was. It was hell on earth. There was a lot of hanky-panky about the business part too, which was difficult.'

Numerous West Coast 'super session men' were credited on the album, giving the impression that the sessions were 'open house'. The producer wanted to include something from each new visitor with the result that many of the tracks sound overproduced. Don agrees: 'It reads like the cast of Ben Hur on that record. You couldn't hear anybody. One or two tracks I felt you didn't know Phil and I were on it. You're vulnerable in those situations. I never go into a studio now with people I don't know. I only do what I want to do. No producer has ever been able to get us any position on the charts and we tried a lot of them, believe me. It seems to me it only worked when we really knew exactly what we thought the people wanted. Once we had the audience listening to us we did what we thought was best, and no producer could change that in the whole twenty-five years we've been recording.'

For some time the Everly Brothers had functioned as a business with little or no contact between the brothers other than on stage or the recording studio. They stayed in separate hotels when on tours and arrived independently at concerts, insisting upon separate dressing-rooms. Ultimately, they even had separate personal managers and friends to the extent that to be in one circle of friends meant that you were automatically excluded from the other. From singing around one microphone, which always added to the visual impact of their shows, they moved to a double mike and ultimately to completely separate microphones. To promote the new album they undertook many chat shows on American TV and radio. By this time, the entertainment industry was aware of the deteriorating relationship between Don and Phil and some of the interviews included questions about it.

The whole of 1972 and the first half of 1973 followed a well-worn path of touring. A second tour of Europe, much longer this time, was arranged for September 1972, following the huge success of the previous year. There were shows in Belgium, Holland and Germany and a four-week tour in Britain. Their most important date was at the famous London Palladium where the Searchers were the support act. Early in 1973 Tim Rice wrote an appreciation of the Everlys for *Zig Zag* magazine. 'When I went to see the Everlys at the London Palladium last autumn, I was more than a little apprehensive. I was convinced I would only be seeing shadows of their former greatness when Don and Phil

stepped out on to the stage. I should have stayed at home, with my memories of their tours during the days when every single with the word Everly on it was a Top Ten certainty. But when they did appear, they soon showed that there was nothing to worry about. The Everlys' sound, balance and stage production were perfect. They kicked off with *Bowling Green* and never looked back. Hit followed hit and they could have played their most famous songs for twice as long without repeating themselves. Their harmonies were as tight as ever, their timing impeccable and it was only on a few songs such as *Til I Kissed You* that the backing reminded one that this was not the original recording.

'Amazing that their sound would stand up so well after so many years. Halfway through the act, they announced some new songs from *Stories we Could Tell*. I thought this is it – the low spot of the act, but the three songs they did from the album (*Mabel's Room, Brand New Tennessee Waltz* and the title track) were as outstanding as the string of proven hits that preceded them.'

This glowing review, by an admitted Everly fanatic, was borne out by the *Financial Times*. It was, without doubt, one of the finest performances the Everlys gave in Britain. It's not the music John McNally of the Searchers remembers 'but, sad to say, the backstage problems the brothers were having'. It seems remarkable that Don and Phil could be at loggerheads with each other off stage and yet put on a flawless performance. Remarkable but not uncommon, says Terry Slater: 'I've never seen them lay a finger on each other, ever. I've seen them arguing their guts off backstage before they go on about something. Either a gig that Don didn't want to do and Phil did or vice versa or maybe something happened during the day that upset Don and his wife or Phil and his wife and they're in a bad mood and they'd sit in the dressing-room and shout at each other and say, "Oh, I ain't gonna do this again" but when they walked on stage they'd forget it. They had to with three, five or ten thousand people out there. I might've known mentally that one of them was unhappy but no one out front would've known.'

One of the songs performed on that tour was the Waylon Jennings/Willie Nelson classic *Good-hearted Woman* which Don explained was included on their

next album. The album, *Pass the Chicken and Listen*, had been recorded in Nashville with old friend Chet Atkins as producer. Instead of West Coast superstars the Everlys were supported by some of the best session musicians in Nashville although only Atkins represented those who had worked with the Everlys before. RCA blamed Don for the delay on *Stories*. 'They said I was dragging my feet. I called up Chet and said, "Let's do an album" and we did one in about a week which is a lot better in the long run, I think. I thought it was an extention of *Roots* and was very good. I figured by then, though, that nothing we did would get us noticed ultimately. There had to be something more than just touring live. It'd been so long since I'd heard myself on radio doing anything new there was no point recording anything. It didn't get played anyway. It was really discouraging and also very expensive. We weren't getting any royalties. We were spending them all in the studio.'

Karen (Don's third wife) and Donald picked out the songs. Phil just sang them. 'That's all. The only song that I think Donald and I connected on was *Lay it Down*. It's the nearest to what we were feeling at the time. They were better than the things we'd been doing on the tail end of Warner's. We were on our best behaviour. We did seventeen sides in three days which at today's rates seems very fast but we just cut fast. We both tried very hard on those RCA albums. It's not like that we didn't bother but they were both difficult to make.'

The album is made up of contemporary songs by writers such as Kris Kristofferson, John Hartford, Guy Clark, Roger Miller and Lee Clayton. *Not Fade Away*, the song Buddy Holly wrote for the Everlys fourteen years previously, is included and John Prine's *Paradise* is given a moving Everly treatment. Understandably so, as it is about the devastation by the coal companies of Muhlenberg County, Kentucky, and mirrors the fate of Brownie, where Don was born.

The album received glowing reviews from all the music press and is regarded as one of their best. It's as if they never left Nashville. Perhaps that is the reason the album works so well. Chet Atkins said of it: 'We thought it was a good album. We recorded it just about like we'd recorded before. We probably did more punching in and correcting mistakes and overdubbing vocals. But it was the same type of work we'd done previously. We all thought it might make it, but it's very hard to bring somebody back like that after they've been cold so long.' The album was to be a fitting swansong for a partnership that had achieved so much. Its lack of success, anticipated by Don, was the final straw. They carried on with their live shows but their days were numbered.

The cracks were beginning to show. On 6 July a date in Frisco, California, was cancelled due to Don being ill. The Everlys were sued for £1m. The following week Don and Phil were due to appear at Knotts Berry Farm in the plush 2,000-seat John Wayne Theatre. Bill Hollingshead was Entertainments Manager at Knotts Berry Farm, Buena Park, California from 1971 to 1976.

Above: *The fateful last show at Knotts Berry Farm, 14 July 1973.*

'I booked Don and Phil five or six times. I always thought of them personally like they were old prostitutes pumping it out for the money with no emotion involved. Their personal managers and their wives and girlfriends all said this was because they'd hated the sight of each other for eight or ten years and they were just performing for the money. Four or five days before the last concert Don told me that it would be the last one that the Everly Brothers would do. I contacted Robert Hilburn of the *Los Angeles Times* and gave him the scoop for an article on the lines of "the end of an era".

'The show didn't go properly from the start. They arrived separately about fifteen minutes before the show and, because of the animosity between them, they had asked for and received separate dressing-rooms. We had a public address system fitted in the dressing-rooms so that we were able to buzz them through two minutes before the show was due to start. Don had drunk Margueritas on an empty stomach but it wasn't until they were on stage that Phil realised that something was amiss. The problem was that when Don began to sing he was singing a quarter note flat. Throughout the show he was missing the phrasing and words and he was saying strange things between the numbers like, "I don't know what you are doing here. You would be better off on a mule ride". You could see that Phil was embarrassed and wanted to end it but didn't know how to. At the theatre we had a water curtain that came down in front of the stage into a pit. It took thirty seconds for the curtain to come

down so as an up-tempo number was nearing its end I told the stage manager who operated the button, to hit it and make an announcement on the lines of, "There they are, ladies and gentlemen, the Everly Brothers" so that Phil would know what was happening. As soon as the number finished, Phil walked off stage and shattered his $1,200 guitar and said, "I'll never get on a stage with that man again." During this time Don was still on stage bowing, thinking he had done a great show. After that, all hell let loose with Phil packing up and leaving the theatre.'

On hearing that the concerts on Saturday 14 July 1973 were to be the Everlys' last together, many fans travelled hundreds of miles to be there. Lynda Harpe of California sums up the show, saying that Don was strained and emotional during the fateful performance. 'Songs that he *must* know backwards and forwards he was singing all wrong, the wrong verses and everything. People were filing out of there; it was so embarrassing! When Phil went off stage Don was wandering around and I thought he'd never go off. I felt really bad for both of them.'

'There's never been a true report of that last show we did,' says Phil. 'Donald had called me and said that he wanted to stop, and thought we ought to take some time off from each other and not speak for at least two years and I agreed with him. We had three shows to do that night – and on the first show I think Donald just overdid the circumstances too much. I did break my

109

guitar on the stage but I put it down like a stukie would put down a weapon. I was through with the war. That was enough for me. The circumstances were too embarrassing and I didn't want to do it any more. I wasn't going to watch the Everly Brothers go out in a sort of a half-ass way like that and so I quit. I mean it sounds like I quit. But I mean it was something that Donald wanted to do and it's fine. It made sense to me.'

Don says of the show: 'It was a great emotional experience, people sometimes misinterpret and read into it. After you've worked with someone for twenty years, plus ten years before that, it can get very emotional.'

Both Don and Phil have spoken about the pressures which brought about the split. Don thought it was like a marriage. 'People that have ever been married and gone through a divorce they can understand what it was like. Now if somebody hasn't had the experience with marriage they won't understand maybe. They'll say "gee whiz, you sang so good together". Well, that's nice but a lot of people sing good together. It shouldn't consume your life, your own personal identity. In the end I said, "I can't do it any more". It was a hard thing to stop, too, because I went out on this tour in 1963 and I didn't get off the road until '73. I've been everywhere so many times I can't even remember. I get them all mixed up. And life's too short to just spend it in an aeroplane and a Holiday Inn or in a motel somewhere. I think that our fights weren't so much to do with each other as the situation we found ourselves in. The job was becoming more important than our personal lives, and I don't think things should be like that. We had a large crew of people working for us and with us and it's hard to take all that apart. We'd been working together since we were kids, and that was our first opportunity to really get out on our own. I mean, we went from being a family act with Mom and Dad to being a duet with each other, and we didn't have any break at all. I always wanted my own career and I was not happy touring especially and we should have quit probably when the records quit selling.'

'The things that caused the split,' according to Phil, 'were the business itself, constant travelling, the constant irritations that go along with music. Making music is the easiest and most beautiful thing in the world to do but getting there, hassles, business, management and they are difficult with music people. Take all that and the normal brother relationship and put us eyeball to eyeball and voice to voice round one mike for fifteen years and you're bound to get some distortion. Loving doesn't come into it. It goes beyond that. It gets into other things involved with humans. The independence of each contributed to the sound and also brought about the eventual end. It was time for Don and I to split. There were family attitudes about it that will never come out but musically we had reached the point when it was time to do other things. We had worked for sixteen years in front of the public and another ten years before that. It's an astonishingly

long time. Normally they give you a gold watch for that service.'

What becomes evident is that from the start there had always been a degree of antagonism between the brothers. Certainly, Don over-emphasized that he was two years older. Perhaps it was normal children's competition pushed to the limit. 'As we both sang and me being the youngest you set out to be good, to catch up,' said Phil. 'As I would run after Donald his abilities would increase and it all came together beyond explanation.'

When Phil and Don were interviewed by Philip Norman in 1972 Phil said: 'You're witnessing the end of one of the greatest sibling rivalries of the twentieth century.' That rivalry had existed before *Bye Bye Love* but Ike and Margaret had ensured each son developed individually by having Don and Phil perform not only duets but solos, trios, quartets and instrumentals which had allowed each to express themselves in their own music. With the success of that record the variation vanished and they were committed to duets. As far back as 1957 they had their own interests and friends. 'They never did get along all that well,' recalls Chet Atkins. 'They seemed to have their own thing going and they just sang together. Before and after the session they went their own ways. I was never around when they had any big fights. I was around when they didn't get on too good and ignored each other once in a while but they were all right most of the time when I was working with them. It seemed to get worse in the later years. I think probably their wives didn't get along and maybe there was some animosity there which was maybe exaggerated between the brothers. I guess Don and Phil are so much alike and that's probably what causes the problems. I know they must love each other very, very much but, you know, you always hurt the one you love and I guess they took their frustrations out on each other.'

Margaret Everly feels that favouritism affected the relationship: 'Women and the managers. I think that they would favour one boy over the other one and that never had been done. They had been taught from babies on up that it was Don and Phil and it wasn't Phil or it wasn't Don.'

Archie Bleyer agrees: 'It was always a question of so many people saying Don was better than Phil. Don came up with this, Don did that. Phil was pushed to the background too much, which wasn't the way it should have been.'

Bill Porter remembers one day the friction boiled over: 'Don and Phil were having an awful argument in the studio which turned into a fight with one hitting the other in the mouth. None of us knew what to do but it was clear that nothing was going to be recorded at that session so we broke up and all came back that same evening and, amazingly, Don and Phil recorded straight off.'

Right from the start Don, with his two years seniority and greater musical talent, was the automatic leader. He always sang the solos and performed the introductions. In the early years this caused few problems, Phil being a laid-back kind of character; but with his growing maturity the situation changed. Perhaps the tour of the UK in 1962 gave him a greater desire to be involved but the real difficulties did not start until the later 1960s when, of course, the hit period had ended. 'They never agreed on too many things but they didn't fight until later years when it got to be a pretty bad problem.' Jack Rael would come home from having dinner with his wife and 'I'd get a call from the road manager that the Everly Brothers were arguing. I don't think they ever had any fisticuffs at any time, but it was argument. It was like Cain and Abel. They just didn't get along and at times I did have to take eight o'clock-in-the-morning planes when they'd be arguing over something and not talking. They both respected me and when it got down to the nitty gritty they did what I told them.

'The TV series did the one thing that Phil always wanted that Don never allowed him to do – that I will probably take the blame for not encouraging. It gave Phil the chance to come into the spotlight and do some introducing and some solos. The writers decided that they would each introduce different acts, that they would banter back and forth. This was something that Phil had wanted for years. He'd always said to me, "Why is Don always like the boss?" It's true, but they were doing that so well for so many years and Phil would not want to bother with it and finally he got married and I guess his wife said, "You're half the act and I think you should do half the talking."

Albert Lee suggests another factor was responsible, in that the brothers 'were on a dead-end circuit, the same old gigs and the Las Vegas thing, which I know Don didn't enjoy, well . . . he just felt he wanted to get away from it. He says "We didn't break up – I left".'

Terry Slater, who is also closely involved with Don and Phil, puts the difficulties into perspective. 'When people ask "Did they argue? Did they fight? Did they throw things?" Of course they did, everyone does, but the whole thing was exaggerated. I was around them very intimately to the extent that I knew all their thoughts, their personal problems separately, I knew their wives' problems, their children's problems, just as they knew mine. They didn't fight any more or any less than anybody else. They were just healthy disagreements sometimes. Don might want to sing a song a particular way and Phil might not but what's wrong with that? If they both walked out like a couple of robots thinking exactly parallel it would be stupid. I can remember on sessions Don hearing a take and saying, "I never want that put on record" and Phil saying "I think it's great" and they'd have an argument and go home and the next day we'd all go out and have a curry together and forget it. Don would say, "I'm not gonna sing that shit, let's forget it" and they'd argue and walk out the studio but another day they'd go in and get three songs and record the arse off it and have a great day so it really was exaggerated and I must stress that because it wasn't that big a deal. They never argued any more than I did with my brother.

'There are many reasons for that blow-up at Knotts Berry. A lot of things had been building up. I think a lot to do with it was different feelings of direction when Phil wanted to do Las Vegas and Don wanted to get into the heavier side of it. That, from my point of view, was the first sign of a break of direction. That's when, in my eyes, the rift really began. Then that friction started and it grew like a disease till in the end it just blew up and neither one of them could take any more.'

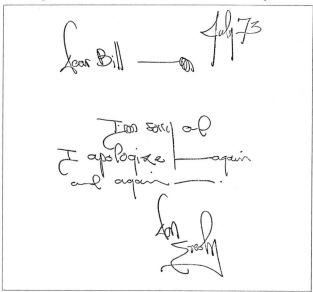

Above: *Don's letter of apology to Bill Hollingshead, after the fiasco of the last Everly show.*

The world did not have to wait long for the first solo set from an Everly Brother. During the first show Bill Hollingshead had to pull the curtain down on the Everlys. 'There were so many people on the grounds of Knotts Berry Farm they had to have a show and Don came up and said that he would do a solo set. I took him over to one of the restaurants and gave him chicken dinner and mashed potatoes and he very quickly pulled himself round. I then auditioned him on my own in the theatre and he performed for fifteen or twenty minutes of non-Everly songs. During this time I got a call from Robert Hilburn asking how things were going and I said, "Do you want another scoop because tonight we are having the première of the Don Everly show?"'

Although Hollingshead says none of the Everly songs were performed, in fact, Don's act consisted of album tracks which had formed part of the stage act in the past, like *Good-Hearted Woman*, *Sing me Back Home* and *Honky Tonk Women*, including *Lucille* which had formed an essential part of the Everly act for years. During one of Don's solo shows, someone in the audience called out 'Where's Phil' Don replied, 'I don't know, have you seen him?' adding, 'The Everly Brothers died ten years ago'. Lynda Harpe, so critical of Don in the first show, was clearly impressed. 'When we heard he was going on by himself, people's reaction was "I've got to see this"! I was really frightened for him, but I have to admit that Don did a couple of really *fine* shows. With the short amount of rehearsal time they had, they really worked well.' Lynda's photographs of those concerts on 14 July show how tense Don is with Phil, and how relaxed and happy he looks performing solo. For a long time nobody believed the break was permanent but the fact of the matter is that for ten years the brothers spoke to each other only briefly and met on one sad occasion.

Ike's resting place in Central City, Kentucky.

That occasion was the death from lung cancer of their father Ike on 22 October 1975; probably a result of the years down the coalmines as a young man and working in the asbestos factory during World War II. The brothers idolised their father and for a short time their common grief brought Don and Phil together when Ike was buried in the family plot in the Rose Hill Cemetery in Central City, Kentucky. Anyone who saw Ike performing with Don and Phil in the early seventies found it hard to believe that such a vibrant personality could be taken at the early age of sixty-seven. Just two months previous to his death Ike and Margaret had celebrated forty years of marriage.

Towards the end of 1975 WEA issued a twenty-track compilation album entitled *Walk Right Back with the Everly Brothers*, a title so evocative of the Everly Brothers' hit period that it was felt to be the most suitable title for this book. The album is a fine collection of the best Warner recordings but also includes some of the re-recordings of the Cadence hits. The continued interest in the brothers' music was evident when the album climbed high in the charts and within a year of release earned the Everlys yet another gold disc – their first for an album. The record is still available today and continues to be a big seller.

Linked with the record's release, the BBC in Britain ran a five part radio series on the lives of Don and Phil. The series included taped interviews with many leading figures from the Everly Brothers story and was narrated by Tim Rice. Although there were omissions, as there will be in any project of that type, the programme did, in the words of researcher Mike Sparrow, 'Tell the story of rock'n'roll. I realised that there was no other act, where most of the people involved were still alive, which could tell the story of the rise and tremendous stardom, the involvement of big business, the decline and final end of the act. The Everlys' story epitomises that of many of the early rock'n'roll stars.'

Closely involved in the project was Nigel Molden,

then of WEA's London office and a committed Everly fan. He sat about putting together an album of unreleased material from the Warner Brothers vaults, *The New Album*, which was issued towards the end of 1977. The material covers a wide spectrum of the Everlys' time with Warner's and shows how Don and Phil were trying to develop their music over the years. Although the album was welcomed by the fans it did not sell in sufficient numbers to encourage Warner Brothers to release any of the remaining unissued tracks. However, two more were released in a boxed set of singles issued in the UK in 1980 by Lightning Records which included all the Everly hits, in many cases with their original couplings.

The Cadence material has been released in many different forms but late in 1982 yet another compilation was released in the UK titled *Love Hurts*. It contains many of the original hits but with the accent on love songs, and earned the brothers another gold disc. It is a remarkable fact that Don and Phil have sold more albums per year over the ten years apart than they did when they performed together.

With such a demand for Everly Brothers records it was inevitable that there would be attempts to bring them back together. Don and Phil split for ten years yet the critics and the public still looked back to the music they produced together. It was a situation Phil understood and was fatalistic about. 'It's more the public that keeps us from working separately. The fact that we did so well and had a broad amount of influence, it's only natural for people to say we should continue together and that's logical but there's no reason we should have to continue to do it. Things didn't evolve that way and just as you can't explain how you evolve to a point of success you can't explain how you evolve to a point of departure. The public must allow Don the freedom to work on his own as finally, at the Palomino, I walked out through a different crowd. It was all right that I was there alone.'

Above left: A strained Phil during the last duets at Knotts Berry Farm and below left: a road-weary Don in 1971. By that time Don was tired of the excessive touring and reperforming of the Everly hits. Below: this strange publicity shot from Warner Brothers from the late 60s could well be prophetic.

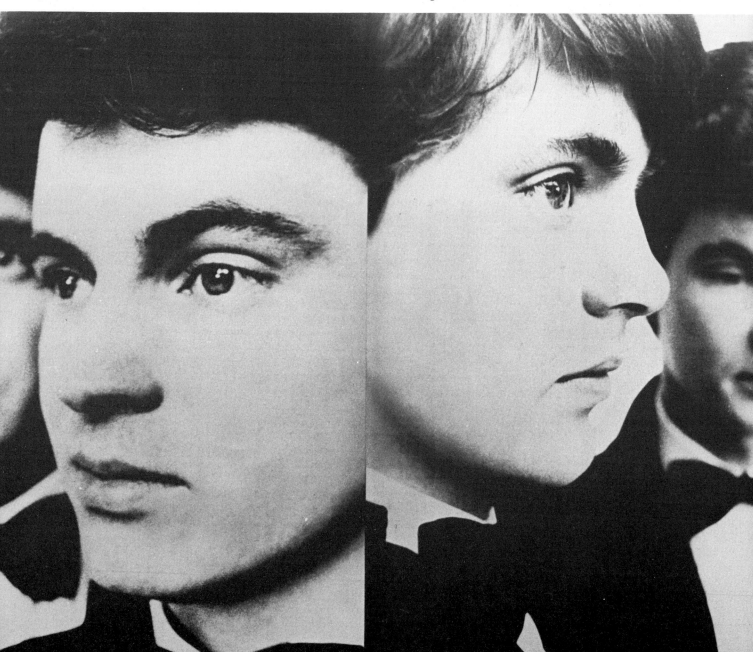

113

11
Don's Solo Career

Don's solo career since 1973 has promised more than it fulfilled. During that time he recorded and performed spasmodically but never with the commitment which would make him a meaningful impact as an artist in his own right. His work has showed many changes of style and material which reflected his constant reappraisal of his music and his striving for new sounds.

Shortly after the split from Phil, Don started working again; not in big auditoriums with his name in lights but once a week in a small saloon called the Sundance in Calabasas, just outside Los Angeles. Word quickly got around there and he would appear before a wildly enthusiastic audience with a scratch band of friends he'd put together. Albert Lee first met Don at the Sundance. 'I was with the Crickets when I met Don. He was my idol really. I was just hanging out at Jerry's house one day when Don called up and suggested we go up to the Sundance. I sat in with Don and he seemed impressed. I played for the rest of the night and after that I used to go out every Tuesday to play with him. We were doing general rock'n'roll stuff – the only Everly Brothers thing was *Lucille*. A bit of a jam really.'

Don had left RCA and started work on a new album for Lou Adler's Ode label. *Sunset Towers* is very much a heads, hands and feet project in that the nucleus of the group were musicians on the sessions, eight of the ten tracks came from the group, and Tony Colton was producer. Albert Lee had by then become a close friend. 'Don had to do an album for Ode and wanted me to play on it but I was back in England when he went into the studio. He did a couple of tracks and it turned into total disaster. I don't think Lou Adler was really into what Don was doing and when I turned up he had more or less handed the whole project over to Tony Colton and lost interest. Tony Colton, being the pushy kind of bloke that he is, took over everything. I really don't know if Don didn't have any songs at the time or if he didn't have confidence in the songs but he ended up doing quite a lot of Tony and Ray's songs and there were just two of his own songs.'

The album materialised from jam sessions in Don's apartment in the Sunset Towers block in Los Angeles (hence the album title) and was recorded over a four-month period at A & M's studios. It can best be described as a fusion of American country rock with British rock; a mixture of Don's country voice and Buddy Emmons' steel guitar with the heavy instrumentals common in British groups in the late 1960s and early 1970s. The backing does tend to burden the vocals and perhaps the album is over-produced. Don admits that he didn't have a good relationship with Tony Colton. 'I didn't get along with him at all. So there I was fighting with this producer I had to work with to get the project down. It was another painful experience. I did get vocally what I wanted on that album. Albert contributed a great deal. I think I'm happier with *Sunset Towers* than I am with *Stories we Could Tell*.' Albert Lee feels that Don's mental approach at the time could have been partly to blame. 'Don didn't really have a lot of input. He more or less let Tony do what he wanted. Tony had a few points there. It was like drawing blood out of a stone trying to push Don to do the vocals this way and that way. Perhaps he was a little unhappy – we all go through the pressures when we're making a record and it's just exhausting. You feel so tied up with it. It's a great album. It wasn't really totally representative of what Don could do. He sang really well on it but, knowing what a great and unusual writer he is, that didn't come across in those couple of songs. He was confused at the time. Actually, it's taken a hell of a long time to get the break-up out of his system.'

Don likes the freedom of being able to be an interpreter of songs. 'My work as a solo artist and writer has generated an enthusiasm for breaking new ground. I'm looking forward to the next LP to generate new tastes and sounds which have grown out of my experience with the first.' There was to be no second album recorded for Ode.

Early in 1975 Don and Karen suddenly disappeared from Los Angeles and appeared shortly thereafter back in Nashville. Rumours are rife of bad experiences he encountered from being with the record company which made him feel that he had to leave L.A. quickly. 'I had a lot of personal problems. Things got so crazy for me in L.A. and I got out.' Up till the end of 1983 Don has never set foot in California again.

His move back to Nashville was to bring Don once more under the wing of Wesley Rose, and he signed a fresh songwriting contract with Acuff Rose. Many were surprised at the tie-up after the previous acrimony, but Don says: 'Wesley's always been a sort of father figure in my life. We've always been good friends and it just seemed the right thing to do. I'm always one of those persons who go on impulse.'

The next year saw Don in self-imposed retirement. He had no inclination to perform and spent his time fishing, relaxing and writing songs when the mood took him. 'I'm back close to my roots. I'm at a time in my life when I have got a chance to just look around and do what I want to do and treat myself the way I want to be treated and not as an Everly Brother. Just to be Don and have a complete identity of my own and make the decisions for myself.'

It was inevitable that Don's involvement with Acuff Rose and with a little cajoling from Wesley would see him back in the studio. On 10 February 1976 he recorded four songs produced by Wesley Rose. He wrote one himself called *Oh! I'd Like to Go Away*;

another was the Fred Rose country standard *Deep Water*. The other two tracks, *Yesterday Just Passed my Way Again* and *Never Like This* were to form Don's first single release on the Hickory label. 'I first went into the sessions to cut *Yesterday Just Passed my Way Again*. I got Sanger Shafer to write another verse for me so I really feel it's my song. It sounded like a hit so that's how it started. We recorded for singles because the jukebox market is very important in country music.'

The record sold well and gave Don a high placing in the Billboard country charts. Don's vocals are superb and he seems more relaxed and at ease on the songs than on the whole of the *Sunset Towers* sessions. The song suits his vocal range perfectly and has become a high spot of Don's live performances, where he introduces it as his favourite.

Further sessions took place in August and November 1976 from which two more country chart entry singles emanated: *Love at Last Sight* and *Brother Jukebox*. The tracks were combined to produce an album entitled *Brother Jukebox* which was issued in the Spring of 1977 to coincide with Don's first major live performance for two and a half years at the Country Music Festival promoted by Mervyn Conn and held at the massive Wembley Arena in London.

Don appeared on the third day of the Festival and was given second billing behind Emmylou Harris and the Hot Band which included, at that time, Albert Lee. There was a great deal of speculation as to what Don would perform considering his often reported objection to singing the Everly hits. Albert Lee knew that Don wanted him to play but it wasn't until the morning of the show that he said, '"Do you want to sing on *Bye Bye Love* and this and that?" and I thought, "Oh, God!" There all of a sudden I was up there doing it with him in England on TV. I never dreamt that I would be on nationwide TV singing Phil's parts. I was really surprised he sang all the old Everly hits but he knew people expected to hear the hits and he seemed prepared to do it.' After two or three years away Don didn't feel quite the same way about the old hits. 'For a while I just didn't want to do them. It was like reading the same book over and over again and always knowing what was coming next.' Don's return to the stage was a triumph and he was one of the hits of the Festival; so much so that Mervyn Conn invited him back the following year.

Don's album was considered a good straight-ahead country music album. For many the outstanding track is Don's autobiographical song *Turn the Memories Loose Again*. The words of the song are clearly meant to put the record straight as to Don's attitude to the Everly Brothers. Don views the album favourably but reveals that he wasn't in agreement with it. 'I have to say there was a time I'd never let it be released but Wesley talked me into it. It wasn't my idea. Surprisingly enough, it comes across as a good album.'

When he was interviewed in 1977 Don clearly had set his sights on a recording career in the country market. 'I love making records. Ever since I was seven years old I've wanted to be on records. And I'm doing

WEMBLEY '77: and the sounds kept movin' on....

A REPORT ON THE NINTH INTERNATIONAL FESTIVAL OF COUNTRY MUSIC BY ALAN CACKETT, TONY BYWORTH & DAVID REDSHAW.

Above: *Don (bottom left) in his first appearance at the Country Music Festival at Wembley, 1977.*

DAILY MIRROR, Saturday, April 23, 1977   PAGE 1E

EXCLUSIVE

WHY I QUIT FOR LOVE

POP☆PAGE

Don explains the real reason for the Everly Brothers split

DON EVERLY quit the world-famous Everly Brothers pop partnership . . . for love. Until now most people thought the split came because he and his brother Phil, the other half of the super-successful singing duo, couldn't get on together.

That was only partly true. The real reason for the break-up was because of his love for a girl called Karen who, doctors said, was dying in a hospital.

Don, idol of the fifties and sixties, on a trip to London, recalled those fateful moments three years ago. . . .

He said: . . . Karen had spinal meningitis. I sat at her bedside, realising the only person who mattered to me was slipping . . .

by STAN SAYER

THE BROTHERS back in 1959 : Big hit.

Your Glass Retailer has some bright ideas in Decorative Glass.

117

Above: *On stage in Bournemouth, 1978, while on a UK tour with the late Marty Robbins.*

that. I'm fulfilling that now in country music. I like it here in Nashville and I like what I'm doing.'

In the spring of 1976 it was felt that Don had established himself as a truly quality country singer. There seemed to be no barrier to a lengthy career for him in what had become a very lucrative market. It did not materialise. There was no follow up to the *Brother Jukebox* LP and, at the time of writing, Don's complete issued output has been one single in 1980. What happened? Wesley Rose thinks that 'He really wants to produce music which is very modern country, more like rock music to me and it was not really material I thought I could help him with.' Don says himself: 'Again it got difficult to work with so I got myself off that deal.' It would seem that there were disagreements regarding Don's musical direction. Perhaps there was pressure on him to join the entertainment rat race. Who knows? The result was that

Don more or less 'retired' for the best part of three years. He made a rare appearance at the BMI Awards in 1977 when he was given an award for one million performances of *So Sad*. This was of special significance because Don is signed to ASCAP and it is extremely rare for a writer to be given an award by the rival organisation.

He visited Britain again in the Spring of 1978 to play Wembley again with Albert, this time backed by British group, Barbary Coast. His Wembley performance was followed by a nine-city British tour with the late Marty Robbins. Barry Fletcher of Barbary Coast remembers the tour: 'I got the feeling that there was another half of Don there somewhere. He clung to Albert Lee like nobody's business. On stage he always seemed as though he'd got to have someone beside him. He was very happy but he seemed to click off on stage. There were a lot of places when he went off into a world of his own but all the time he'd be there looking for someone.' Albert backs up that comment: 'Don was very nervous. It surprised me he never

Above: *Don with Paul McCartney, Wings and the Crickets at the Buddy Holly Memorial in London, 1979.*

drank when he was doing a gig. He loves a drink – we all do – and I think he would've eased up a bit if he had had a beer before he went on. He was a little bit nervous and still, and very self-conscious.'

Throughout the next couple of years Don made regular visits to the UK to undertake TV shows or festivals. Perhaps the most satisfying date for Don during this period was in October of 1979 when he appeared on the show that climaxed the Buddy Holly week arranged by Paul McCartney. Don joined the Crickets and Albert Lee and his performance was the high spot. At the end of the show Paul McCartney and Wings were on stage with the Crickets and Don joined Paul McCartney to harmonise on *Maybe Baby*.

Don did not perform in the United States from 1976 until 1980 and the shows he did in England gave Don the chance to visit the country which was fast becoming his second home. Don missed the 1979 Wembley Festival but was booked again in 1980. Albert was with him again. By this time the Festival had changed in concept and was organised in various European cities so that the artists toured from show to show. Once again Don's show followed that of his 1977 and 1978 sets and drew comments from some critics that it was time for a change. That change was already on the way. Don's relaxed lifestyle in Nashville had led him to Jack Clements and, within the creative atmosphere of Clements' studio, Don started putting together his own band which he called the Dead Cowboys. 'because it seems that everything these days has the word "cowboy" in the title somewhere!' The four-piece band was cosmopolitan but with a strong pedigree: Philip Donnelly from Ireland on lead guitar, Rachel Peer on bass, Englishman Tony Newman (formerly with the Nashville Teens and Jeff Beck's group) on drums, and Lamar Hill on keyboards. The band was put together for a tour of

Holland, France and Britain in July and August 1980. Don suddenly decided he wouldn't do it again 'unless I had my own band because without your own band you're limited. I could do some familiar country stuff but I felt it was time for me to do more than that.'

Before leaving for Europe the group undertook some rehearsal concerts in Nashville and received rave reviews. The fans in Europe were soon to see why. Don was revitalised by the music. The act was still primarily Everly Brothers hits and songs from Don's *Brother Jukebox* album, although there were interesting additions in *When will I be Loved, Sweet Dreams* and Blondie's *Dreaming*. The outstanding change was that all the music had been put to new arrangements which gave each of the musicians the chance to shine. The act produced many highlights but a ten-minute version of *Til I Kissed You* must rank among the best.

The tour ended at the Venue in London where Don and the Dead Cowboys played their new show for a capacity audience and received a tremendous reception. 'It was one of my most successful evenings in show business. We'd worked the whole month in France and enjoyed it but we said, "Wait till we get to London. We'll show them what we can do." I loved the response at the Venue. I really enjoyed that evening.'

Back in the United States Don and the Dead Cowboys went into the studios to pull together material and a musical style suitable for the group in order to get a recording contract. A number of studio-recorded demo tracks of essentially new songs written by Don were submitted to different companies. Polydor in the UK expressed strong interest. Don and the band returned to the UK in May of 1981 to appear for a week at the Diamond Club in Caerphilly, South Wales, but unfortunately Polydor weren't ready to release any material to coincide with the visit. Ultimately, they released two of those demo recordings (*Lets Put our Hearts Together/So Sad*) on a single in August by which time Don was back in Nashville. The record sank

Above: *Backstage at Hammersmith, 1979, with Albert Lee and his wife, Karen. Don is playing the prototype Gibson he gave to Albert.* Opposite: *Playing electric guitar for the first time in the UK, The Venue, 1980.*

without trace. Don was less than pleased with the company's lack of promotion: 'I thought I could've got the group over and done some television. I could've got something done but they didn't do that. I was over in the UK with the group but they wouldn't put the record out and then they put it out when we'd come back to the States. It was illogical.' At Don's request the recording contract was dissolved.

Don and the Dead Cowboys continued to perform on a regular basis in Nashville at the Sutler Saloon. 'The owner's a dear friend and I regard it as my local. It's the most suitable place to perform here in Nash-

ville and I get satisfaction from it. I'm really happy with the group. They're very good. I want to keep them together but it's very hard. We work to keep the wolf away from the door but they've got other gigs to do.'

Even so, Don's life remained fairly low key. He did not perform, other than in Nashville, for over a year. He concentrated his efforts on his songwriting and following his hobbies. 'I carry cameras with me wherever I go on the road. I have a Nikon, a Leika, a Rollaflex, a small Olympus and a Minox like an old German spy camera. I'm a regular tourist on the road and more so as the years go by. I still like to sit down to a nice dinner in a nice restaurant, or cook it myself, and a nice big bottle of wine. I belong to Les Amis du Vin. My lawyer and I started the chapter here in Nashville. It's become a source of great satisfaction. Over the past

Above: *Don with Albert Lee at Don's Nashville home, presumably in mid-winter!* Opposite: *A typical shot of Don, taken at Lincoln in June 1982. He and the Dead Cowboys topped the Country Music Festival bill.*

five years I've shared my time between Nashville and England and now I'm captivated by the Gulf of Mexico where I go fishing. I love it down there and have decided to go back there frequently. Those three places I can really get the best of all I need. I like travelling to other places too. I like Australia. I want to see the Orient again. I see it becoming an important part of my life again over the coming years.'

At the beginning of 1983 Don was enthusiastic about the future. 1982 had been a traumatic year with his marriage to Karen breaking up and, as a result, was artistically non-productive. Karen had been acting as his manager but Don re-signed with Jack Daley and spoke positively about his plans and ambitions. 'I've never really pushed my solo career until now. I've really done nothing for the past five or six years. My writing is better than it ever has been and Jack Daley is negotiating a record deal with a major company at the

moment. The record business is my future. I hope that with an album out or a single, *that* will create the audience for me. I'll try it again and see what happens. I really would like to think that I gave myself a real good shot at my solo career.'

The record deal did not materialise because plans were afoot for a much more ambitious venture – the reunion of the Everly Brothers. So, at least for the time being, Don's solo career has been put on ice. During the ten years he performed alone, Don showed with his intermittent activity that he has tremendous ability as a writer and performer. His greatest testimonial comes from his brother. 'Don is very talented. He is possibly, if not the best singer in the world, close to it. When he wants to, there is no one that can out-sing him and nobody can out-play him – when he really wants to do it. He was the larger piece of the Everly Brothers. He could always out-sing me and out-play me. He was just a great creator. If he doesn't let everybody get in his way, if he goes straight out and doesn't use everybody else to carry the situation and decides to go himself, there's no one can touch him. I know this better than anybody because I'm his brother. I've seen him sing all his life.'

12
Phil's Solo Career

Phil's solo career had a flying start, although accidentally, with an album issued by RCA just before he and Don split up, titled *Star Spangled Springer*. Phil has come to regret both the title and his note to the fan club that is reproduced on the back cover: 'I'm taking this opportunity to thank you for your interest in my brother Donald and I over the years, and to dispel any rumours that deny the continuance of the Everly Brothers.' 'I thought the title of the album up! That was over a bottle of wine at a restaurant in Laurel Canyon and there was this picture of a springer spaniel with a cute expression on its face. I bought that picture and I came up with that tongue-twisting title. I got a letter from someone saying that they liked the album but the guy who created the cover should be shot. Obviously you'll never see me write something on the back of an album again because it turned out to be absolutely stupid. What that really said is "This doesn't mean, because I'm singing by myself, that I want to quit". But the circumstances were different then.'

The album is a superb set of songs and is arguably the best solo work produced by either brother to date. All the songs are written by Phil and Terry Slater with the exception of Albert Hammond's *The Air that I Breathe*. Phil's performance shows that he is an expressive singer who makes the song not only the outstanding track on the album but also one of the most memorable of all Everly recordings. Albert Hammond regards Phil's version as definitive and it should have been issued as a single. Phil explained: 'The reason it wasn't was that Duane Eddy, who produced the album, wanted to put it out and I said "No". So I have no one else to blame but myself and I must admit that for the benefit of any Duane Eddy fans that might read this. I knew it was a great song – it was the only one I didn't write! – but I thought it was too slow and wouldn't make it.' The song was issued as a single in the UK but by that time Don had left RCA and Phil was obliged to leave too in order that the contractual obligations could be finalised. The company were not behind Phil to the extent he warranted and the single failed to sell.

The self-penned numbers were a comment on Phil's life and views at that time ranging from family, rock'n'roll patriotism, and the divorce from his first wife. *La Divorce* is an unusual song which moves from

Right: *On stage at the Palomino, May 1981, and* opposite: *Phil in London in 1974, launching his solo career.*

124

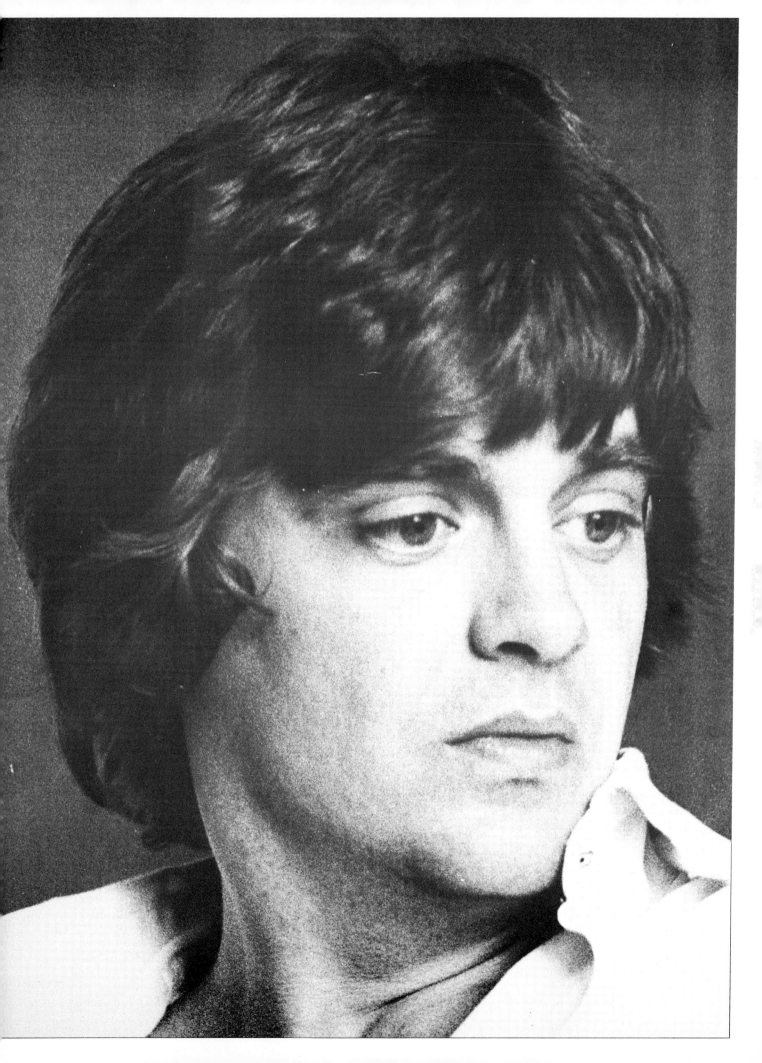

a slow sweeping ballad with a notable string arrangement to a brisk up-tempo country song dual tracked by Phil. The song leans heavily on Phil's experiences. 'I was looking at the divorce document and the opening line is "In the Superior Court . . ." and I put that in the song. The bit I liked was "He can send the cheque from hell or heaven" because I had to insure my life in case I should die so that the alimony got paid. That's the standard form but I always thought that it was crazy. Alive or dead you're going to pay. It's hard to sing that song.'

Snowflake Bombadier is, in Phil's opinion, one of his best songs. 'The song tells my life story as well as giving my philosophy on life. It was very difficult to write. I wrote thirteen verses but only three survived. Warren called me up after he'd written the string parts and he said: "It's Grammy time!".' The song fades with a brief glimpse of Duane Eddy's distinctive guitar work and provides a suitable closing to the album.

It is unfortunate that the release of the album coincided with the hiatus caused by the split. While RCA may not have had much incentive to promote an act in the throes of leaving them, neither was Phil inclined to undertake an extensive promotional campaign. After the break with Don, he did not undertake a live show for well over a year. He spent the rest of 1973 taking it easy. 'It was a change getting up in the morning, looking at the tomatoes and feeding the dog. It was a normal kind of life and, no matter how much money you have, you can't buy that.'

Although he wasn't singing publicly, Phil was maintaining an involvement in showbusiness, writing songs and trying his hand at writing TV scripts and movie production. His first television performances were as a host on a late-night music show called *In Session* which was broadcast across the United States in the early part of 1974. The show obtained a cult following among rock music fans because of the sound quality that was achieved. 'It was a concept that I had dreamed up. I had seen that the music quality on TV wasn't good and I had the idea of doing a show from a recording studio. I presented it to the two producers and they tried to do the show without me but it didn't work because I knew the relationship between me and the singers would be different than if the presenter was a disc jockey or something like that. I felt that the performers would relax more and learn that they would be treated with respect instead of indifference. That's why I did that – plus it seemed it was good at the time.'

The show had an impressive guest list, including Poco, B. B. King, Don McLean, John Prine, José Feliciano and Linda Ronstadt. Although Phil's role was primarily that of host, which involved him interviewing the guests, there were opportunities for him to sing. He concentrated on his solo material.

Once the taping of the shows was complete Phil and his wife Patricia travelled to England to enable Phil to record on album for the British Pye label under a worldwide distribution deal he had signed to produce three albums. On leaving RCA, Phil had a few contract offers from the major record companies but he had strong reservations about joining a big corporation. This was due, in part, to his experience with RCA. 'My own album for RCA had me worrying and organising my own distribution. I had to get my own people out on the streets to promote the record. All I should have to worry about is the music. You just can't make music with the great big unwieldy corporate organisation that is just strangling the business in the States. The problem is the big corporations can afford to "lose" records because they have such a lot of product.'

The album was recorded over a number of weeks during the Spring and Summer of 1974. Patricia had to return to California before Phil as she was expecting their first child, a boy, Christopher Isaac, who was born on 25 September. His birth coincided with Phil's first release for Pye. *Invisible Man* (inspired by Phil's separation from Patricia) was issued in the UK as a single and generally obtained good reviews. It was seen as an encouraging sign for the new album which was released at the beginning of 1975. In Britain the album was titled *Nothing's too Good for my Baby* after the old Eddie Cantor song included on the album and *Phil's Diner* in the United States. The American sleeve was different to the British issue and had a picture of Phil standing outside a restaurant called Phil's Diner. Why different titles? Why Phil's Diner? Phil explains: '*Star Spangled Springer* was my title and after that I quit choosing titles. The restaurant was a place I just ran across. I did think about buying it but it was owned by six lawyers so I gave that up. You'll never get six lawyers to agree on anything. I now own a place jointly with my old friend, Tommy Geas, straight up the street from Phil's Diner and I still think I might make it down the flat one day.'

Of the eleven tracks on the album, nine were co-written by Phil and Terry Slater (with Warren Zevon having joint credit on one of the tracks) and one was an Albert Hammond/Lee Hazlewood song *We're Running Out*. The most interesting aspects of the album are the varied styles of music and the development of Phil's lyrics. Pye classified the album 'middle of the road' but its music styles encompassed calypso, the 1930s, ballads, country, rock'n'roll and straightforward commercial pop.

The release of the album motivated Phil towards performing again. In March he appeared for two nights at the famed Palomino in North Hollywood. Among his back-up musicians were old friends Warren Zevon and Sammy McCue. They were his first live shows for close on two years and also his first at a venue that has become his main performing outlet since. The act at that time concentrated on his solo material including only *When Will I be Loved* and *Let It Be Me* of the Everly Brothers hits.

Phil was back in England in August to record his second album for Pye which was released in the Autumn as *Mystic Line*. Once again, it was a team

Opposite: *In London, 1974, publicising his first release for Pye. All three albums for Pye were recorded in London.*

effort with Phil and Terry Slater co-producing and Warren Zevon writing all the arrangements. By this time Warren was an artist in his own right. His involvement was fortuitous. 'Phil caught me en route home from Spain and I spent a month in London, working on that album.' This time all ten songs are written by Phil; either alone or with Terry and Warren, and the material is extremely varied. Warren's emerging style is particularly evident and *When Will I Be Loved* was re-recorded with a reggae beat. Also included was *Patiently* written by Phil in 1960 for the Everly Brothers. 'That was probably directed at my first wife. I wrote almost all of my songs from what I could feel. I need a catalyst to write a song.' Phil's unique ear for harmony has given him a flair for melody and he is prepared to double track his own voice if he feels it enhances the song. *Words in Your Eyes* is an outstanding song about the break-up of a relationship. 'That song became a kind of turning point in my life. I wrote something and six months to a year later I was living it. Perhaps subconsciously we see things that we choose not to see.'

The album was released to good reviews, not least from the *Los Angeles Times* which described the performance as 'Disarming and versatile'. Phil's life at this point was positive. His solo work had been well received, he had a settled life with which he was clearly content and, perhaps most important, his songwriting had been vindicated. During 1975 Linda Ronstadt had a massive hit with *When Will I be Loved* which resulted in Phil (along with publishers Acuff Rose) being awarded the Robert J. Burton award by BMI for the most played country song of the year. He attended the award ceremony in Nashville, with Patricia and his mother Margaret, as the guest of Boudleaux and Felice Bryant.

Despite the favourable reaction to his Pye albums, Phil was not happy with the arrangement. He felt that he was not getting the support he deserved. 'It looked like a good situation but I expected a lot more than was delivered.' Phil asked to be released from his contract before completing the third album. 'We hadn't had any real success with it and I didn't want to burden myself or them. The combination wasn't working and I'm a believer that if everything works right it will be successful.' Six months later the Pye organisation in the United States was closed down.

Shortly after *Mystic Line* was recorded Phil was suffering his second broken marriage. His separation and subsequent divorce from Patricia were extremely painful and still affect Phil today. He retreated from the public gaze. He stopped performing live. 'I felt compelled, pressured, and I wasn't satisfied. I don't want to sing like that. It took that much time for people to get over Don and I having stopped singing – and I don't think everybody's over that yet.'

For the next three years Phil's life was extremely low key. He concentrated on song writing, either alone or with friend Joey Paige, and undertook an occasional guest appearance on an album. Throughout this dark period Phil was surrounded by his close friends and

Above: *Phil with Wesley Rose, after receiving an award for 'the most played country song' of 1975.*

gradually they began encouraging him to reactivate his career.

The 'rehabilitation' began in 1978 with a cameo performance in the film *Every Which Way but Loose* where Phil sang a duet with Sondra Locke of a song he'd written with Joey Paige *Don't Say You Don't Love Me No More*. Snuff Garrett was responsible for producing the music for the film and the soundtrack album: 'I had two weeks to make *Every Which Way But Loose* and I picked up the phone and called Phil and asked him to come in and sing on the song he had written for the picture. So I said, "Why don't you go in and sing on the film at the same time?".' The film version of the song is not complete so Phil's appearance is fleeting. 'Don't go out to get some popcorn or you'll miss me! I enjoyed doing that. Clint Eastwood and the whole cast and crew had a family atmosphere. I did a song for the sequel *Any Which Way You Can* and I'm in the background on some of the shots in the Pal', but I didn't sing that time.'

Phil's re-entry into the world of performing followed shortly afterwards. In February 1979 Phil travelled to East Berlin to perform on a television show with Dean Read. 'Dean's a really good friend going way back to the early 1960s. We met at the Warner Brothers studios where we were both acting students. We don't share the same political views but he's still an honest and interesting man to me.' Phil included Everly hits and a new song *Ich Bin Dein* in his part of the show and all were well received.

Phil was equally pleased of the awareness of the East Berliners to the hits of the Everly Brothers. Encouraged by their acceptance of his new material, he became positive about recording again. It was suggested that he would be signing with another British company but ultimately he joined forces with Snuff Garrett and recorded an album for Elektra. The album was titled *Living Alone* and contained ten songs written by Phil. With the exception of the title track, all were written jointly with either Joey Paige or Garrett Music staff writer, John Durrell. The album reflects Phil's traumatic life with the break-up of his marriage to Patricia. 'I was not really emotionally sound. I had been getting a lesson in life and I was still a little sick, a little not together with the divorce back and forth. Usually, if I've written the songs by myself, it's straight from what I've lived. If I've written with somebody, I'm maybe doing a piece of specialised material with a little essence of what I think. The songs could've been done better – I do them better on stage and so I know I could've recorded them better and that's not a reflection on Snuff but it's a reflection on me because Snuff can't get me to do what I couldn't do at the time.'

The album was not a commercial success. In fact, US sales were so disappointing that the album was soon deleted and it was not released in the UK. Despite Phil's personal criticism of his performances, the record stands up to scrutiny. Phil shows once again that he has the ability to impose deep feeling into his lyrics, particularly on the ballads such as *Living Alone,* and *Love will Pull us Through* as well as producing songs which are well suited to his use of harmonies. The album was a good beginning for rejuvenating Phil's career and should have been built upon but it was not to be. 'There are fate things that get in the way of things. There was a business situation that arose between Elektra and me and the producer and that, therefore, kept us from following through. The president of the company changed and all kinds of things happened. You know, those are things that are beyond you. It's like the sign is wrong on the road for a lorry driver and he makes the wrong turn. That's exactly what happens. You can't explain that, as you can't explain it if that album had been successful. I couldn't have given you a reason either way. You just have to do the best you can for the best reasons at the time the opportunity presents itself.'

Phil had enough incentive in his work to begin performing again. On 1 December 1979 he appeared at the Palomino and during the next year he was to perform there six more times, including a charity show in May with Jerry Lee Lewis and Emmylou Harris for the benefit of disabled children. He also appeared for a week in Lake Tahoe N.V. 'I decided that it was time to play live again. So I went and played at the Pal' just to see how I felt. Before that show I just didn't want it bad enough to do something about it. But it was fun and I had a good time.'

In 1981 Phil spoke of the special relationship he had with the audience at the Palomino. 'I play there about every two months. I like saying that's the only place I play. We have a following in Los Angeles that is kind of an underground situation. I only play Friday and Saturday and we do ten days to two weeks of rehearsal. When I open I feel like my blood's really up and I'm really excited. We play only four shows, that's all there's going to be, and we set out to bring the audience to their feet. Anything less than that would not be enough. I love to get people to sing along and on Saturday nights I bring my kids up and they sing. I get Eden, Don's boy, up too. It's really a two-day party, and that's how we approach it. It costs more than I make to do it, but it's worth it because I feel good about it. I've found that I'd rather sing something brand new and move on than to sing something I have cut already. It is just part and parcel of the creative process, I guess. I try to write at least two new songs every two months that I'm going to perform. It forces me to write the song, forces me to make the song really good, because you're going to stand in front of people and either succeed or fail on it, so the song has to be good. When it works there's nothing like the excitement I get from that. The crowd is so nice, I'm only against myself, I'm up against my own expectations of what I want to achieve. Once, I did *Dream* on the stage and the feeling of the warmth was such that I called it again and everybody in the Pal' sang it. It was the most wonderful sound in the world because I could listen to them singing back at me and it was just great. Those are the rare moments and you can't get that hawking your stuff around the country – I can't, anyway. I feel good because I can drive straight home and sit in my house and feel good. When I pour a glass of champagne it's not like I'm in the Holiday Inn or somewhere.'

The beginning of 1981 saw Phil sign up with Curb Records for whom he produced two singles, *Dare to Dream Again* and *Sweet Southern Love*. Each had a great deal of airplay and reached high positions in the Billboard Adult Contemporary Charts and Country Charts. There was an indication from Phil that he was approaching things differently with Curb. 'Because they didn't sell, my solo albums are failures as far as I'm concerned. As I wrote all the songs – I've made a joke many times that if Phil Everly keeps writing these songs and they don't sell I'm going to quit using his material. I now write more honestly about how I live. The new things I'm doing like *Dare to Dream Again* are more hopeful and more structured. This time I'm going to approach it more of a singles attitude and I may get some outside material because I want it to be commercially successful. It's no good to sing things that you think have meaning and have no one to hear it. I'm not interested in that. It really is important that it is widespread. Otherwise it's not valid.'

Above: *At the San Diego Animal Park in 1981, with Jay Lacey, Joey Paige and Pat Anthony.*

Paradoxically, at the same time Phil was reflecting that success for him had more to do with reaching his audience with his lyrics than obtaining huge success through shallow material. 'The type of song I try to do is something that will relate to what people really live, to what life's really about. The only thing I can do is sing and if I don't get down to the essence of my life and my heart, then what have I really done? Nothing. I have a song called *In Your Eyes*, and if I can affect one couple with my song I'm satisfied. That's what counts to me. The rest of it would be wonderful – to have millions of people listening to it – but if not, I can understand that, too. I'm fatalistic about it. I may never have another large hit and that's all right. I have no complaints coming at all because we had a tremendously successful career.'

Dare to Dream Again was issued in Britain on Epic and Phil visited London to promote it. The record made the lower reaches of the pop charts but the sales were not sufficiently high to tempt Epic to release the follow-up single. The Curb contract gave an option for three singles and an album but Phil's relationship with Curb ceased before either was released. 'I let it all slide. Mike Curb is a very nice man and the people there were very good to me but Curb Records is a sub label of Columbia and they just weren't big enough to promote the singles properly which was a pity really

because I got a good response to *Dare to Dream Again*. I think it was one of the best things I've done.'

The visit to England also enabled Phil to make a guest appearance on a Cliff Richard TV documentary series which had Cliff singing songs which reflected his musical career from rock'n'roll to Gospel. Cliff has long been a fan of the Everly Brothers and invited Phil to join him for the show to recreate the rock'n'roll era. Phil was the only other artist to perform in the four-part series. He duetted with Cliff on *When Will I Be Loved*, *All I Have to Do Is Dream* and a medley of rock'n'roll classics. The response of the audience was so great that the two men agreed that it would be fun to record together.

Throughout the remainder of 1981 Phil performed spasmodically with his group. He performed regularly at the Palomino and in July and August undertook a short Californian tour. One of the dates was in San Diego at the Wild Animal Park which was booked by Bill Hollingshead, formerly of Knotts Berry Farm, whose own production company is responsible for artist booking at a number of Californian entertainment centres. 'When I booked Phil a year after the split there were hardly no Everly Brothers songs in his act,

130

Above: *A relaxed Phil, on stage at the Palomino in May 1980. 'I like to say it's the only place I play.'*

although he did one or two to satisfy the fans. I booked him again this year in San Diego and he was introducing a lot more Everly music into his act. He's a businessman. He knows what the audiences want.'

Phil had put together a tight band which worked well together. Apart from Joey Paige who played bass and provided back-up vocals, Jay Lacey was on lead guitar. He had been part of the Everly Brothers trio in 1967, and Phil says: 'I would say there is nobody in the world could touch his interpretation. When he sets a tone and it's melodic, I will fluff inside.' As for the rest of the band: 'There are two brothers playing drums and bass. They go by different names. One is named Pat Anthony and the other is Angelo Don De Vito. The pianist is a really fine young musician named Dicky Thompson.'

Phil signed a contract early in 1982 with Capitol Records and in May and June was in London to record under the supervision of Stuart Colman. Four songs were recorded in those sessions. In line with the concept Phil adopted at Curb, they were aimed at the singles market. One song was regarded by all as particularly strong, *Louise*, written by Ian Gomm, and it was released in Britain and Northern Europe in Sep-

tember. Phil visited Britain to promote the single and also visited Holland to undertake interviews. The record spent a number of weeks in the British charts and reached the lower forties. Phil also recorded more tracks to complete a début album for Capitol to be released in the Spring of 1983. Among the songs recorded were two duets with Cliff Richard and at the beginning of February 1983 one of these tracks, *She Means Nothing to Me*, was released as a single. It is a catchy up-beat song with a driving guitar riff provided by Everly fanatic Mark Knopfler of Dire Straits. The record received a great deal of radio airplay and soon showed in the pop charts. It rose steadily, peaking at Number Nine on 16 March, thus becoming Phil's first UK Top Ten record since 1965. This is a remarkable achievement because it received no direct promotion by the two stars. Moreover, Capitol had felt the cost of a promotional video was not justified at a time when every major record release was backed in this way.

It is good to see that, in these times when pop music success depends as much on the appearance of the artist or a particular fashion to catch the imagination of the adolescent audience, a top quality pop record can become a sizeable hit on the strength of its sound alone and it is also a pleasure to see success coming to two artists who between them had clocked up fifty-one years in the rock industry. There are bound to be those who say that Phil's UK success was due to his teaming with Cliff Richard but that would be decrying Phil's abilities and professionalism. His work with Stuart Colman has showed an awareness of the UK record market and the success of the single with Cliff was achieved on the strong foundation created by *Louise*. This has carried through to his album *Phil Everly*, a strong collection of commercial material appealing to all age groups.

While the releases in the UK concentrated on the tracks produced by Stuart Colman, Capitol in the United States appeared to be directing Phil's career towards a different market. At the same time as *She Means Nothing To Me* was being released in the UK, Capitol were releasing *Who's Gonna Keep Me Warm* backed by *One Way Love*. Both sides were recorded in May 1982 under the direction of Capitol staff producer, Kyle Lehning, and, as with the Curb singles, quickly showed in the Billboard Country Chart and, slightly later, in the Adult Contemporary lists.

The increase in activity and radio play seemed, at the beginning of 1983, to suggest a change in approach in Phil's solo career. The many years touring as an Everly Brother had given him a circumspect view of his life style. 'I've done all the gruelling I want to do, I enjoy a home life, a non-travelling life. I like it nice, peaceful and quiet. I live in a home and not in a hotel room. In the last nine or ten years I've seen my children grow up and that's something I couldn't have done without the situation surrounding the split from Don. My contract with Capitol is making me come out. I'm only now at a stage where I can get away from the house and enjoy myself. Terry said only recently that he didn't think I was fully ready to make the commit-

Opposite: *With Cliff Richard, to promote their UK Top Ten single* She Means Nothing To Me. *Phil was a guest on Cliff's TV show and Cliff duetted on two songs for Phil's album.* Above: *A scene from* Every Which Way But Loose.

ment a year ago when I came over to promote *Dare to Dream Again*. Now, well, I've got a twenty-year friend, my closest friend and when he says, "Come over and promote the record. It will help," I believe him, so I expect I'll be coming over more and more often. I don't anticipate a lot of live work. I don't want to get back on the road too much. Not four or five months a year. I don't want it running my life again. I don't mind doing some, particularly if I can take my boys with me and show them the world. I'm quite happy the way things are. I get out of the house now but I still love to get back there.'

Phil's many years in the business with all its ups and downs have also provided him with a self-effacing attitude in an industry renowned for its egotism. He carries with him an aura of content. 'You finally have to realise that what is really important is your own life. If I'm going to use as a criteria for my happiness someone else's opinion of what I'm doing and their rejec-

tion of what I think is good then I'm going to be very unhappy. It's not like, "Damn the torpedoes, full speed ahead" because my desire is to please. I would be happier if people liked my music.'

Despite a burgeoning solo career with Capitol Phil, like Don, was constantly plagued with the same question. '"When are you going to get together again?" I've been asked the question so many times, especially in England, that I'm now semi-forced to re-evaluate what I've thought about it.' Consequently, when Don contacted Phil about reforming he received a more receptive response than he might have expected. Phil was ready to settle his differences with his brother.

The resulting concerts have returned Phil to the limelight and it will be interesting to see how he manages to compromise his desire for a quiet life, stated so firmly some eighteen months ago, with the higher degree of touring that will be required as one of the Everly Brothers.

As for ambition, Phil is very clear. 'I haven't got those career ambitions. I never did have them. I'd like to sing with Jason one time on stage. I'd also like to win a Grammy. I'd rather sing with Jason (his son) than win a Grammy. I've had a good life and I've no gripe. That's probably the greatest gift that God has given me.'

13
The Reunion and
After

When I started this book some three and a half years ago I intended that it would be published to mark the twenty-fifth anniversary of the release of *Bye Bye Love*. This proved to be fortuitous because as the book was being finalised it became increasingly evident that Don and Phil were to re-unite and it seemed logical to delay publication to cover such an historic event.

There was general surprise that Don and Phil were contemplating working together again after a ten-year break. 'There is a desire on both our parts to do it which is brand new and that's the big point,' explained Phil. 'I don't want to end my life on negative terms with my brother. It's important that Don and I get back together and sing together. The main reason is that if my Dad was still alive it would please him greatly and I think it will please us too.'

Initially the concerts were proposed for February 1983 but were postponed again and again as the scale of the project mushroomed. 'It's wound up being very complicated because there's obviously been more interest than even I expected,' says Phil. 'Don and I would probably be better singing together in the back garden of his home or my home but as we had a public parting I think we should have a public gathering.'

Finally, two concerts were arranged for 22 and 23 September at the Royal Albert Hall in London. The brothers decided independently on doing the show there. As Don put it, 'It's a special place for us. We have very fond memories of the Albert Hall. It was the last place we appeared with our Dad.' The 7,000-seat capacity was quickly taken up by fans who had given up hope of ever seeing Don and Phil on stage together again. Although they had many offers from all over the world, the Everlys limited their performances to the two shows.

'It's basically an event for us,' Phil declared. 'I'm not one for touring overmuch and neither is Don and so I don't see us wanting to do a lot of touring. After this length of time it's really a personal thing we're settling up. Harmony singing is one of the most intimate things for two people to do. We mean for it to be good. The old pro comes out and you want to be as good as you can be, personally and for the people.'

The Everlys settled 'the big Southern feud', as they both call it, with a bear hug when they finally met in Nashville in the early Summer. They used the occasion to go into a studio with some session musicians. 'Those sessions were just for their benefit,' said Terry Slater. 'They got together so that they could

Reunion masks anger

A BITTER 20-year-old pop feud was still festering last night — behind the scenes of a glittering comeback show by the legendary Everly Brothers.

Showbiz insiders say Phil, 45, and Don, 46, continue to get on so badly that they:

BOOKED into separate London hotels for their two reunion concerts at the Albert Hall;

REFUSED to travel in the same car—even on their way to the shows; and

LAUNCHED into a blazing back-stage row after their first concert which ended with Phil storming out.

Grim-faced Don even refused to sign a shaken fan's autograph book because Phil's signature was already on the page.

Enemies

The rockin' brothers' concerts on Thursday and last night were their first for ten years.

The veteran duo, who had massive hits like Bye Bye Love, have been rowing since 1963 and became bitter enemies when Don got hooked on drugs.

The Sun Says—Page Six

Phil . . . he stormed off after a row

Don . . . he refused to sign autograph

. . . Phil and Don in London yeste...

Everlys–harmony

NEARLY 10 years after the Everly Brothers last appeared together on stage, Phil Everly has been speaking about a possible reunion.

The brothers—Phil and Don—one of rock 'n' roll's biggest and most influential acts during the Fifties...

Everly two a winner!

BY ROBIN EGGAR

TEN YEARS after the Everly Brothers last sang "Bye Bye Love, Hello Happiness," they are coming back—and their first concert is to be in Britain.

They are to make two TV specials for the US and Britain at London's Royal Albert Hall.

When they split up in 1973, Don and...

Rock

Everly Brothers
Albert Hall

You had to half-close your eyes, but then it all came back: 1958, *The Perry Como Show*, two boys with strange greased quiffs and matching tuxedos, hoisting identical black-top jumbo guitars and sharing a microphone as they chopped the chords and sang in siren harmony about how Johnny had kissed the teacher.

Every kid whose life was turned around by pop music in the period between Elvis and the Beatles feels something special for the Everly Brothers. Sometimes they were great rock 'n' rollers and sometimes they were great country ballad singers, but at their most perfectly realized – in "Bird Dog", "When Will I Be Loved" or "Cathy's Clown" – they defined a new kind of ultra-pop.

In 1973, after a decade of mutual rancour, they called it quits; last night's concert represented their first appearance together since the parting. Filmed and recorded for posterity, it may not have carried the cultural punch of that flickering black-and-white performance on a nineteen-inch screen 25 years ago, but certainly felt like history of some sort being made.

The evening was heavy symbolism. They arrived on stage from separate staircases, opened with a song they wrote together ("The Price of Love") and brought the show to a close with the reconciliatory "Let It Be Me".

A skilled band including guitarist Albert Lee, pianist Pete Wingfield, backed them with the encouragement superbly idiomatic accompaniments, ranging in the of the show from the rock riffing of "Lord through the sub meldrama of "Take Mary", to the unrestrained ecstasy of Don Everly's Parents of the...

NOW: Don and Phil Everly, together again for a...

THEN: The Everly Brothers. Phil scarcely...

exercise their voices and learn the songs again.' The sessions were fairly relaxed affairs and it became more of a jam. Don wasn't really nervous about it. 'We had both been singing various things over the years but not like we had before. We just walked up to the microphone and said, "Right, it's *Bye Bye Love* in the key of A". Everybody knew it and away we went.' Phil thought the 'first couple of notes was like jumping into a pool. You don't know how cold the water is. I didn't know if I could hit the high notes. The sound was pretty much the same – a little older maybe.'

The Everlys journeyed to London in early September to undertake intensive rehearsals with the musicians booked to support them. The make-up of the band had been a matter of great speculation, as Phil acknowledged earlier. 'There has been some debate about it and even Don and I have tried to talk about it but it winds up getting sticky. Each of us has a group and I could happily sing with Don's people and I'm sure he'd be just as happy with mine. Then there's

people who have said they'd like to be involved. I have to keep an open mind and leave it to the natural flow of events.' 'There were so many possibilities,' explained Terry Slater. 'In the end it became so complicated and they'd be so many people who would've been offended if we'd picked others that it was decided to leave it to me. Albert Lee had played with Don before and both Don and Phil respected his playing so they picked him but I put the rest of the band together.' Albert didn't know that he was to be part of the band until a month before the rehearsals started in London. 'Don had mentioned it but then nothing happened. I heard all sorts of rumours about the people likely to do it, Dire Straits and James Burton were mentioned, but I think in the end they wanted someone on the stage they knew and felt comfortable with and my name came up.'

Albert led a group of top British session musicians who between them have an impressive pedigree in rock music: Martin Jenner on guitar and steel guitar,

136

Mark Giffiths on bass, Graham Jarvis on drums and Pete Wingfield on keyboards. Over a ten-day period Don and Phil worked with them three hours each day getting the act together. Don and Phil were determined that the shows were going to be extra-special; so was Terry Slater. 'They decided to do what they always did best and that's their hits including some, which was nice, that they'd never ever done on stage before. They wanted to do a show which really demonstrated what the Everly Brothers were all about.'

Both had included a fair proportion of the hits in their solo acts but, in line with their differing musical tastes, their approach varied enormously and it must have been a problem to return to the disciplined style required of harmony singing. Albert Lee explains the difficulties: 'The rehearsals were hard work. It was a case of everybody wanting to get it right; how the songs will finish; how the guitar solos will fit in. I wasn't around them when they had problems together but I got an idea of what it must have been like. At the beginning it wasn't coming off right and the band was really depressed. Every song was gone into and Don would suggest this and Phil would say that. Then Phil didn't come into the rehearsals for a couple of days and seemed happy enough to leave it to Don and it needed that give and take to get it right on the night. When Don was in the rehearsals on his own he was just like the old Don we've come to know and love over the past ten years with his varied vocal phrasing but the minute Phil came in and walked up to the mike Don keyed straight back into the tight vocals necessary to make the harmony come through.'

Don and Phil overcame their different approach to the hits by looking at the songs afresh. 'The Everly Brothers style is their voices and that never changes,' according to Terry Slater. 'The arrangements though were just born as we rehearsed. Everybody knew the songs and so the arrangements are based on the originals but as they rehearsed everybody had ideas and Don or Phil would say, "That sounds good", and the sound gradually came together.' It is interesting that Don and Phil still use the same method that they did in their first recording sessions over twenty-five years ago.

There must have been a great strain on the relationship between Don and Phil as the concerts approached and it may have been the creative tension why Phil was not involved in all the rehearsals. It would be naïve to think that they are now the closest of friends just because they've had ten years apart. Their relationship has always been strained and by the time of the split there was extreme tension between them which ten years of non-contact was unlikely to have eased. It has been a softly-softly reconciliation, with close friends creating an important buffer. At the same time there has been a marked change in approach. 'We don't argue now,' says Don. 'When you have a serious dispute it makes you stop and think about what you say and how you react to each other. The trouble was that I blamed the Everly Brothers. If it wasn't for that I could go and do this or go and do that but now I can't use that as an excuse for my unhappiness. At this point the brothers come first and the act second.' Now Phil thinks 'there is creativity and power in a disagreement which helps make the end product good. You have to come to a point to harmonise but you can start at different points. It's where you wind up that counts. It's a process we're better able to handle now whereas before it was divisive.'

As the day of the first concert arrived, Everly fans started arriving from all over Britain and the Continent. Some even made the long journey from the United States. Friendships were renewed and contacts made while the buzz of anticipation grew. Don and Phil had stipulated that the prime seats should be reserved for the fans who had remained loyal to them over the years; all were in position long before the show began.

After Phil Brady, the supporting act, had entertained the audience, the Everlys' backing band began preparing for the arrival of Don and Phil. The Royal Albert Hall was full to overflowing and the atmosphere was electric.

Don and Phil surprised everyone by appearing unannounced – Phil from high to the left of the stage, Don from the right. They were wearing matching tuxedoes with high wing collars which accentuated Phil's litheness and Don's rotundity (reflecting his continued enjoyment in good food and wine!). Each had a black Everly guitar slung around his neck. The applause welled up around the circular auditorium as they were recognised and built up into a lengthy standing ovation which clearly surprised Don and Phil. During rehearsals Albert Lee had been discussing their entrance. 'They thought they would come out to the guitar riff of the opening number like they always had done. Someone suggested they come unannounced and let the audience just enjoy seeing them and welcome them. Don said, "Do you think there'll be a big enough response?" and I said, "Are you kidding? They'll go mad".' Terry Slater didn't 'think they were surprised as such by the reception. They'd forgotten. It had been a long time. It was more a case of, "Oh wait a minute, this is how it was".'

Once the audience settled down, Don strummed the introduction of *The Price Of Love* which set the tone for the rest of the evening. Hit followed hit in an exciting evening of memories; yet the strength of the show was not one of nostalgia, but of visual excitement linked with singing and playing of the highest order. The whole performance was so strong it would be impossible to find a highspot. Old favourites from the Everlys' live performances as *Walk Right Back* and *So Sad (To Watch Good Love go Bad)* sounded fresh and alive. It was exciting to hear *Temptation*, *When Will I be Loved*, *Crying in the Rain* and *Claudette* done live. There was one song new to the Everlys – Sam Cooke's *You Send Me* – which Don introduced as being their feelings towards the fans. There were interesting montages such as *Devoted To You*, *Ebony Eyes* (without the recitation) and the magnificent *Love Hurts*. Each was complete in itself and yet blended together. Halfway through, the band left the stage and Don and Phil sat on stools to sing a selection of songs from the *Songs Our Daddy Taught Us* album which had everyone who was at the Albert Hall in 1971 remembering the vibrant performance Ike gave on stage with his sons. It was clearly also in Don and Phil's minds.

Each show lasted for well over two hours and included just about every major hit of the Everlys' career (*Problems*, *Like Strangers* and *Poor Jenny* being the notable omissions). But this was not the perfunctory performance that the Everlys were sometimes criticised for in the late 1960s and early 1970s. Don and Phil were enjoying singing together. They had power. They were singing as much for each other as for the audience. The backing group provided splendid support. Albert Lee had produced a tight band within a very short period and yet each had the opportunity to impose his individual character to the evening. Phil summed them up: 'They're sensational. They've made it a delight.' At the end of each evening Don and Phil received a tumultuous standing ovation and performed three encores. On the second night they showed their appreciation of the other musicians by bringing them out to share the applause.

The concerts were a magnificent triumph for the brothers who managed to bring to its feet the entire audience made up of aficionados, ageing rock'n'rollers, today's pop stars and young people experiencing their music for the first time. Terry Slater thought it was first class. 'You never have any fear about their singing. They're probably the most professional people in the music business. There was never any fear that they wouldn't be good.'

The concerts have put the Everlys back in the top league and big money is involved. They were filmed by Delilah Films Inc in association with MGM/UA through whom a home video cassette is available. The concerts were shown in Britain on the BBC, on HBO Cable Television in the United States, and in many other countries. A live double album has been released world-wide by Impression Records. The BBC will be screening a major documentary on Don and Phil in the form of a profile on their roots and the background of their music which was filmed in Kentucky and Nashville when the brothers first got back together.

They are both quick to dispel any suggestion that the financial aspects of the reunion were the prime object in getting together. 'Money is a nice motivation but we wouldn't do the shows just for that,' says Don. 'We've had loads of offers over the years for quite phenomenal sums; much more than we ever got when we were together. Every day someone would say "Why don't you do it again?" but it never felt right. But the times change. You change. Maybe we had enough time alone and time away from the road so it seems exciting again.' 'If it was just for the money,' Phil says 'we would've chosen a bigger venue and done a world tour and made a lot of money. There's money in it, of course, but we're not fools!'

Although the reunion was primarily an event for Don and Phil and their fans, the success of the shows was such that offers flooded in from all over the world. While this stretched into years of work they purposely made no plans for the future. 'A lot of energy and work has gone into this project,' said Terry Slater at the time. 'We started in April or May and Don, Phil and I have all put an enormous amount into it, so while it's physically over, there's still a lot going on. They're going to digest it all over a period of months. Maybe after Christmas we'll all sit down to discuss the future. They may or may not wish to tour around the world or do more solo work or records or a TV special. Who knows? A year ago we didn't know we'd be playing at the Royal Albert Hall and maybe next year we'll be playing there for a week.'

Early in the New Year it was announced that Don and Phil had signed a recording contract with PhonoGram International and in the Spring they travelled to London to record an album with Dave Edmunds. 'We have a lot of respect for his work,' says Phil, 'and we share a similar appreciation of basic rock'n'roll.' It is an extremely strong set of songs, for despite being very much of the 1980s Dave Edmunds has managed to capture and maintain the strength of the Everly harmonies, while recreating the freshness that is the hallmark of the early Warner Brothers recordings. The strongest track is quite definitely a Paul McCartney song written specially for Don and Phil, *On the Wings of a Nightingale*, which has been chosen for the initial single. In addition there are songs from Frankie Miller, Jeff Lynne, Paul Kennerly and three from Don. A version of Bob Dylan's *Lay Lady Lay* is included, which is ironic bearing in mind that Don and Phil rejected the song when it was first written.

PhonoGram are very enthusiastic about the record and are preparing a substantial promotional campaign. Videos have been prepared for four of the songs on the album and yet another is under consideration. The material will form a thirty minute programme on American Cable TV's Album Flash series and of course

the separate films can be used for promoting the singles that are released. Bas Hartong was responsible for signing Don and Phil to PhonoGram, and 'grew up with their music. It's timeless to me. The prospect of having the Everlys excited me because their music has always been legitimate and never relied on nostalgia. They stayed away until they were ready to come back with something new. The interest in the project is amazing and the enthusiasm both within PhonoGram and generally is beyond my wildest expectation. The Everlys are filling a gap in this company's roster because now we have an act that can appeal to an older audience and yet still reach the top 40.'

Recording time for the album was limited because Don and Phil had to return to the USA to commence rehearsals for their first tour in eleven years. The itinerary is extensive by anyone's standards: in ten weeks they will be playing thirty-three venues in the United States and Canada at such notable auditoriums as the Worlds Fair in New Orleans, The Pier in New York City and The Greek Theatre and Pacific Amphitheatre in California. At the time of writing the tour has been extremely successful indeed, with the vast majority of dates being sellouts. After a short break Don and Phil will visit the UK for a month-long tour taking in fifteen cities, while plans are being made for additional promotional dates in the UK and Europe.

For these two extensive tours Don and Phil had hoped to keep the reunion band together, but the commitments of three of the band to Cliff Richard has meant that recruitment has been necessary to augment their close friends Albert Lee and Pete Wingfield. Joining them are Phil Donnelly from Don's Dead Cowboys on guitar, together with Nashville session men Larrie Londin on drums and Phillip Cranham on bass, thus continuing the long line of superb bands that have supported Don and Phil on tour over the years.

So far their new career together has followed a logical progression, taking each step as it comes. As to the future, Don and Phil appear to have accepted that they will always be a stronger force together than they are individually. Don regards the album as a new beginning after a ten-year vacation and Phil also feels that it is important for their music to mature.

They can look forward with enthusiasm. Their status in the industry has been enhanced over the past twelve months by the confirmation of their abilities as exciting performers, producing an album of songs which are valid today and do not rely on past glories. Terry Slater, so important in bringing them back together, shows how he sees the future: 'After ten years it felt right for them to get back together. Their songs are living on as they will forever but they can't recapture what they were, the whole industry has changed since those days, but they can go out to be something different. They're still the Everly Brothers but they're delivering to a different generation and getting back to the music again. Now there isn't so much of the tension around them it gives them so much power to come back.'

An evening of nostalgia at the Royal Albert Hall

The Everlys turn the clock back and London loves it

LONDON (AP) — The Everly Brothers have made a triumphant comeback at London's Royal Albert Hall, ending a 10-year split that broke up one of the top acts in rock 'n' roll history.

The audience, mainly middle-aged, sang and clapped along as the brothers — Don, 46, and Phil, 44, sang non-stop through their old hits from Bye Bye Love to a jazzy Blues Stay Away From Me.

It was the first of two sell-out reunion concerts at the Albert Hall, normally one of London's top classical music venues. The 6,000-seat auditorium was packed with now mainly middle-aged fans.

The Everly brothers, once the teenage favorite of a generation, split in 1973 after an emotional act when Phil came to his guitar halfway through the show and stormed off the stage. They blamed the growing period by declining popularity.

Both performed solo concerts that won critical acclaim with commercial success.

Little seems to have brought them together again.

They were joined by Terry Slater, bass player and long-time friend, one of their close friends during British times of the 1960s. Thousands of the once-in-a-night of nostalgia Monday sent women fans laid flowers on the stage and danced in the aisles of the famed auditorium as the brothers sang their unique harmonies backed by a five-piece band.

The guitars were accompanied by pedal steel guitar the Al Anderson and fiddle and by Albert Lee.

Phil said to tears and a wonder I last thought you might ask if we've really made up.

"Well, we're friends again." Halfway through the show, the two brothers sang country songs they were taught on acoustic guitar. They played their final Hall 10 years ago during the final days before they were overwhelmed by the Beatles and other British groups who took over the world.

Their songs of high school angst and the passion of adolescent love seemed a little strange after all these years, but one seemed to find the right chords as they sang along on two incredible sounding melodies of teenage and chorus too-old.

In the audience were Paul McCartney, Ringo Starr, Eric Clapton and a now a top ten ex-Monkees and is now producer on stage and television producer.

14
The Influence of the Everly Brothers

During their six-year run as a world-wide top selling act, the Everlys were unique. No one else sang two-part harmony with a close country feel. Moreover, the numerous copyists who emerged did not have the instantly recognisable voices of the Everlys. They communicated to young audiences with songs that might sound like sentimental ballads to anyone hearing them for the first time in the 1980s, but in the late 1950s they were perfectly tuned to the way things were for teenagers then, coping with school, parents, new or broken love affairs.

Added to their unique sound and their good songs were their appearance and professionalism. They are both handsome men who have been aware of changing dress styles. In those early years they were in a position to design their clothes and by doing so influenced the dress sense of their contemporaries. They were at the forefront of any changes of styles as Chet Atkins remembers: 'I remember they used to wear these trousers with the legs so tight. I think they put them on and then sewed the legs together.' At all times they have dressed impeccably and with style.

Whether on stage, in the recording studio or in interviews, Don and Phil have always been the ultimate in professionalism. An Everly Brothers record guarantees quality and value for money. Right from the start they were committed to issue only the best material, recorded in the best possible conditions. On stage they established a charisma that didn't require decibels or lights to create excitement. They always worked with a small tight group, never more than four musicians, and with a sound level that meant that the harmonies could be heard. Don and Phil always insisted on top quality back-up musicians who were able to recreate the sound on the records while remaining unobtrusive.

Visually they were perfectly matched – Don singing his soulful solos with little movement, while extrovert Phil would retain a visual impact before coming in close to link in with the harmony. It is a pity that they finished their time together working off separate microphones because the excitement generated by the merging of bodies, guitars and voices around one microphone was immense. Their stagecraft, however, was not limited to their work together. Anyone who has seen Don performing with the Dead Cowboys and Phil with his group at the Palomino will vouch for the remarkable stage presence they each still have. They belong on stage and are acutely aware of what is expected of them as performers. It is an instinct built

into them over all the years they have been professional singers. They are superb entertainers and this quality, a unique sound, excellent songs, attractive appearance and professionalism, are essential to build and maintain a successful career in the pop music industry. They do not in themselves explain the longevity of the Everlys' career or their influence. That is in the material they recorded.

Don and Phil were just one of many acts to explode on the music scene in the late 1950s which are now regarded as the pioneers of rock'n'roll. Most of them have not had the creative influence of Don and Phil. Apart from Elvis, the Everlys were the most consistently successful act of all the early rock'n'roll performers both sides of the Atlantic. Their period of success lasted much longer than any other act. Here, I believe, lies the principal reason for the extent of the Everlys' influence on future musical tastes. Whereas the majority of acts maintained a style that had proved successful, the Everlys were innovative and were always striving for new sounds. Compare *Bye Bye Love* with *Til I Kissed You* and *Cathy's Clown* and *Temptation* and *The Price of Love* and the extent to which their music developed becomes clearly evident. It is my belief that it was their ability to produce new fresh sounds that inspired the newer generation of musicians.

During my preparation for this book I came across many references to the influence of Don and Phil both from people associated with the Everlys and other artists. In addition, I either spoke or wrote to various personalities asking for their own views on the importance of Don and Phil in the development of rock and country music. It is not possible to include all – that would take a book in itself. It is a mark of the esteem the industry holds for Don and Phil that so many people were prepared to comment on the debt they owe to the Everly Brothers.

Bob Dylan . . . 'We owe these guys everything. They started it all.'

George Hamilton IV . . . 'The Everly Brothers were one of the main pioneers of rock music. I have a high regard for them, both as talented individuals and also as human beings.'

John McNally (of the Searchers) . . . 'The Everly Brothers from the first hearing on Radio Luxembourg 208 of *Dream* influenced the band, not only vocally but the guitar sound as well. They did at that time tune their Gibsons slightly higher and used open chord tunings which gave them that lovely rhythm sound for the likes of *Bird Dog*.'

Buddy Holly (in an interview shortly before his death) . . . 'Since I've been touring across the country I've been privileged to meet some very talented entertainers indeed. The Everly Brothers – Phil and Don – they're very special friends of mine. And boy they just seem to get better and better every record they make. Take *Bird Dog* now, that one's just dynamite.'

Graham Nash (of the Hollies) . . . 'Twenty-five years since *Bye Bye Love*, hey? Well, that's one of the points of my life when I definitely knew I wanted to have the effect on people that *Bye Bye Love* had on me. I remember in the late fifties attending a local school dance with Allan Clarke walking across the dance floor hearing *Bye Bye Love* and stopping, trying to figure out why it felt so good. So I can say the Everly Brothers have definitely influenced me. They were the main inspiration for me and I think almost everyone in rock'n'roll owes a great deal to them. Singing actually on microphone with Phil Everly was one of the greatest things that ever happened in my life. Probably the biggest influence on the way I sing has been Phil Everly. I thank God he put them on the planet.'

Stevie Nicks . . . 'I remember when I was in the fourth grade laying on my bed listening to *All I Have to Do is Dream* and immediately singing harmony. I learned to be a second harmony singer from Everly Brothers records and so to this day whenever I hear anything on the radio I immediately sing as Everly Brothers harmony. When Lindsey and I first started singing together we were both such Everly Brothers fans that, since I don't have a terrifically high voice and he doesn't have a terrifically low voice, it wasn't that different from two guys singing as far as ranges went. So we sang those very close tight harmonies that Don and Phil sang.

Chuck Berry . . . 'I don't think Elvis Presley was as good as the Everly Brothers and I don't think the Beatles were either.'

John Stewart . . . 'I had a song that is really written in the style of the Everly Brothers. I am one of their biggest fans. One of the first songs I ever learned to play was *Dream* and I wanted to write a song with that feel to it. I thought "Who better to have than Phil Everly to sing the harmony on it?" He showed up and . . . the nicest guy. Absolutely not an inch a star. Was a pro all the way. He was harder on himself than I was and within forty minutes he had it knocked out. What amazed me, we were playing the song for the first time and he started singing along with it. I said, "Phil, you've never heard the song." He said, "I know. I don't know how I do that." To hear that golden voice coming over the speakers was worth the four months in there.'

Don Arden . . . 'I think that they were particular personalities. They were a household name, more or less covering all the aspects of show business. Everybody around accepted that they were talented and unique. Their sound was recognisable everywhere in the world. Nobody could ever copy them successfully. I don't think anybody tried.'

Snuff Garrett . . . 'Anyone who was around in the late fifties and early sixties will tell you that there was no one better than Don and Phil Everly. They were one of a kind and no one since that day has topped them. Two guys just can't get together and sing like Don and Phil Everly did. They created a style all their own and I've never heard it matched again.'

Warren Zevon . . . 'I don't think anybody can deny that their influence was profound and all-pervasive. Phil often blended rock'n'roll harmony of a particular kind. A white kind . . . just rock'n'roll and I think you hear it everywhere. The Beatles surely were influenced by them. Well, since everybody who wasn't influenced by the Everly Brothers was influenced by the Beatles, I should think the influence went everywhere.'

Albert Lee . . . 'I think what was so special about the Everlys in the late fifties and early sixties was that they had a unique sound and such an incredible blend. It was something we weren't exposed to at the time. They did everything on one microphone and it sounded perfect. It was so natural for them to sing together. They didn't have to compensate here and there. Today there are so many things you can do with the equipment to achieve the same result but they did it naturally. If you hear Phil's voice today he still sounds like a little kid it's so high. It's such a perfect harmony voice to Don. You would think that their voices would've evened out as they got older. Both their voices have dropped but that difference remains.'

Glen Campbell . . . 'I did a lot of sessions with them in the mid sixties. They were real fun to do. They're great guys. I like them a lot.'

Frank Ifield . . . 'Everything that's being generated today has come about because of our influences in the past and among those influences are the Everly Brothers. You couldn't see that I was influenced by the Everly Brothers. Even if you heard me sing an Everly Brothers song you wouldn't see that I was influenced by them but I always have been. It's there in the back of my mind. Maybe in a totally different song I'll come up with a little Everly Brothers phrase that gives it a little hook in the middle.'

Kris Kristofferson . . . 'I learned to sing harmony off old Everly Brothers records. I loved them. Hey! Where are they? We need them today. They were the best and they'd make it big today. Just like in the past.'

Keith Fordyce (compère on such shows as *Ready Steady Go!* **and** *Pop Inn* **in the 1960's)** . . . 'They both seemed shy and reserved but always exhibited a most agreeable sense of warmth and friendliness as well as consistent courtesy. To have them as guests on a show was always a thrill because the excitement and reaction of the audience was always

guaranteed. It is a considerable tribute to the quality and intelligence of their work that the recordings that they made still sound fresh today, entertaining and modern and that cannot be said for most of the stars of that era.'

Earl Hensley . . . 'To me the Everly Brothers are the epitome of rock'n'roll harmony. I don't think any two people, be they brothers, sisters, related or whatever, have the actual harmony that Don and Phil have. You know everybody's singing Everly Brothers songs now. They're coming back. With the right material and at the right time I believe that the Everly Brothers will be back. This will be because they are the best at what they do. They're the tops in the field of music.'

Chet Atkins . . . 'They were a great influence. They came along with something different. Two brothers singing harmony was new in the pop field or rock field whatever you want to call it. They were the best ever.'

Joe Smith . . . 'As a DJ on a radio station I found their music was the easiest to play. It found instant audience, nothing very subtle about it and it was melodic and they sang well. They were instant on the ear and I felt that they had touched a chord with young people, especially with their music and their songs and their simplicity. I'd say the most important thing they did, if Elvis Presley added an energy to rock'n'roll, the Everly Brothers did that for country music without the Presley touches but made it simple and the most important contribution was the sound vocally. That was the keynote for so many groups and still is today and I guess that's the biggest contribution, a vocal sound like nothing ever heard before.'

Buddy Harman . . . 'I think that between them the Everlys and Elvis played the biggest part in the development of country music to what we have today.'

Wesley Rose . . . 'The Everlys came at the best time in the world for country music. What they have contributed is that they brought a lot of new young fans to country music. They started a complete new trend and a complete new type of material which was aimed at the young. On the road they were always so professional. They had the "boy next door" wholesome image, very clean-cut, which the parents of the kids accepted so there was never the animosity towards them as there was towards Elvis Presley. Their harmonies were magic and have never been topped.'

Boudleaux Bryant . . . 'They probably had more influence than the Beatles because they stamped a style on the whole business that will last for generations. That is not belittling the importance of the Beatles at

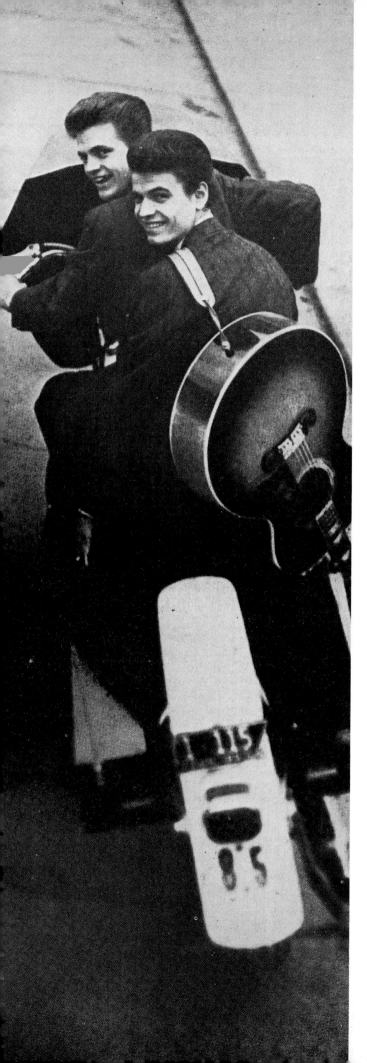

all but the Everlys were in at the start when rock music was not widely accepted. They were the bridge to the Beatles who developed the sound further. The Beatles could not have achieved all they did if the foundations had not previously been laid by Don and Phil, and all the others. The Everlys made the general public, as well as the aspiring artist, aware that harmony was a very merchantable commodity. Quite a few harmony acts came out at that time and then that eventually spread into larger groups which were influenced by having heard the Everly Brothers, by having listened to them, by having listened to the songs and the structure, particularly some of the ballads. I think that they did exercise a tremendous influence on what has become our contemporary pop music.'

Terry Slater . . . 'The Everlys were the pioneers of the music business today. They were unique. There will never be another Everly Brothers. They did beautiful songs that still stand up today, and I don't think you can measure their contribution to the music industry. I had the pleasure of sitting in a dressing-room with Bob Dylan and seeing Bob just look at them and say how much they meant to him and that's fantastic. I've sat down with Neil Diamond and seen Neil looking up to the boys and I've looked out from the stage many times and seen Graham Nash sitting there in complete admiration. Robert Plant was at many of our shows. I can mention the major names in show business today that have sat in front and watched Don and Phil and just adored them, because they're unique and they are just beautiful people and fantastic singers.'

Boudleaux Bryant and Terry Slater between them sum up the importance of Don and Phil. The list of artists who began their careers trying to copy the Everly' harmonies is never-ending. Not already mentioned but just as important are: Paul McCartney, Gram Parsons, the Byrds, the Mamas and Papas, Rodney Crowell, the Bellamy Brothers, the Eagles, Nick Lowe, Francis Rossi of Status Quo, John Sebastian of the Lovin' Spoonful, Simon and Garfunkel (who have included *Bye Bye Love* and *Wake Up Little Susie* in their stage act for many years by way of tribute to Don and Phil), Barbara Dickson, Mark Knopfler, and even Brian May of Queen has acknowledged Everly influences in the form of their song-writing and there are many many more.

It seems only right that the last word on the subject should be a personal view from Don and Phil's mother, Margaret. 'It makes me feel very humble to have had two boys who have done what they have. When I was over at the Albert Hall in England in 1971 and in Holland as well, I stood and watched the people. How thankful I was to see people who didn't know my children and see how much they loved them. That was a fantastic feeling and well, the tears came and my husband felt the same way.'

147

November 20, 1981

Thank you for your letter, Roger.

I would be happy to participate in the book you are
compiling on the history of the EVERLY BROTHERS.

It would be impossible to fully evaluate the impact
of the Everly Brothers on contemporary music.
Impossible, because that impact and influence continues
still. I will say this ... when you realize that musical
giants no less the stature of the Beach Boys and the
Beatles openly point to Don and Phil as early influences
on their style and career, you get some measure of their
far flung impact.

On a more personal note, having been around since the
virtual dawn of rock and roll, I can say without hesitation
that I enjoyed their magnificent harmonies the first time
I heard them ... and would run, not walk to listen if I
knew they were joining forces once again. They are unique
artists and rare individuals. I like them a lot.

I hope this information will be helpful to you.

Much good luck with the book.

Sincerely
Dick Clark
DICK CLARK

DC:pa

Mr. Roger E. White

NATIONAL SPINAL INJURIES CENTRE
AYLESBURY AND MILTON KEYNES HEALTH DISTRICT
(BUCKINGHAMSHIRE AREA HEALTH AUTHORITY)

TELEPHONE
AYLESBURY 84111

STOKE MANDEVILLE HOSPITAL
MANDEVILLE ROAD
AYLESBURY
BUCKS.
HP21 8AL

The first time I met the Everly Brothers was in Hollywood - my
first every visit to Glitter town and I was not only silenced
by the enormity of what Hollywood ment to us Show-Biz types,
that It quite stunned me and my first interview was with
Don and Phil.

Imagine my horror therefore, when suffering a mental block,
I forgot which was Don and which was Phil and had just been
given the cue to start the recording for the interview.

We survivors are made of strong stuff and despite this slight
hitch I opened the interview with "so here we are in Hollywood
with the one and only Everly Brothers - Gentlemen - introduce
yourselves to all your loyal fans in Britain. Don spoke first
and said "hello, this is Don Everly etc etc." and from then on
it was plain sailing, but it is funny how a mental block cane mak
you forget faces that you have known and loved for years.

JIMMY SAVILE O.B.E

As far as I am concerned the Everly Brothers were a very necessary
part of Rock and Roll. Most things progress because new things are
injected into it; there's no doubt that when rock and roll first
started it was pretty basic and in fact when you listen to the early
Sun sessions with the Elvis Presley group, you could hear it being
built up from just rhythm guitar and a bit of slap bass coming in
and the drums coming in and it's amazing to listen to that album.
What the Everly Brothers did was to bring a melodic harmonious sound
to what was really an aggressive form of music and I can remember
hearing 'Dream' and some of the other stuff and thinking that it was
a whole new realm to rock and roll; it just broadened it out and
the best exponent of that style of rock and roll, which was the
harmony and thirds, was the Everly Brothers.

I have always believed that if you like something then you are influenced
by it somewhere along the line. For instance, one can hear a drum sound
or something on someone else's record and maybe in a couple of albums
time you'll have a similar sound on yours and that's quite bona fide;
it's quite legitimate to do that.   But, the influence that the
Everly Brothers had on me was a more of a total kind of influence; in
that I loved their music so much that I wanted to sing their stuff; but
of course I couldn't because I only had one voice. Now, with technical
advancement one can quite easily make an Everly Brothers type record
oneself, singing both Phil and Don's parts. In those days what it
led me to - because the Everly Brothers not only brought harmony to
that rock feel, they also had that kind of country ballad side to
their career which was so sensational, and Boudleau & Felice Bryant writing those
very melodic ballads - they triggered off my desire to sing that kind
of beautiful melody.

A lot of people think that rock and roll is a tempo, but it's not;
it's a musical culture, so that I can now sing "Miss You Nights" and
although I can't say directly that the Everly Brothers influenced
me when I chose that song, there's no doubt looking back that the first
real melodic sort of songs that I remember listening to were Everly
Brothers songs. So I feel now that if I ever sing a song that people
like and it's a ballad, somewhere along the line I have to say thanks
to the Everly Brothers for being an influence upon me in that section
of my music.

Having sung with Phil on my recent T.V. show, it was a great thrill
for me, one of the highlights of my career. There I was standing
on the stage singing with someone who had this terrific power on me
when I was first getting into rock and roll and to hear his voice
soaring above mine was a great joy, so I can't say enough and speak
highly enough of the Everly Brothers, I think they were and still are
terrific.

Roger White
is invited to
The Everly Brothers
World Reunion Press Conference
Monday, September 19, 1983   B.A.F.T.A.
191/195 Piccadilly,
12:00 Noon   London W.1.
                               c/op Tony Brainsby Publicity
Admission by this invitation only   01 834 8341

Hi! The shows are
going well, The boys
are singing better
than ever, band sound
good too! looking forward
to England, hope the shows
are selling, good luck
with the book
Albert

Roger White

England....

CLIFF RICHARD

Cliff Richard

P.O. BOX 46C, ESHER, SURREY, KT10 9AF.   TEL: ESHER 67752

EVITA RECORDS LIMITED
118-120 WARDOUR STREET,
LONDON, W1V 4BT
01-437 3224/5

23 February 1982

R. E. White Esq.

Dear Roger :

I am delighted to respond to your request for a few brief thoughts about the Everly Brothers.

They were undoubtedly a very important part of my teenage years - in fact their second hit in England "Wake Up Little Susie" hit the chart two days before my thirteenth birthday. They enabled me to appreciate vocal harmony, immaculate production and perhaps above all, their songs (including the ones they wrote themselves) always had simple, direct, but very effective, lyrics.

I still enjoy their records today as much as I did back in the fifties and sixties. Of course it is a great pity that they are not still making music together but I certainly appreciate the problems of a long and close working partnership with just one other individual.

I have recently had the honour of meeting Don on more than one occasion and as he had a lot to live up to in my eyes, I am delighted to report that I was in no way disillusioned or disappointed after I had met one of my great heroes and music influences.

Best wishes.

Yours sincerely

TIM RICE

DIRECTORS: ANDREW LLOYD WEBBER   TIM RICE   DAVID LAND
Reg. No. 1033070 England.   Reg. Office: 118-120 Wardour Street, London W1V 4BT

BRUCE WELCH MUSIC LIMITED

64 Stirling Court, Marshall Street, London W1V 1LG Telephone (01) 434 1839

9th December 1981

Mr. Roger White,

Dear Roger,

In the late 1950s, there were only about seven truly international Rock 'n' Roll acts; Elvis, of course, Buddy Holly, The Everlys, Little Richard, Bill Haley, Fats Domino and Jerry Lee Lewis, and they all had an enormous influence on those of us involved in music here in the UK.

The Everlys were unique. Being brothers, they had a perfect voice blend and they used unusual harmony techniques which showed particularly in the beautiful melodies of their slower songs. Added to that, they had wonderful songs written for them at the beginning and then, of course, wrote their own hits which suited their style perfectly. As a record producer now, I can appreciate the quality of the recordings, produced in primative conditions by today's standards, with the perfect balance between the voices, the acoustic guitars and the tight electric guitar solos provided by the likes of Chet Atkins.

I saw the Everlys at the New Victoria when they toured the UK in 1960 and, unlike some American stars, they enhanced their record image. They were completely professional on stage, they recreated their harmonies perfectly, looked very good and had a marvellous backing group in the Crickets. They were an inspiration to all of us in the business.

When Hank and I came to London in early 1958, we used to go to the 2Is coffee bar and were known as the guys that sang the Everly songs while Hank's main claim to fame was that he wore glasses like Buddy Holly and could play all the Holly guitar solos perfectly!

The Everlys have influenced performers of the 1960s who used harmony vocals and that influence on people like Graham Nash and the Byrds has flowed through to the three and four part harmony used by the groups of the 1970s like Crosby, Stills and Nash and the Eagles.

I am sorry that Don and Phil no longer perform together as I feel that there are enough good songs around which could give them recognition now that stars of their stature deserve.

Best regards,

BRUCE WELCH

Directors: Bruce Welch Peter Gormley
Registered in England No: 875595. Registered Offices: 7 Staple Inn, Holborn Bars, London WC1V 7QN

Dave Edmunds
...field Road, London S.W.6

THERE ARE MANY OTHER ARTISTS, BUT, IF PRESSED I WOULD HAVE TO ADMIT THAT THE EVERLY BROS. HAVE HAD MORE INFLUENCE ON MY MUSIC THAN ANYONE ELSE. THE WAY DON SANG THOSE SOLO PASSAGES SO BEAUTIFULLY STILL SETS ME. BUT MOST OF ALL IT WAS THEIR ACCURACY IN SINGING TOGETHER. I ONCE ASKED DON IF THEY USED TO SPEND A LONG TIME WORKING ON THEIR PHRASING TO ACHIEVE SUCH PERFECT SYNCRONIZATION ON EACH OF THE MANY RECORDS THEY MADE OVER THE YEARS, TO WHICH HE REPLIED, "NOPE, WE JUST SANG 'EM." WHEN I LISTEN TO THEIR RECORDS EVEN NOW, HIS ANSWER STILL PUZZLES ME.

DAVE'S RAVE

VETERAN rocker Dave Edmunds has been telling me about his work as producer on the long-awaited Everly Brothers reunion album.

"It was a dream come true," he says. "It put me in the enviable position of being able to approach the world's great songwriters for contributions.

"I took the plunge and asked Paul McCartney and he was delighted. Dylan gave us some unfinished songs, but they weren't really right. The Everlys have included Lay Lady Lay because Dylan originally wrote it for them, but they turned it down at the time!"

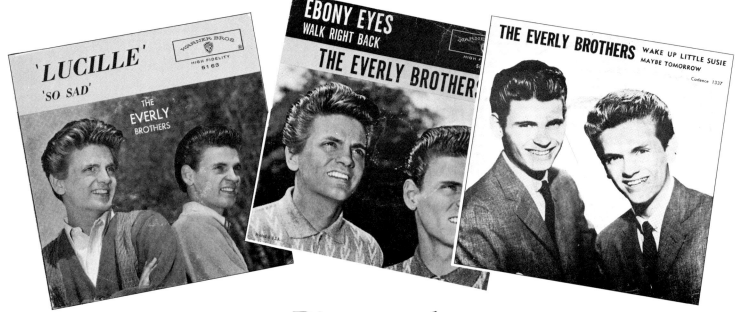

Discography

The length of the Everlys' recording career and the constant release of compilations makes it impracticable to include a full discography and it is necessary to limit the following to US and/or UK issues (with the exception of foreign language issues). The details provided include all regular single and LP releases for Cadence, Warner Brothers and RCA. Only compilation albums of particular interest are included. For Don and Phil's solo careers singles have been detailed where either or both tracks are not available on albums.

Date Recorded	US No.	Title	UK No.	Date of Release
COLUMBIA				
9.11.55	21496	Keep A Lovin' Me	–	Early 56
9.11.55	21496	The Sun Keeps Shining	–	
CADENCE				
1. 3.57	1315	Bye Bye Love	HLA 8440	May 57
1. 3.57	1315	I Wonder If I Care As Much	HLA 8440	
16. 8.57	1337	Wake Up Little Susie	HLA 8498	Sept 57
16. 8.57	1337	Maybe Tomorrow	HLA 8498	
12.57	1342	This Little Girl Of Mine	HLA 8554	Jan 58
12.57	1342	Should We Tell Him	HLA 8554	
6. 3.58	1348	All I Have to Do Is Dream	HLA 8618	Apr 58
6. 3.58	1348	Claudette	HLA 8618	
10. 7.58	1350	Bird Dog	HLA 8685	Aug 58
10. 7.58	1350	Devoted To You	HLA 8685	
13.10.58	1355	Problems	HLA 8781	Nov 58
13.10.58	1355	Love Of My Life	HLA 8781	
2. 3.59	1364	Poor Jenny	HLA 8863	Apr 59
2. 3.59	1364	Take A Message To Mary	HLA 8863	
7. 7.59	1369	(Til) I Kissed You	HLA 8934	Aug 59
7. 7.59	1369	Oh What A Feeling	HLA 8934	
15.12.59	1376	Let It Be Me	HLA 9039	Jan 60
13.12.59	1376	Since You Broke My Heart	HLA 9039	

Early 58	1380	When Will I Be Loved	HLA 9157	Jul 60
18. 2.60	1380	Be Bop A Lula	HLA 9157	
18. 2.60	1388	Like Strangers	HLA 9250	Jun 61
Early 58	1388	Brand New Heartache		
Early 58		Leave My Woman Alone	HLA 9250	
8.58	1429	I'm Here To Get My Baby Out Of Jail	–	Oct 62
8.58	1429	Lightning Express	–	

WARNER BROTHERS

18. 3.60	5151	Cathy's Clown	WB1	Mar 60
18. 3.60	5151	Always It's You	WB1	
24. 3.60	5163	So Sad	WB19	Aug 60
8. 7.60	5163	Lucille	WB19	
1.11.60	5199	Ebony Eyes	WB33	Jan 61
17. 9.60	5199	Walk Right Back	WB33	
1.11.60	5220	Temptation	WB42	May 61
27. 7.60	5220	Stick With Me Baby	WB42	
1. 6.61	5501	Muskrat	WB50	Oct 61
30. 5.61	5501	Don't Blame Me	WB50	
14.11.61	5250	Crying In The Rain	WB56	Dec 61
14.11.61	5250	I'm Not Angry	WB56	
14.11.61	5273	That's Old Fashioned	WB67	Apr 62
30. 3.62	5273	How Can I Meet Her	WB67	
20. 9.62	5297	No One Can Make My Sunshine Smile	WB79	Oct 62
11. 9.62	5297	Don't Ask Me To Be Friends	WB79	
27. 1.63	5346	So It Always Will Be	WB94	Mar 63
27. 1.63	5346	Nancy's Minuet	WB94	
5. 3.61	5362	It's Been Nice	WB99	Jan 63
28. 1.63	5362	I'm Afraid	WB99	
6. 9.63	5289	The Girl Sang The Blues	WB109	Oct 63
6. 9.63	5389	Love Her	WB109	
19. 2.64	5422	Ain't That Lovin' You Baby	WB129	
19. 2.64	5422	Hello Amy	WB129	
13. 5.64	5441	The Ferris Wheel	WB135	Jun 64
13. 5.64	5441	Don't Forget To Cry	WB135	

13. 5.64	5466	You're The One I Love	WB143	Sep 64
13. 5.64	5466	Ring Around My Rosie	WB143	
13. 5.64	5478	Gone Gone Gone	WB146	Oct 64
13. 5.64	5478	Torture	WB146	
10. 7.60	5581	Made To Love	–	1965
13. 7.60	5581	Donna Donna	–	
2.12.64	5600	You're My Girl	WB154	12.1.65
2.12.64	5600	Don't Let The Whole World Know	WB154	
3.12.64	5611	That'll Be The Day	WB158	24.2.65
2.12.64	5611	Give Me A Sweetheart	WB158	
4. 4.65	5628	The Price Of Love	WB161 (Decca)	21.4.65
4. 4.65	5628	It Only Cost A Dime	WB161	
4. 4.65	5628	It Only Cost A Dime	WB5628 (Pye)	
4. 4.65	5639	I'll Never Get Over You	5639	Aug 65
4. 4.65	5639	Follow Me	5639	
Sept 65	5649	Love Is Strange	5649	Oct 65
Sept 65	5649	Man With Money	5649	
12.11.65	5682	It's All Over	5682	1.12.65
12.11.65	5682	I Used to Love You	5682	
22. 1.66	5698	The Dollhouse Is Empty	–	Feb 66
22. 1.66	5698	Lovely Kravezit	–	
20. 6.63	5778	Release Me	–	1966
20. 6.63	5778	Sweet Dreams	–	
3. 2.66	5808	Power of Love	5743	Mar 66
3. 2.66	5808	Leave My Girl Alone	5743	
2. 6.66	–	I've Been Wrong Before	5754	
3. 6.66	5833	Hard Hard Year	5754	22.6.66
3. 6.66	5833	Somebody Help Me	–	
3. 6.66	5857	Like Every Time Before	–	14.9.66
3. 6.66	5857	Fifi the Flea	–	

6. 1.67	5901	Devil's Child	–	1.2.67
6. 1.67	5901	She Never Smiles Anymore	–	1.2.67
5. 1.67	6074	Oh! Boy	6074	
5. 1.67	6074	Good Golly Miss Molly	6074	
22. 3.67	7020	Bowling Green	7020	Mar 67
22. 3.67	7020	I Don't Want To Love You	7020	
28. 4.67	7062	Mary Jane	7062	Jul 67
21. 6.67	7062	Talking To The Flowers	7062	
14. 9.67	7088	Love Of The Common People	7088	Oct 67
10. 5.67	7088	A Voice Within	7088	
21. 3.68	7192	It's My Time	7192	3.4.68
21. 3.68	7192	Empty Boxes	7192	
7. 7.68	7226	Milk Train	7226	31.7.68
7. 7.68	7226	Lord Of The Manor	7226	
20. 7.68	7262	T For Texas	–	22.1.69
17. 9.68	7262	I Wonder If I Care As Much	–	
15. 4.69	7290	I'm On My Way Home Again	–	7.5.69
9. 4.69	7290	Cuckoo Bird	–	
15. 7.69	7326	Carolina On My Mind	–	6.8.69
1. 4.69	7326	My Little Yellow Bird	–	
11.11.69	7425	Yves	7425	Oct 70
9. 1.70	7425	Human Race	7425	

RCA

	0717	Ridin' High	2232	
	0717	Stories We Could Tell	2232	
	–	Lay It Down	2286	
	0901	Not Fade Away	2286	
	0901	Ladies Love Outlaws	–	

IMPRESSION RECORDS

23. 9.83		The Price of Love	IMSI (7″)	18.11.83
23. 9.83		Devoted to You/Ebony Eyes/Love Hurts		
23. 9.83		Devoted to You/Ebony Eyes/Love Hurts	IMSTI (12″)	18.11.83
23. 9.83		Baby What You Want Me To Do		
	880–213–7	On The Wings Of A Nightingale	MER170	10.8.84
	880–213–7	Asleep	MER170	10.8.84

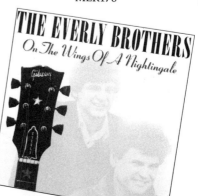

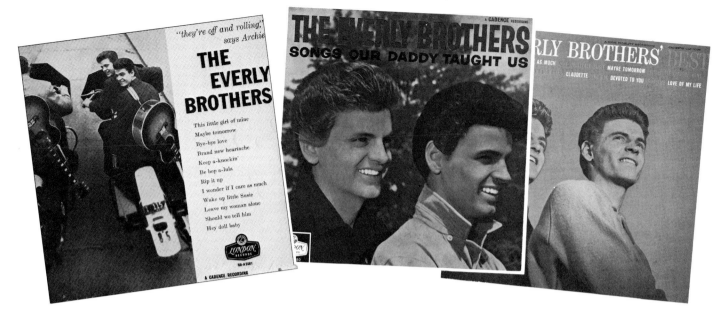

THE EVERLY BROTHERS Cadence CLP 3003
Rel April 1958
This Little Girl of Mine/Maybe Tomorrow/Bye Bye
Love/Brand New Heartache/Keep A Knocking/Be Bop A
Lula/Rip It Up/I Wonder If I Care As Much/Wake Up Little
Susie/Leave My Woman Alone/Should We Tell Him/Hey
Doll Baby.

Issued in UK on London HAA 2081

SONGS OUR DADDY TAUGHT US Cadence CLP 3016
Rel Dec 1958
I'm Here To Get My Baby Out Of Jail/Down In The Willow
Garden/Long Time Gone/Barbara Allen/Oh So Many
Years/Kentucky/Lightning Express/Rovin' Gambler/Who's
Gonna Shoe Your Pretty Little Feet/That Silver Haired
Daddy Of Mine/Rockin' Alone In An Old Rockin' Chair/Put
My Little Shoes Away.

Issued in the UK on London HAA 2150. In the USA it was
reissued in 1962 as Folksongs By the Everly Bros on
Cadence CLP 3059 (CLP 23059). In 1976 the album was
reissued in the UK on Philips 6467 500 with the addition of
Love Of My Life, Brand New Heartache, Since You Broke
My Heart, and Should We Tell Him. In 1983 the original
album was released in the UK on Ace CH 75

THE EVERLY BROS BEST Cadence CLP 3025
Rel March 1959
Bye Bye Love/I Wonder If I Care As Much/Wake Up Little
Susie/Maybe Tomorrow/Should We Tell Him/This Little
Girl Of Mine/All I Have To Do Is Dream/Claudette/Bird
Dog/Devoted To You/Problems/Love Of My Life.

Not issued in the UK

FABULOUS STYLE Cadence CLP 3040 (CLP 25040)
Rel May 1960
Like Strangers/Since You Broke My Heart/Let It Be Me/Oh
What A Feeling/Take A Message To Mary/Brand New
Heartache/When Will I Be Loved/Rip It Up/Til I Kissed
You/Hey Doll Baby/Poor Jenny/Be Bop A Lula.

Issued in the UK on London HAA 2266 with

All I Have To Do Is Dream/Claudette/Love Of My
Life/Devoted To You/Bird Dog and Problems replacing
Since You Broke My Heart/Let It Be Me/Brand New
Heartache/Rip It Up/Hey Doll Baby/Be Bop A Lula

15 EVERLY HITS Cadence CLP 3062 (CLP 25062)
Rel 1962
Wake Up Little Susie/All I Have To Do Is Dream/Bird
Dog/Devoted To You/Till I Kissed You/I Wonder If I Care
As Much/Claudette/Oh! What A Feeling/Let It Be Me/Bye
Bye Love/Take A Message To Mary/Problems/Maybe
Tomorrow/When Will I Be Loved/Poor Jenny.

Not issued in the UK

IT'S EVERLY TIME Warner Bros W (WS) 1381
Rel May 1960
So Sad/Just In Case/Memories Are Made Of This/That's
What You Do To Me/Sleepless Nights/What Kind Of Girl
Are You/Oh True Love/Carol Jane/Some Sweet
Day/Nashville Blues/You Thrill Me/I Want You To Know.

Issued in UK on WM 4012 (WS 8012)

**A DATE WITH THE EVERLY BROS Warner Bros W (WS)
1295**
Rel Oct 1960
Made To Love/That's Just Too Much/Stick With Me
Baby/Baby What You Want Me To Do/Sigh Cry Almost
Die/Always Its You/Love Hurts/Lucille/So How
Come/Donna Donna/A Change Of Heart/Cathy's Clown.

Issued in UK on WM 4028 (WS 8028)

BOTH SIDES OF AN EVENING Warner Bros W (WS) 1418
Rel Aug 1961
My Mammy/Muskrat/My Gal Sal/Grandfather's
Clock/Bully Of The Town/Chloe/Mention My Name In
Sheboygan/Hi Lili Hi Lo/Wayward Wind/Don't Blame
Me/Now Is The Hour/Little Old Lady/When I Grow Too
Old To Dream/Love Is Where You Find It.

Issued in the UK on WM 4052 (WS 8052). A souvenir 7"
sampler was issued along with this album on PRO 135 on
which the Everlys introduce 10 of the numbers on the

album. A 10" single sided record was made available to
radio stations (PRO 134). The record has shortened versions
of five songs from the album

INSTANT PARTY Warner Bros W (WS) 1430
Rel Jan 1962
Step It Up An Go/Love Makes The World Go
Round/Jezebel/True Love/Bye Bye Blackbird/When It's
Night Time In Italy/Oh My Papa/Trouble In Mind/Autumn
Leaves/Long Lost John/The Party's Over/Ground Hawg.

Issued in UK on WM 4061 (WS 8061) but with *Temptation*
replacing *Love Makes The World Go Round*

THE GOLDEN HITS OF THE EVERLY BROTHERS
Warner Bros W (WS) 1471
Rel June 1962
That's Old Fashioned/How Can I Meet Her/Cryin' In The
Rain/I'm Not Angry/Don't Blame Me/Ebony Eyes/Cathy's
Clown/Walk Right Back/Lucille/So Sad/Muskrat/
Temptation.

Issued in the UK on WM 4018 (WS 8018)

CHRISTMAS WITH THE EVERLY BROTHERS (AND
THE BOYSTOWN CHOIR) Warner Bros W (WS) 1483
Rel Oct 1962
*Adeste Fideles/Away In A Manger/God Rest Ye Merry
Gentlemen/What Child Is This/Silent Night/Hark The
Herald Angels Sing/*Angels From The Realms of
Glory/Deck The Halls/Bring A Torch Jeanette Isabelle/*O
Little Town Of Bethlehem/We Wish You A Merry
Christmas.

Issued in the UK on WM 4116 (WS 8116). The album
doesn't feature the Everly's singing on *Away In A Manger*
and *Angels From The Realms Of Glory*. It was reissued under
the same title on Harmony HS 11350 in 1969. Tracks
marked * omitted

SING GREAT COUNTRY HITS Warner Bros W (WS) 1513
Rel Oct 1963
Oh Lonesome Me/Born To Lose/Just One Time/Send Me
The Pillow/Release Me/Please Help Me I'm Falling/I Walk
The Line/Lonely Street/Silver Threads and Golden
Needles/I'm So Lonesome I Could Cry/Sweet Dreams/The
Last Song I'm Ever Going To Sing.

Released in the UK on WM (WS) 8138

THE VERY BEST Warner Bros W (WS) 1554
Rel Aug 1964
Bye Bye Love/Til I Kissed You/Wake Up Little Susie/Crying
In The Rain/Walk Right Back/Cathy's Clown/Bird Dog/All I
Have To Do Is Dream/Devoted To You/Lucille/So
Sad/Ebony Eyes.

Issued in the UK on WM (WS) 8163. Cadence hits
re-recorded

GONE GONE GONE Warner Bros W (WS) 1585
Rel Jan 1965
Donna Donna/Lonely Island/The Facts Of Life/Ain't That
Lovin' You Baby/Love Is All I Need/Torture/The Drop
Out/Radio And TV/Honolulu/It's Been A Long Dry
Spell/The Ferris Wheel/Gone Gone Gone.

Issued in the UK on WM (WS) 8169. The album was
reissued in stereo in the UK in 1970 on Valiant VS 109

ROCK'N'SOUL Warner Bros W (WS) 1578
Rel March 1965
That'll Be The Day/So Fine/Maybelline/Dancin' In The
Streets/Kansas City/I Got A Woman/Love Hurts/Slippin'
And Slidin'/Susie Q/Hound Dog/Outskirts Of
Town/Lonely Weekends

Issued in the UK on WM (WS) 8171

BEAT'N'SOUL Warner Bros W (WS) 1605
Rel Aug 1985
Love Is Strange/Money/What Am I Living For/Hi Heel
Sneakers/CC Rider/Lonely Avenue/Man With
Money/People Get Ready/My Babe/Walking The Dog/I
Almost Lost My Mind/The Girl Can't Help It.

Issued in the UK on WM (WS) 1605

IN OUR IMAGE Warner Bros W (WS) 1620
Rel April 1966
Leave My Girl Alone/Chained To A Memory/I'll Never Get
Over You/Doll House Is Empty/*Glitter And Gold/The
Power Of Love/The Price Of Love/It's All Over/*I Used To
Love You/*Lovely Kravezit/June Is As Cold As December/It
Only Costs A Dime.

Issued in the UK on W (WS) 1620. Reissued on Harmony in
1970 under the title Chained To A Memory. Tracks marked

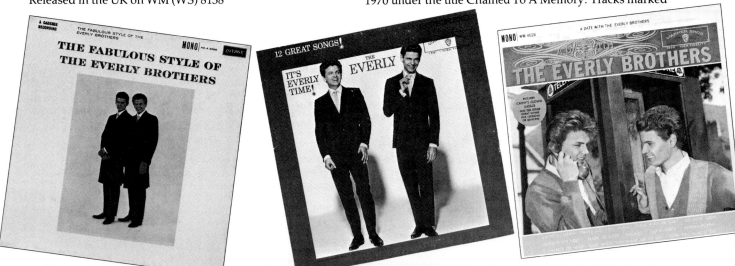

TWO YANKS IN ENGLAND Warner Bros W (WS) 1646
Rel July 1966
Somebody Help Me/So Lonely/Kiss Your Man
Goodbye/Signs That Will Never Change/Like Everytime
Before/Pretty Flamingo/I've Been Wrong Before/Have You
Ever Loved Somebody/The Collector/Don't Run And
Hide/Fifi The Flea/Hard Hard Year.

Issued in the UK on W (WS) 1646

THE HIT SOUND OF THE EVERLY BROTHERS Warner Bros W (WS) 1676
Rel Feb 1967
Blueberry Hill/I'm Movin On/The Devil's Child/Trains And
Boats and Planes/Sea Of Heartbreak/Oh Boy/Legend In My
Time/Let's Go Get Stoned/Sticks And Stones/House Of
The Rising Sun/She Never Smiles Anymore/Good Golly
Miss Molly.

Issued in the UK on W (WS) 1676

THE EVERLY BROS SING Warner Bros W (WS) 1708
Rel Aug 1967
Bowling Green/A Voice Within/I Don't Want To Love
You/It's All Over/Deliver Me/Talkin' To The Flowers/Mary
Jane/I'm Finding It Rough/Do You/Somebody Help Me/A
Whiter Shade Of Pale/Mercy Mercy Mercy.

Issued in the UK on W (WS) 1708

ROOTS Warner Bros W (WS) 1752
Rel Dec 1968
The Everly Family 1952/Mama Tried/Less Of Me/T For
Texas/I Wonder I I Care As Much/Ventura
Boulevard/Shady Grove/The Everly Family
1952/Illinois/Living Too Close To The Ground/You Done
Me Wrong/Turn Around/Sing Me Back Home/Montage
Everly Family 1952/Shady Grove/Kentucky.

Issued in the UK on W (WS) 1752. Warner Brothers issued a
7" promotional EP titled The Everly Family (1952) Parts 1
and 2 (PRO 306). The record contains the tapes of the Everly

Family radio show in Shenandoah, Iowa, extracts of which
are used on the 'Roots' album

THE EVERLY BROS SHOW Warner Bros 2 WS 1858
Rel July 1970
Mama Tried/Kentucky/Bowling Green/Til I Kissed
You/Wake Up Little Susie/Cathy's Clown/Maybelline/Bird
Dog/Rock'n'Roll Music/The End/Aquarius/If I Were A
Carpenter/Price Of Love/The Thrill Is Gone/Games People
Play/Baby What You Want Me To Do/All I Have To Do Is
Dream/Walk Right Back/Susie Q/Hey Jude/Lord Of The
Manor/I Wonder If I Care As Much/Love Is Strange/Let It
Be Me/Give Peace A Chance.

Issued in the UK on WS 1858

ORIGINAL GREATEST HITS Barnaby BGP 350
Rel July 1970
Bye Bye Love/Problems/Let It Be Me/Maybe Tomorrow/Be
Bop A Lula/Bird Dog/Love Of My Life/Keep A
Knockin'/Leave My Woman Alone/A Brand New
Heartache/Wake Up Little Susie/Like Strangers/Rockin'
Alone In An Old Rockin' Chair/Long Time Gone/All I Have
To Do Is Dream/Til I Kissed You/Poor Jenny/Should We
Tell Him/Lightning Express/Rip It Up.

Issued in the UK on CBS S 66255

END OF AN ERA Barnaby ZG 30260
Rel Jan 1971
Take A Message To Mary/Roving Gambler/This Little Girl
Of Mine/I Wonder If I Care As Much/Kentucky/When Will I
Be Loved/Down In The Willow Garden/Barbara
Allen/Devoted To You/Oh, What A Feeling/That Silver
Haired Daddy Of Mine/Since You Broke My Heart/I'm
Here To Get My Baby Out Of Jail/Put My Little Shoes
Away/Oh, So Many Years/Hey Doll Baby/Who's Gonna
Shoe Your Pretty Little Feet.

Issued in the UK on CBS S 66259

The entire Cadence catalogue was issued on these two
double LPs

STORIES WE COULD TELL RCA LSP 4620
Rel 1972
All I Really Want To Do/Breakdown/Green River/Mandolin
Wind/Up In Mabel's Room/Del Rio Dan/Ridin'
High/Christmas Eve Can Kill You/Three Armed Poker
Playin' River Rat/I'm Tired Of Singing My Song In Las
Vegas/Brand New Tennessee Waltz/Stories We Could Tell.

Issued in the UK on SF 8270

PASS THE CHICKEN AND LISTEN RCA LSP 4781
Rel 1973
Lay It Down/Husbands And Wives/Woman Don't You Try
To Tie Me Down/Sweet Memories/Ladies Love
Outlaws/Not Fade Away/Watchin' It
Go/Paradise/Somebody Nobody Knows/Good Hearted
Woman/A Nickel For The Fiddler/Rocky Top.

Issued in the UK on SF 8332. RCA issued a one sided 7"
promotional record titled Don Everly Talks about Pass The
Chicken and Listen RCA SP 45-409

WALK RIGHT BACK WITH THE EVERLY BROTHERS K 58168
Rel 1975 in the UK only
Walk Right Back/Crying In The Rain/Wake Up Little
Susie/Love Hurts/Til I Kissed You/Love Is Strange/How
Can I Meet Her/Temptation/Don't Blame Me/Cathy's
Clown/All I Have To Do Is Dream/Lucille/So Sad/Bird
Dog/No One Can Make My Sunshine Smile/The Ferris
Wheel/The Price Of Love/Muskrat/Ebony Eyes/Bye Bye
Love.

THE NEW ALBUM K 56415
Rel 1977 in the UK only
Silent Treatment/Dancing On My Feet/Gran
Mamou/Burma Shave/Nancy's Minuet/He's Got My
Sympathy/Little Hollywood Girl/Omaha/Empty Boxes/I
Can't Say Goodbye To You/Nothing Matters But
You/When Snowflakes Fall In The Summer/I'll See Your
Light/Why Not.

Previously unreleased material

THE SENSATIONAL EVERLY BROTHERS Readers Digest RDS 9703/4
Rel Feb 1979
Bye Bye Love/Wake Up Little Susie/All I Have To Do Is
Dream/Claudette/Bird Dog/Devoted To
You/Problems/Take A Message To Mary/Poor Jenny/Til I
Kissed You/Let It Be Me/When Will I Be Loved/Be Bop A
Lula/Keep On Knockin'/Oh What A Feeling/Maybe
Tomorrow/Hey Doll Baby/Like Strangers/Rip It Up/Leave
My Woman Alone/Cathy's Clown/This Little Girl Of Mine/I
Wonder If I Care As Much/So Sad/Lucille/Walk Right
Back/Ebony Eyes/Temptation/Muskrat/Don't Blame
Me/Crying In The Rain/Love Hurts/How Can I Meet
Her/Thats Old Fashioned/No One Can Make My Sunshine
Smile/The Price Of Love/Love Is Strange/The Ferris
Wheel/If I Were A Carpenter (Live)/Games People Play
(Live).

LOVE HURTS K-Tel NE 1197
Rel Dec 1982
All I Have To Do Is Dream/Til I Kissed You/So Sad/Let It Be
Me/Problems/Love Of My Life/No One Can Make My
Sunshine Smile/Devoted To You/Take A Message To
Mary/When Will I Be Loved/Love Hurts/Walk Right
Back/Memories Are Made Of This/Like Strangers/Brand
New Heartache/Since You Broke My Heart/Love Is
Strange/Crying In The Rain/Donna Donna/Cathy's Clown.

These compilation albums are the only ones issued to
include both Cadence and Warner Brothers recordings

THE EVERLY BROTHERS REUNION CONCERT
Impression Records IMPDI
Rel Nov 1983
The Price of Love/Walk Right Back/Claudette/Crying In The
Rain/Love Is Strange/(Medley) Take A Message To Mary –
Maybe Tomorrow – I Wonder If I Care As Much/When Will
I Be Loved/So Sad (To Watch Good Love Go Bad)/Bird
Dog/Be Bop A Lula/Lightning Express/Put My Little Shoes
Away/Step It Up And Go/Bye Bye Love/Gone Gone
Gone/All I Have To Do Is Dream/Wake Up Little
Susie/(Medley) Devoted To You – Ebony Eyes – Love
Hurts/Cathy's Clown/(Til) I Kissed
You/Temptation/Lucille/Let It Be Me/Good Golly Miss
Molly

NICE GUYS Magnum Force MFLP 1028
Rel Sept 1984 in the UK only
Trouble/What About Me/Eden To Cainin/Chains/Meet Me
In The Bottom/In The Good Old Days/Nice Guy/Stained
Glass Morning/Dancing On My Feet/Mr Soul/Don't You
Even Try/Kiss Your Man Goodbye.

This album consists of tracks recorded for Warner Brothers
and never before released

EB 84 Mercury 422–822–431–1
Rel Sept 1984
On The Wings Of A Nightingale/Danger Danger/Story Of
Me/Taking My Time/First In Line/Lay Lady Lay/Following
The Sun/You Make It Seem So Easy/More Than I Can
Handle/Asleep.

Issued in the UK under the title *The Everly Brothers* on
MERH44

OTHER SIGNIFICANT EVERLY BROTHERS RELEASES

The Singles Set issued as a Collectors Limited Edition by
Lightning Records in the UK in 1980 consisting of 15 singles
in picture sleeves and booklet.

Tracks are:

Bird Dog/Devoted To You
Bye Bye Love/I Wonder If I Care As Much
Wake Up Little Susie/Maybe Tomorrow
All I Have To Do Is Dream/Claudette
Problems/Love Of My Life
Poor Jenny/Take A Message To Mary
(Til) I Kissed You/Oh! What A Feeling
Let It Be Me/Since You Broke My Heart
When Will I Be Loved/Be-Bop-A-Lula
Like Strangers/Should We Tell Him
Cathy's Clown/Temptation
So Sad/Lucille
Walk Right Back/Ebony Eyes
The Price Of Love/Crying In The Rain
You're Just What I Was Looking For Today/Whatever
Happened To Judy (previously unreleased)

Nashville Tennessee 9 Nov 12″ EP containing four original
Columbia tracks:

The Sun Keeps Shining
Keep A Lovin' Me
If Her Love Isn't True
That's The Life I Have To Live

Issued in 1981 by Bear Family Records ESP 13443

Bootleg Albums

BACK WHERE IT ALL BEGAN
Everly Family Radio Show 1952/The Sun Keeps
Shining/Keep A Lovin' Me/Souvenir Sampler – Both Sides
Of An Evening LP/Don't Ask Me To Be Friends/No One
Can Make My Sunshine Smile/(So It Was . . . So It Is) So It
Always Will Be/Nancy's Minuet/I'm Afraid/The Girl Sang
The Blues/Love Her/Hello Amy/Don't Forget To Cry/You're
The One I Love/Ring Around My Rosie/Things Get Better
With Coca Cola (Take 2 & 3)

COKE, CHRYSLER 'N COUNTRY
You're My Girl/Don't Let The Whole World Know/Give Me
A Sweetheart/Follow Me/Love Of The Common
People/Empty Boxes/Milk Train/Lord Of The
Manor/Chrysler/Plymouth Commercial/Coca Cola
Commercial/It's My Time/I'm On My Way Home
Again/Cuckoo Bird/Carolina In My Mind/My Little Yellow
Bird/Yves/Human Race.

These albums were issued in the late 1970s and include in
the main Warner Brothers recordings which had not been
issued on previous albums

PHIL EVERLY
RCA
STAR SPANGLED SPRINGER No. APL 0092
Rel June 1973
That Air That I Breathe/Sweet Grass County/God Bless
Older Ladies (For They Made Rock & Roll)/It Pleases Me To
Please You/Lady Anne/Red, White and Blue/Our
Song/Poisonberry Pie/La Divorce/Snowflake Bombardier.

Issued in the UK on SF 8370

PYE
PHIL'S DINER No. 12104
Rel Dec 1984
Sweet Music/Goodbye Line/Feather
Bed/Summershine/Too Blue/There's Nothing Too Good

For My Baby/Invisible Man/Caroline/We're Running Out/It's True/New Old Song.

Issued in the UK under the Title 'There's Nothing Too Good For My Baby' on NSPL 18448

MYSTIC LINE No. 12121
Rel Oct 1975
Patiently/Lion And The Lamb/Mystic Line/January Butterfly/You And I Are A Song/Words In Your Eyes/Better Than Now/When Will I Be Loved/Back When The Bands Played Ragtime/Friends.

Issued in the UK on NSPL 18473

ELEKTRA
LIVING ALONE No. 6E 213
Rel 1979
I Was Too Late For The Party/Ich Bin Dein (I Am Yours)/You Broke It/Living Alone/Buy Me A Beer/California Gold/Love Will Pull Us Through/I Just Don't Feel Like Dancing/Charleston Guitar/The Fall of '59.

Not issued in the UK

CURB
Singles
Dare To Dream Again/Lonely Days Lonely Nights, ZS65401 Nov 1980.

Issued in the UK on EPIC EPC 9575.

Sweet Southern Love/In Your Eyes, Z56 02116.

Not issued in the UK

CAPITOL
Singles
Who's Gonna Keep Me Warm/One Way Love, B 5197.

Not issued in the UK

PHIL EVERLY Capitol Est 27670
She Means Nothing To Me (with Cliff Richard)/*(i) God Bless Older Ladies/Sweet Pretender/Never Gonna Dream Again/I'll Mend Your Broken Heart (with Cliff Richard)/** (ii) Better Than Now/A Man And A Woman/Louise/When I'm Dead And Gone/Sweet Suzanne/Oh Baby Oh (You're The Star).

* Re-recordings of songs previously recorded for RCA *(i) and Pye **(ii)

DON EVERLY
ODE
Single
Tumbling Tumbleweeds/Only Me, Ode '70 66009 Nov 1970.

Not issued in the UK

LPs
DON EVERLY No. SP 77005
Issued Dec 1970
Tumbling Tumbleweeds/Eyes Of Asia/Don't Drink The Water/Safari/Omaha/February 15th/When I Stop Dreaming/My Baby/Thinking It Over/My Friend/Sweet Dreams.

Issued in the UK on A & M Label No. AMLS 2007

SUNSET TOWERS No. 77023
Issued 1974
Melody Train/Jack Daniels Old No. 7/Warmin' Up The Band/Helpless When You're Gone/Did It Rain/Brand New Rock & Roll Band/Takin' Shots/The Way You Remain/Evelyn Swing/Southern California.

HICKORY
BROTHER JUKE BOX No. AH 44003
Issued 1977
Brother Jukebox/Love At Last Sight/So Sad (To Watch Good Love Go Bad)/Lettin' Go/Since You Broke My Heart/Deep Water/Yesterday Just Passed My Way Again/Oh, I'd Like To Go Away/Oh, What A Feeling/Turn The Memories Loose Again.

Issued in the UK on DJM No. DJF 20501 with addition of 'Never Like This'

POLYDOR (UK)
Single
Lets Put Our Hearts Together/So Sad, POSP 315 issued Sept 1981.

Acknowledgements

If you, having read this book, feel that I have achieved my aim of giving an insight into Don and Phil, then credit must be given to the following individuals who supplied material which has been incorporated into the text. I would like to thank John Tobler, Pete Frame, Richard Wootton and Mike Sparrow (of BBC Radio London who gave me access to the transcripts of the interviews he undertook when compiling The Everly Brothers Story, transmitted by BBC Radio 1). Thanks also to Roy Burchell of *Melody Maker*, for his help in the early stages of this project, and Graham Barker and Robert Ellis for their photographic donations. To this list should be added Spencer Leigh, Philip Norman, Peter O'Brien and Bruce Pollock, whose articles about the Everlys have proved an important source of material for this book. The rarity of many of the photographs, and the limited availability of the KMA Guides in particular, has meant that a great deal of behind-the-scenes activity has been necessary to ensure sufficient material was available for the book. The quality and quantity of the pictorial material is due to the efforts of freelance photographer Ian Tilbury, who gave up much of his busy time to help me on this book. The exclusive photographs of the reunion concerts were also provided by him, and I feel extremely lucky to have found someone as committed to the subject as I am. My sincere thanks go to him. Finally, thanks to Tony Gale at Pictorial Press.

As a member of the Everly Brothers International Fan Club, I was able to draw upon the resources of the members – which proved invaluable in the research for the book. Tom Lewis of Australia was the first to respond to my cry for help and sent all his valuable papers to me on trust. Martial Bekkers of Holland allowed me access to his vast collection of scrapbooks and Mary Ann Bailey and Margaret McNie of the USA provided research material and photographs. David Thorpe and Bob Isaac of England respectively researched the chart information and worked on the discography with me. I would also like to thank Fan Club Co-Presidents Laura Williams (who donated photographs) and Sue Goodwin. Others who provided great assistance and warrant special mention are Albert Lee, Margaret Everly, Terry Slater, the kind people of Shenandoah, Iowa and particularly Evalyn Saner of KMA, Earl Hensley of Chicago, Nona Thomas of House of Bryant, Dean May of Acuff Rose and all the celebrities that gave up their valuable time to write to me or undertake interviews.

To all the other people too numerous to name who have provided assistance, advice and those who have merely shown an interest I say thank you: and my apologies to anyone who feels he or she has been forgotten. I would also like to thank everyone at Plexus: Sandra Wake, Terry Porter and particularly Lisa Hardy and Ken Kitchen for all their hard work and patience during the finalisation of this book.

Finally, I would like to pass on my grateful thanks to Don and Phil, not only for the open and candid way they answered my questions (which were often on a far more personal level than they would expect) but also for the pleasure they have given – both together and separately – as recording artists and performers over the period of their career. It has been a thrill to have produced this book and I hope and trust that both of the Everly Brothers will look at the book with pride and that you, the reader, will regard it as a fitting tribute to two of the most outstanding performers of the rock'n'roll era.

The author's royalties are being donated to the Jimmy Savile Stoke Mandeville Hospital Appeal.